Jaguar
E-type

To my father

Motor cars have played a significant role in almost every aspect of my life since a very early age. As a young boy, my father would pack me off to the race track in East London, South Africa, where we would regularly see the likes of Clark, Hill, Bonnier, Piper, Attwood, John Love and many others.

It was through my father's encouragement that my interest in cars, and sports cars in particular, flourished. Although he died many years ago, I would like to dedicate this book to the memory of Hamilton, who did so much to stoke the fires of enthusiasm in my love for cars.

Glen Smale

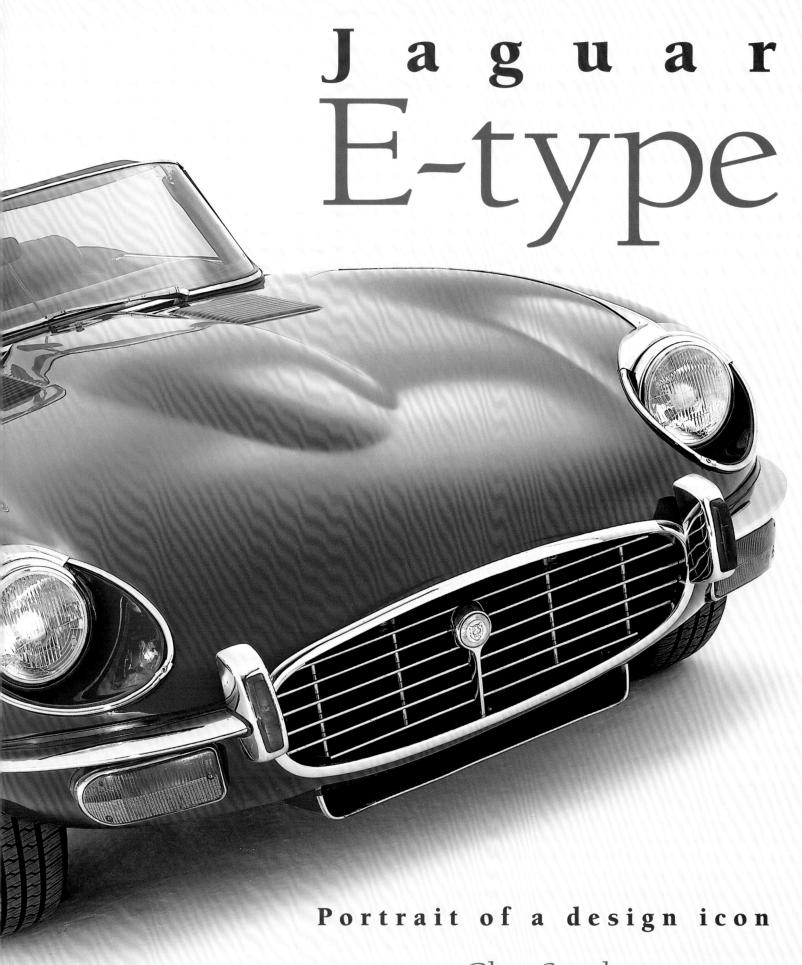

Jaguar E-type

Portrait of a design icon

Glen Smale

A catalogue record for this book is available from
the British Library

ISBN 978 1 84425 338 8

Library of Congress catalog card number 2006935975

Published by Haynes Publishing,
Sparkford, Yeovil, Somerset BA22 7JJ, England
Tel: 01963 442030 Fax: 01963 440001
Int. tel: +44 1963 442030 Int. fax: +44 1963 440001
E-mail: sales@haynes.co.uk
Website: www.haynes.co.uk

Haynes North America Inc.
861 Lawrence Drive, Newbury Park,
California 91320, USA

Design and layout by Lee Parsons, Richard Parsons

Edited by Ken Smith

Printed and bound in Great Britain by
J. H. Haynes & Co. Ltd

PHOTOGRAPHS

Author: 51-52, 72, 79, 102, 106, 107 top, 129 bottom, 134 bottom, 161 bottom,
163 top, 164 bottom, 165 top, 166, 168-170, 171 bottom, 178, 183-184, 188-189, 203,
207 top, 208, 210 bottom, 211, 213, 217, 221-223, 225
Automotive Research: 18 bottom, 118 top, 121, 123 top, 143 top, 152, 186-187,
190-191, 193-197, 200-201, 202 bottom, 206, 210 top, 214 top, 215, 226 bottom, 227
Castrol/BP Archives: 132-133
John Colley: cover, 58-59, 66-67, 70-71, 74-76, 86-87, 103, 107 bottom, 110-111,
114-117, 119, 120 bottom, 122, 123 bottom, 124-125
Geneva Motor Show Press: 89 top right
John Higginson/Cogent: 212
Jaguar: 19, 22 top, 32 top, 38, 42 top, 101, 143 bottom, 156, 171 top, 172-173, 179,
185, 192, 198-199, 202 top, 204-205, 207 bottom, 214 bottom, 216, 218-220, 226 top

Jaguar Archives USA: 118 bottom, 120 top
JDHT: 27-28, 30-31, 32 left, 37, 40-41, 42 bottom, 43, 45, 50, 56 top, 60, 63-65, 77,
88, 89 top left, 94-100, 112-113, 128, 129 top, 130, 138, 140-141, 150 bottom, 153,
161 top, 167, 175-177, 178 bottom, 181 bottom
LAT Photographic: 16-17, 18 top, 20-21, 22 bottom, 23, 26, 29, 32 right, 33, 36,
48-49, 53-55, 56 bottom, 57, 61-62, 89 bottom, 90-93, 126-127, 131, 134-135 top,
139, 142, 174, 181 top, 182, 224
Barry Lategan: 7
James Mann: 6, 9, 11-15, 24-25, 34-35, 108-109, 136-137, 228-229
MIRA: 81
Tom Wood: 2-3, 10, 46-47, 68-69, 73, 78, 80-85, 104-105, 144-149, 150 top,
151, 154-155, 157-160, 162, 163 bottom, 164 top, 165 bottom, 209

Contents

Foreword

By Stephen Bayley

If the history of the British car were limited to the years between 1959 and 1962 we would not be disappointed. In fact, we would be very pleased because not a great deal before or after those three short years could rival in significance, charm, ingenuity or glory what occurred in between.

In 1959 there was Issigonis' Mini, perhaps the most ingenious and influential car ever. In 1962 came Ford's Cortina which brought a measure of Detroit glamour (if that's the right word) to the yearning consumers of bleak suburbia. And in between came the ineffable Jaguar E-type, simply the most exciting and beautiful car ever designed for mass production.

The E-type was launched at the Parc des Eaux Vives, a swish hotel restaurant on the shores of Lake Geneva, close to, but culturally very distant from, the scrum of the 1961 Salon de l'Automobile. People were almost tearfully astonished by its winning combination of sensuality, technology and availability. In terms of culture, they commented on its erotic morphology: the E-type seemed to predict the democratisation of pleasure that was the keynote address of the sixties. Philip Larkin wrote in his *Annus Mirabilis*:

> *Sexual intercourse began in 1963 (which was rather late for me)*
> *Between the end of the Chatterley ban and The Beatles' first LP*

The Jaguar, an automobile equivalent of sex, was two years ahead of the poet.

Design of the E-type drew on a glorious backlist of expressive shapes, although they were often derivative. The inimitable handwriting of founder Sir William Lyons could be found in the SS90 and SS100, although these were perhaps inspired by Mercedes-Benz. The XK120 was an enhanced copy of Carrozzeria Touring of Milan's pre-War BMW 328 Mille Miglia. But then Jaguar began to take an independent direction.

To Lyons' inspired borrowings was now added the empiricism of aerodynamicist Malcolm Sayer. Technically, his D-type had an aeronautical type alloy centre section with a tubular truss to carry the engine.

Aesthetically, it showed a brilliant awareness of the art and craft of penetration. Then his E2A prototype went a stage further. In the translation of this prototype, this technical essay by a man in a brown coat, into the almost salacious E-type for a passenger in a mini skirt, it is irresistible to see, again, the bravura hand of Lyons. The E-type was what a later Jaguar designer, Geoff Lawson, called 'the optimum expression of steel'.

Curves are what matter in car design. 'There are,' Lawson added, 'fat rounded cars and thin rounded cars: the difference between a curve that is muscular and one that is anorexic is about 3mm.' That glorious E-type shape mediates between the two. It is both masculine and feminine all at the same time and this, philosophically, is what gives it such allure. As a result the E-type is regularly voted the most beautiful car ever made. The only production car on display in New York's Museum of Modern Art (the others are a 1947 handmade Cisitalia and a Grand Prix Ferrari), its feline presence makes the gallery sculpture of the sixties look ham-fisted.

To be honest, Sayer and (more likely) Lyons may have been slyly influenced by Touring's Disco Volante for Alfa Romeo, another design which took the ovoid form to extremes. But Pollock is not diminished because he was influenced by Picasso. Anyway, as the latter said, 'great artists don't borrow, they steal'. But this act of car theft promoted the original idea to something very near perfection.

There is a simple check-list to assess the quality of a car's aesthetics: 1. Stance, 2. Proportion and Composition, 3. Details and 4. Symbolism.

The E-type's stance is both elegant and aggressive, a winning combination. Its (phallic) proportions amaze, but are moderated by sober and balanced composition, especially in the front and rear elevations. The details – that orifice, those lights – are unforgettable and, in terms of symbolism, the E-type will always be remembered for its easy suggestions of sex and speed.

The 1961 Jaguar E-type is proof, if proof were needed, that cars can be sublime works of art.

Acknowledgements

Jaguar cars have always played an important role in my life, from as far back as I can remember. It is therefore with a great deal of pride that I have been able to compile this book, in what is most certainly the realisation of a lifelong dream for me. In particular, the E-type is a car that I have admired since I was a small boy and I have vowed to own one at some stage of my life.

For now though, I must be content with writing about these wonderful cars, but that too would not have been possible without the help of a great many people from numerous sections of the industry – current Jaguar staff, retired personnel, public relations and advertising staff and also those who have moved on to other fields of work.

In the design studio at Jaguar, I would like to thank Ian Callum and Julian Thomson for their time in what must be a very busy and demanding work schedule. The Jaguar Daimler Heritage Trust (JDHT) of course played an invaluable role in sourcing information and photographs and here I am most grateful to Executive Director, John Maries, who thought that my interview questions more closely resembled a doctoral thesis. In the JDHT Archives, Anders Clausager, Chief Archivist, and Karam Ram, Photographic Archivist have tolerated countless requests for assistance and I thank them for their swift responses every time. Other JDHT staff, Julia Simpson, Tony O'Keefe, volunteers Derek and Margaret Boyce and Penny Graham have all contributed in a meaningful way and I am very thankful for their assistance.

I am also indebted to Michael Quinn, grandson of Sir William Lyons and Mrs Patricia Quinn, daughter of Sir William, for kindly answering my many questions and identifying several key photographs in this book.

In the Jaguar press department, Jonathan Griffiths has been most helpful and across the Atlantic in Jaguar's American archives, Mike Cook has been extremely cooperative in providing material. I would also like to thank Jane Stewart, Brand PR Manager, Jaguar Cars Ltd and Susannah Gammell, Account Executive for Jaguar's ad agency, Eurorscg, for their assistance in sourcing Jaguar ad material and obtaining permission to use this.

As the designer of some of Jaguar's most admired sports cars in recent years, Keith Helfet was able to offer an insight into how Jaguar design worked while Sir William Lyons was still alive, right up until Keith's departure in 2002. Although Keith is a freelance design consultant today, his enthusiasm for the marque shows no sign of decline and he has been extremely patient in explaining the complex world of automobile design to a complete novice. I am most grateful to Keith for the many hours spent in his charming company.

Sometimes, the most knowledge and experience is to be found with those who were actually at the coalface during the years of the E-type's infant years. I spent many valuable hours in the company of Jim Randle, Geoff Turner, Brian Martin, Tom Jones, Pat Smart and the inimitable Norman Dewis. Collectively these gentlemen contributed enormously to my research and I would like to express my gratitude to them all. Tommy Sopwith, Jaguar dealer and owner of the Equipe Endeavour race team, also provided a valuable insight into the early days of Jaguar E-type racing.

In order to obtain an accurate account of how the E-type was covered in the media during those heady days of 1961, I am most grateful to Anne Hope, Michael Kemp, Graham Macbeth and Stuart Blaydon, all of whom are members of the Guild of Motoring Writers. They provided me with numerous fascinating stories from those exciting days leading up to, and just after, the launch of the E-type. I would also like to express my thanks to Katherine Grimes, Arts Publicist, BBC Publicity, for allowing me to use material from their BBC 2 television programme, The Culture Show.

My grateful thanks also go to Dennis McVey who was able to locate an important photograph of the E-type on test during those early pre-launch days at the MIRA test facility, Nuneaton, Warwickshire in England.

Some of the gorgeous photographs in this book only came about thanks to the generous actions of certain E-type owners. To Jeff and Pam Harrison, John Burton, Gordon Turner and Christopher J. Scraggs, I would like to extend my grateful thanks for providing their stunning cars and allowing them to be photographed. I would also like to express my gratitude to Jaguar Drivers Club members, Ken Wilson and Roger Whalley who provided valuable assistance in various ways.

And last, but by no means least, I would like to express my heartfelt thanks to my editor at Haynes Publishing, Mark Hughes, who has shown great patience and offered endless encouragement throughout this project. Designers Lee and Richard have demonstrated passion and understanding for the subject in accurately illustrating the book's message while Christine Smith has handled all administrative issues in her usual friendly and professional manner. Derek Smith requires special mention as he has provided valuable support and guidance in pulling the whole project together. Many thanks guys.

Glen Smale
April, 2007

Introduction

So much has been written on the subject of Jaguar, and in particular the E-type, that one could be forgiven for wondering what else there could be to write about on the subject – and yet there is still so much that is unknown about the E-type, one of the most influential sports cars in the history of sports-car design. It is this state of affairs which has prompted this dedicated study into the inspiration behind the E-type's development and design, and which will offer an explanation into the influence that this iconic car has had over the design of its successors.

The Jaguar E-type was created at a time when the approach to modern automobile design was advancing at an extraordinary rate. This development in design technique effectively loosened the control traditionally held by a company's owner or founder in this area, as the role of automobile design became a far more sophisticated and specialised function within the car-making industry. The E-type's designer, Malcolm Sayer, joined Jaguar in 1950 and immediately introduced a far more specialised, mathematical approach to automobile design that took into account aerodynamic surface technology and streamlining,

considerations which at that time were only being used in the aero industry. Not only did he incorporate this state-of-the-art approach in his design philosophy, but he also introduced advanced construction methods in the cars he was responsible for creating.

The evolution of the E-type's design history is very closely linked to the progressive demands of the car buyer at the time of its development and launch, and research in this field has revealed some of the design influences of the pre-E era as well as the reasons for the car's eventual replacement. Given that cars are designed and made by people for people, it was inevitable that by studying the E-type in this way, it would produce many interesting factors that had had an impact on the designers' thinking and style of work during the late 1950s and early 1960s.

It is significant that it was the E-type that was chosen by the author for this study, as this car, more than any other, marked a turning point in contemporary sports-car design in the 1960s. This was a time when creative flair was allowed to develop freely and an automobile designer could express his skill

through challenging the boundaries of convention, thereby pushing the envelope of engineering possibilities.

For many, the creation of the E-type also represents a period when societal values in Britain were being liberated in the most alarming fashion, as the Baby Boomer generation really got things rocking. Economic prosperity and affluence in the United States were growing at a meteoric pace, which enabled Jaguar to exploit the lucrative market across the Atlantic. It was into this market that the Jaguar E-type was welcomed with open arms in trendy London or New York, as it was seen to be sleek, sexy, outrageously fast and above all affordable to a larger group of swinging youngsters than ever before.

The Jaguar E-type stands alone as probably the only volume-production sports car ever to be modelled directly from a thoroughbred race car. The significance of this factor cannot be overemphasised, as the complexity of designing and developing a road-going sports car from a racer is an expensive process because of the differences in manufacturing and assembly techniques. Not only did Jaguar achieve this remarkable

milestone, but in the process they created one of the most successful and recognisable sports cars of all time.

During the research for this book it was established that most of the original E-type chassis engineering and development records had unfortunately been destroyed many years ago, so there is much that may never be known about the car's early pre-launch development. With this in mind, the author interviewed several Jaguar designers and engineers, both past and present, in an effort to establish the motivation and inspiration behind the E-type's design and packaging for the market. Through this work, it has also become apparent that although the industry today has access to the most advanced computerised design aids, model testing facilities and market research techniques, designers frequently make reference to past icons, the E-type in particular. While this may speak volumes for the genius of the E-type's design back in 1961, one is left wondering where the inspiration for future iconic designs is going to come from.

Had Malcolm Sayer not been taken from us in the prime of

his life, and at a time when he was embarking on a brave new direction in Jaguar design, we can only imagine what other groundbreaking cars he might have produced had he been given the opportunity. We can, however, enjoy the legacy that Malcolm Sayer established that started with the creation of the D-type back in 1954 and which eventually led to the introduction of the Jaguar E-type. Through the design excellence, technical brilliance and affordability that this car represented, the E-type will undoubtedly go down in automotive history as one of the most iconic sports cars ever designed. This book is a celebration of that success.

Author's note

Given the development timeline of the E-type and the various prototypes and race cars which preceded it, there has been some unavoidable repetition of details due to the overlapping nature of these events. Some minor repetition has been retained in order to ensure continuity in the explanation of certain models at various points in the book.

Glen Smale
April, 2007

Jaguar's early sports cars

'Sports cars should trigger different emotional responses to normal cars. They should be much more exciting, they should reflect the adrenalin in the character of the driver.'

**Julian Thomson – Chief Designer,
Advanced Studio, Jaguar Cars**

1935	1937	1945	1948	1954	1957
S.S.90 2½-litre introduced	SS100 3½-litre introduced	Jaguar moves to Browns Lane	XK 120 Open Two Seater launched	October, XK 140 launched	May, XK 150 launched
S.S.100 2½-litre introduced					

Some pre-war history

Today, the name of Jaguar conjures up thoughts of speed and power, of low-slung and sleek sports cars, but it wasn't always that way. In fact, the company founder, William Lyons was more interested in producing higher-volume family saloons than a small number of sports cars, but he was also acutely aware of the prestige that came with having a sports model in the range.

In the early twentieth century, the town of Blackpool, Lancashire, on the north-west coast of England, was better known as a popular holiday destination for thousands of tourists and located not far from Lytham St. Anne's, home of the world-famous golf course of similar name. However, in the early 1920s, another commercial activity was born that would eventually become a household name in much of the modern world.

A partnership between William Walmsley and William Lyons in 1922 was to see the start of a sidecar manufacturing company, Swallow Sidecar Company, which was eventually to become the springboard for Lyons's dream, to produce his own car. Swallow Sidecar and Coach Building Company (in 1926), later the Swallow Coach Building Company (in 1928), was just the beginning for the partners and was to prove a valuable stepping stone for the young Lyons in his quest.

A move to new premises in the Foleshill district of Coventry in 1928 was necessary in order to cope with the burgeoning business. As car production continued to grow, Lyons increasingly found that while he wanted to expand markets and increase production, Walmsley was content to stay small and manage what they had. 1935 proved to be a significant year in the company's history as the two founders finally decided to go their separate ways, which simultaneously ushered in a new phase in the growth of the business with the introduction of 'Jaguar' under the S.S. name.

In March 1935, S.S. Cars Ltd introduced the new S.S.90, a low-slung, two-seater sports car for the well-to-do driver looking for something with a little more zip, and which would attract the attention of most passers by. By all accounts, company co-founders Lyons and Walmsley had produced a winner, and at a very affordable price to boot.

Based on a shortened version of the S.S.1 chassis, the S.S.90 was the company's first production sports car. More affordable to the average car owner of the day, a sports car capable of 90mph was certainly a new development in the market and all for just £395. Although the numeral '90' was meant as an indication of the car's potential top speed, this was slightly ambitious for the 2,663cc standard-six engine, as reported in the press at the time.

1935 was a busy time for the company, as Bill Heynes joined the firm in April of that year, just in time to get stuck into the S.S.90's replacement model, the SS100. No doubt the '90' provided the engineers with good experience and the

An early SS100 pictured in Park Lane, London, by *Autocar*. Many thought that this was where such cars belonged, but the competition victories soon began to mount up.

many lessons learned were then applied to the new SS100. By now the full-stops had disappeared from the 'SS' name as they no longer stood for Standard Swallow, or Swallow Sport, depending on your preference, a debate which has never really been resolved, and will no doubt continue to be the subject of many fireside discussions. Ernest William (Bill) Rankin, who went on to become Jaguar's chief advertising executive, started with the company in 1934 and was tasked with selecting a new name for the upcoming range of sports cars. Rankin, together with the company's advisers, Nelson Advertising Agency, proposed the name of 'SS Jaguar' which was accepted by Lyons.

The 2¹/₂-litre SS100, launched in September 1935, was every driving enthusiast's dream, and the new car was introduced at the same price as the car it replaced, the S.S.90. But it was the 3¹/₂-litre SS100, launched in September 1937, which really set the sports car world alight. The SS100 with its 125bhp 3,485cc engine was a really handsome car, capable of that magic 'ton' and all for 'just' £445. To put this figure into

perspective, the average gross weekly wage for males in Britain in 1938 was £3.45, which was roughly £180 per annum, or around two and a half years of gross wages if you wanted to buy an SS100.

In pre-war days, the usual social and working routine for the sports car owner might have included the regular office run from Monday to Friday, while the weekends were reserved for some sporting action at the local track or a swift run through the country roads nearby. A sports car was to be driven, not wrapped up in cotton wool or limited to the shopping run. The very nature of a pre-war sports car meant that it could be driven to a racing circuit and there prepared for some competitive action. It would have fenders, bumpers and most often a windscreen that could all be removed by the owner once at the track in order to reduce its weight, thereby making it more competitive. A small aero screen could then be fixed in place and the car was more or less ready for some amateur track action. This flexibility was the very essence of a sports car, its name

↑ The SS100 3½-litre cut a handsome picture wherever it stood.

Such sports cars had developed into more dedicated racing machinery and it became less usual to find a car that could double as a normal daily vehicle yet be quickly transformed at the track come the weekends.

Thus it was that sports car owners became split between those who were more professionally intentioned and those who just wanted a car that was sporting in character and appearance. The role of the sports car had evolved, resulting in more-purpose-built racing machinery on the one hand, and a more comfortable, although still capable, performance-orientated sports car for everyday use on the other. Those who chose the non-professional route were more typically owners who could afford to indulge their fantasy or passion, and therefore opted for more comfort and a sleek and attractive style of sporty-looking car. Thus was born the performance car for the 'general market' where good sporting looks and the stylish and trendy aspects of car ownership helped to identify an owner's position in society, granting them greater acceptability amongst their peers.

↑ SS100s (nos. 24 & 12) line up at Donington awaiting the start of an SS Club event in 1938, while an older SS1 is farthest from the camera.

being derived from the competitive or sporting activity for which the car was made.

With the passing of hostilities in 1945, the company moved again, to its better-known home at Browns Lane, Coventry. It would still be some time before organised sporting activities once again became a regular part of the motoring scene, but when this did come about, the playing field had changed somewhat. Towards the end of the 1940s and the beginning of the 1950s, a far more sophisticated sporting car, needing more attention to prepare, was required in order to be competitive, and it became more expensive to participate at a high level.

XK 120

One of the first steps in this direction for Jaguar was the introduction of the new XK engine. Developed under the beady eye of Bill Heynes, Jaguar's director of engineering, the new double overhead-cam (DOHC) motor was mostly the work of Wally Hassan and Claude Bailey. Intended for the

↓ This was the aluminium-bodied XK 120 show car displayed at the 1948 Earls Court Motor Show.

new Jaguar Mark VII saloon, the new power unit needed a test bed and so the XK 120 was born. The story of the creation of the XK 120 is as remarkable as any in the company's history, when one considers that it took a mere two weeks for the body shape to be formed, under the supervision of Bill Lyons.

For the 1948 Earls Court Motor Show, a standard Mark V saloon chassis and running gear were adapted for the new XK engine and '120' body work. Originally fabricated out of aluminium, because this was relatively cheap and plentiful after the War and not subject to rationing as steel was, the first show car was made ready in around six weeks. Bill Lyons anticipated an initial run of only 200 XK 120 open two-seaters (OTS) with additional small runs to follow should the demand be sufficient. In fact, such was the reaction from the public that even before the show was over Lyons had made arrangements with Pressed Steel of Oxford to manufacture the steel pressings for the XK 120 body, as increased production was clearly going to be necessary.

Brian Martin, an apprentice in the experimental shop in 1949 recalls: 'Sir William Lyons saw the XK 120 basically as a means of proving the power unit to go in the big saloon, and the big saloon was going to be the money spinner, the Mark VII.'

However, it would be almost twelve months before the first production cars would be available for the public in the latter half of 1949, but not before a group of journalists had been shown what the new sports car could do. Such was the state of the sports car market at the time that most journalists and public alike did not believe that a production car could achieve the claimed 120mph top speed without fouling its plugs on the one hand, while not being very driveable at town speeds on the other. Jaguar demonstrated to an assembled throng of media and general onlookers on the Jabbeke motorway in Belgium in 1949 that the car could in fact match the factory claims on both counts, achieving a two-way average in excess of 125mph in almost standard trim. This was truly a remarkable achievement for a car costing a basic £998, and a little over £1,263 fully taxed in Britain.

↑ This contemporary press photograph of the aluminium-bodied XK 120 shows off the striking lines of the sports car. It is said that the XK 120 eventually earned the company US$40-million in export sales, not bad for a car that was intended merely as a test bed for their new engine.

↑ Ian and Pat
Appleyard attend
the most famous
XK 120 of all
time, NUB 120,
which they drove
in many rallies.

In the XK 120, the customer got a far more comfortable, spacious and altogether easier car to live with than in the pre-war style of sports car, such as the SS100. The XK 120 was also much larger, had a far more practical boot for travelling, and was fitted with the all-new XK DOHC engine giving improved performance. This was a car that looked like a show-stopper, and therefore commanded a far higher price than the SS100.

The majority of the early, aluminium-bodied XK 120s ended up going to America, and when the steel-bodied version started to come off the production line, most of them headed west too. Not only did William Lyons stick to his end of the steel allocation agreement with the Board of Trade, requiring him to export most of his production, but he had no difficulty in selling his cars Stateside either. The actor Clark Gable would end up buying three XK 120s, and when people like that buy your products with such enthusiasm, it is good publicity for the company whichever way you look at it. Motorsport victories also attracted the attentions of celebrity

buyers, and as successful people were highly visible in society, this was a boon for Jaguar publicity.

Brian Martin again: 'I don't think anybody, perhaps even he [Sir William Lyons] himself, anticipated that the XK was going to be so successful, particularly in the American market which is where most of them were sold to start with. I can remember, when we first started building the XKs, it was very, very rare that you saw a right-hand-drive car going down the assembly line and I remember rows and rows and rows of cars waiting to go to the docks, and they were all American spec.'

The American car buyers were big on names for cars, such as the Ford Sportsman, Lincoln Continental, Studebaker Starlight Coupe, Cadillac Eldorado and many others. Max Hoffman, the self-styled New York-based foreign-car importer, always claimed that Americans didn't like numerals or letters as model identifiers, they preferred to have a name for their cars and he tried to get foreign motor manufacturers to comply. So why was it that the Americans embraced the name XK 120, which to the uninformed really meant nothing at all? The origins of this title started way back in the experimental department at Jaguar, where the 'X' stood for 'experimental' and the 'K' was simply the next sequential letter assigned to that line of experimental engine development, hence the prefix 'XK' referred originally to the engine and not to a car at all. The '120' was a reference to the potential top speed of the car which in 1948/49 appealed to just about anybody, because it was really only racing cars that could achieve such a top speed. To have a road-going sports car with that kind of performance, readily available to anyone in the market who had the money in the late 1940s, was almost unheard of.

For the average man in the street, and in very simplistic terms, most sports cars were the same, with four wheels and four mudguards, two seats and a windscreen. But with the XK 120 the whole package was so totally different from anything that had ever been produced before. Factory staff at the time felt that the Jaguar XK 120 was 25 years ahead of anything else on the market.

Brian Martin recalls: 'It was such a beautiful shape, and most other sports cars that were being made, and I can think of things like the TR and probably the early Austin Healeys, but certainly British sports cars were pretty blunt and not very interesting to look at, they have become more interesting in an historical vein rather than what they were at the time. That's the way it was; and that's always been in my estimation

nights at an average speed of 100mph. Although many were sceptical at first, the company prepared a car for the attempt in August 1952 and four drivers, Leslie Johnson, Stirling Moss, Jack Fairman and Bert Hadley rose to the occasion, averaging 100.31mph for the seven-day period. The importance of this accomplishment was well noted in the vital American market, as the record results were published in the November 1952 issue of *Auto Speed and Sport*. This was a significant coup for Jaguar in that the car ran in almost standard trim apart from certain modifications for endurance purposes such as the installation of a Pye two-way radio for contact with the pits.

Following the early success of the 120 open two-seater (OTS), Jaguar introduced the XK 120 fixed-head coupé (FHC) in March 1951, and the drop-head coupé (DHC) two years later in April 1953. For a car that was never really intended for series production, the total of a little under 12,000 vehicles must have made pleasant reading for Sir William, all the same.

XK 140

There were many Jaguar admirers and enthusiasts who took a dislike to the XK 140 when it was introduced at Earls Court on 15 October, 1954. The truth of the matter is that it was never intended as a replacement at all for the very successful XK 120, which, as we have seen, was itself not intended as a

Tyrone Power, one of Hollywood's great romantic swashbuckling stars of the mid-twentieth century, stands beside his XK 120.

When launched on 15 October, 1954, the XK 140 was immediately offered in all three body styles – open two seater (OTS), fixed head coupé (FHC) and drop head coupé (DHC).

where Jaguar's success has been.'

Not only did William Lyons have a superb eye for design, but he was an excellent publicist as well, and when a young British engineer by the name of Leslie Johnson approached the company to do a record run at Montlhéry in France, Lyons listened. Having just completed a personal test at the same track in a stock XK 120, achieving an average speed of over 130mph for an hour, Johnson came up with the ambitious plan to run at the banked French track for seven days and seven

volume sports car from the outset. An altogether more sleek and elegant sports car was planned as a replacement for the 120, but with the factory running at full stretch on all fronts, there was simply no spare capacity with which to design, retool and produce a completely new car. Rare factory shots of this still-born replacement show it to be much lower than the XK 140, with a very simple and smooth shape.

When it was realised that the replacement model, which hadn't even been named at that point, was not going to go

→ The new Jaguar XK 140 DHC was seen as a stop-gap model as the company had insufficient resources with which to tool up for a complete XK 120 replacement. Powered by the 190bhp XK engine, the '140' was capable of speeds of up to 140mph.

ahead, plans were put in place to update the 120 for the market. This more than kept the factory humming along and demand for the updated sports car continued. Although the 140 did continue with its predecessor's stunning theme, as a hastily prepared replacement the new model did suffer from a bit of an inferiority complex. From the beginning of the 140 model line, it was offered in all three body forms, the open two-seater, fixed-head coupé and drop-head coupé.

The bulky Mark VII saloon bumpers made the car appear much heavier, and the wider gaps between the grille slats also detracted from the car's earlier elegance. With the heavier bumpers came matching front and rear overriders which actually increased the car's overall length by around three inches. However, one important difference with this model was that its engine was moved three inches forward on its chassis, thus allowing far greater interior cabin space, as well as better handling. Though it was a car that was never planned for, a little over 9,000 vehicles were produced which certainly helped to amortise the company's costs.

XK 150

As is so often the case, the first car of a range is usually the best. In the case of the XK 150, introduced in May 1957 in both FHC and DHC form, it is perhaps a little unfair to criticise

↓ The higher waistline of the XK 150 made the car appear more bulky, although it offered improved interior accommodation.

what was by all accounts a fine car, but it had certainly become a little more bulky and heavier looking. The apparent weight gain occurred as a result of a tidying up of the car's styling, achieved by raising the waistline, which no longer had such a pronounced dip around the door area. Gone were the evocative and shapely curves of the XK 120/140, and a smoother although more bulbous look was achieved. The effect of this was to provide a huge increase in interior space at around shoulder level. Other styling improvements included a full-width, wrap-around windscreen and a one-piece rear bumper which replaced the split bumpers of the XK 140. With more power on tap, a wider grille was required to improve cooling, which gave the new model a bigger 'mouth' than its predecessor.

Bulky or not, the 150 offered a more refined ride and greater comfort with increased power, while still retaining that unmistakable 'Lyons' feel. With more seductive curves than the classic shape of the 120 and 140, the XK 150 was to some customers the ultimate Jaguar sports car. Announced on 2 October, 1959, the XK 150S was fitted with the larger 3.8-litre engine as used in the Mark IX saloon. Introduced in all three body forms (OTS, FHC and DHC) and fitted with triple two-inch SU carburettors, power output was boosted to 265bhp with a top speed of 136mph. Some 9,400 XK 150s of all variants were made and production of the final variant, the XK 150S, ceased in late 1960.

With Jaguar having successfully experimented with more-modern methods of sports car construction in the D-type, and on the saloon-car side with the Mark I series, the future of the traditional separate chassis and body construction method was surely limited. By the late 1950s, Jaguar realised that significant changes would be required and that meant in the design, pressing and assembly processes as well. Anders Clausager, chief archivist at the Jaguar Daimler Heritage Trust (JDHT) confirms this: 'The XK 150 went out of production in the autumn of 1960; I cannot believe that there was any serious consideration given to continue this car.' ■

↑ The Jaguar XK 150 was a handsome car even with its hood raised, and commanded respect wherever it was seen.

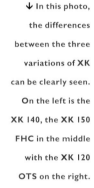

↓ In this photo, the differences between the three variations of XK can be clearly seen. On the left is the XK 140, the XK 150 FHC in the middle with the XK 120 OTS on the right.

Racing cars to production prototypes

Jaguar: Panthera onca – *a member of the cat family, the largest found in the western hemisphere and known for its speed, stealth, power, grace...and beauty.*

Author

1950/51	1953	1954	1955	1956	1957	1958/59
Malcolm Sayer arrives at Jaguar, 1950	C-type wins 1953 Le Mans	XK 140 launched at Earls Court	William Lyons knighted for contribution to UK exports	Jaguar ceases racing as a works activity	D-type sweeps to victory in Le Mans 24-Hour (1st, 2nd, 3rd, 4th & 6th)	E1A prototype undergoes testing
C-type wins 1951 Le Mans			D-type scores Jaguar's first works victory		E1A breaks cover	

Malcolm Sayer arrives at Jaguar

In 1948, a very youthful Malcolm Sayer was contracted to establish the Faculty of Engineering at Baghdad University. Two years later, Jaguar technical director, Bill Heynes hired the young but experienced Sayer fresh back from his short stint in the Middle East, where he had learnt some interesting design methods and interpretation skills from a German engineering professor he had met in Baghdad. Sayer's time spent at the Bristol Aircraft company earlier had taught him many valuable lessons in the aerodynamic efficiency of surfaces and shapes, and this, together with his automobile engineering diploma from Loughborough College (Leicestershire, England), endowed him with the ability to interpret the concept of airflow and surface resistance better than most in the motor industry.

The 1950 Le Mans 24-Hour race had seen two XK 120s finishing twelfth (Peter Clark/Nick Haines) and fifteenth (Peter Whitehead/John Marshall in JWK977), a result which showed that mechanically the cars could stand up to the rigours of twenty-four-hour racing. It also held out the possibility of a higher-placed finish given a more suitable, lighter body. In view of this performance with near-standard machinery, William Lyons was persuaded that a dedicated Jaguar race car could bring them the most prestigious crown in long-distance racing.

Although Lyons had not been terribly keen to go racing, once the decision had been taken to participate in motorsport, the company opted to use people from within the company who had the relevant experience. That group included Wally Hassan, who had worked for Bentley and the English racing team ERA, Lofty England who had been with ERA and on motorbikes before the War, as well as Malcolm Sayer and Phil Weaver who had come from Bristol.

'We had a nucleus of people who knew about motor racing, but it wasn't a new department that was formed with somebody in charge. Basically, William Lyons said: "England, you have got a job to run the service department, but as well as doing that you can look after the motorsport side as well".' remembers Brian Martin.

↑ 'JWK 977', one of the early aluminium-bodied XK 120s, achieved significant success on circuits around England, and finished 15th overall in the 1950 Le Mans 24-hour driven by Peter Whitehead/ John Marshall in near-standard trim.

26

Martin, who joined Jaguar as a 16-year-old straight from school in April 1949, recalls: 'Jaguar knew that if they were going to go seriously into competition, they had to have a car that was more competitive than the heavy chassised XK 120 and I suppose this is where Lofty England's influence in motor racing and Phil Weaver in particular from Bristol had helped, and the methods of construction that were used then in sports racing cars was to have a lightweight steel frame with an aluminium body clothing it. Malcolm just brought the shape.'

Upon Malcolm Sayer's arrival at Jaguar, he was assigned the job of optimising the XK 120 for competition, a project which had only been partially worked on by Bill Heynes at that stage. The difficult task facing Sayer was to take the existing XK 120 mechanicals and running gear, and to design a body which would retain elements of the 120's style, but at the same time be light enough to compete on the international stage. Jaguar wanted a car that could challenge the supremacy of Ferrari, Aston Martin, Mercedes-Benz and the other big-name racing cars that had been dominant since before the war. That sounds like a fairly straightforward undertaking in the motor industry, but in a relatively small manufacturing concern such as Jaguar in 1950, you ran the risk of treading on someone's toes, somewhere along the line. However, in this case, it wasn't Malcolm Sayer who was in danger of treading where he shouldn't. Due to his superb efforts in producing a winning car, some friction began to occur between the two departments responsible for the manufacturing and maintenance of these cars.

Lofty England was the service manager in charge of customers' cars, but he was also the service director on the Jaguar board. As this function included looking after Jaguar's racing customers, Lyons appointed Lofty as the company's racing manager as well. This arrangement brought Bill Heynes and Lofty England, who according to Jaguar personnel there at the time, 'didn't get on', into conflict with one another. Bill Heynes was responsible for manufacturing the cars, which included responsibility for the competition shop, while Lofty looked after the servicing of those cars, which covered general as well as racing customers. It is not difficult to see how the responsibilities of the racing and manufacturing managers might collide when something urgent was required for a racing car, a task which needed to be carried out by the competitions department.

'That arrangement caused a lot of conflict between the people, the side of the company that built motor cars and the side of the company that used motor cars, particularly in motorsport. How we built competition cars and how we looked after them was nothing to do with how they were raced, so occasionally there was this sort of friction between the responsibilities', recalls Brian Martin.

The responsibility of maintaining the race cars was, for Lofty and Jaguar, an extremely important one, and one which William

Le Mans 1953 – Lofty England discusses some racing issue with Duncan Hamilton seated in the car. Tony Rolt is partly obscured behind.

Lyons relied on increasingly heavily to generate good publicity for the company. Top racing drivers like Duncan Hamilton, Peter Whitehead, Peter Walker and others, owned their race cars but had them serviced by the factory. Martin explains: 'They were cars that were owned by other people not cars that were owned by the factory. The "Old Man" was very keen that what he was there to do was to sell motor cars, not to have motor cars hanging around that somebody hadn't bought.'

The C-type takes shape

When Sayer arrived at Jaguar, according to Brian Martin who had worked on the pre-production XK 120 aluminium-bodied cars: 'The C-type wasn't in existence; it was still in the design stage.' Although the concept of a lightweight race car had just got underway, Sayer still had to complete the design, oversee the construction and dress the new racing frame created by Heynes and his team.

In line with Jaguar's model identification protocol, the 'X' stood for experimental and as history has shown us, the 'K' referred to the six-cylinder double-overhead-cam engine development which powered the XK 120 sports car. Internally, Sayer's initial prototype racing car which used XK 120 mechanicals and running gear, was named the XK 120C or XKC, where the letter 'C' stood for competition.

Having dispensed with the extremely heavy steel chassis of the XK 120, a substantial degree of body strength and

stiffness was achieved through the fabrication of the racer's new lightweight tubular space frame. To reduce weight still further, the frame was constructed from tubing of varying thickness depending on the load to be carried at particular points in the frame. Sayer's method was then to stretch an aluminium skin over a welded tubular space frame which served merely to clothe the frame, not to strengthen the structure in any significant way.

However, in an attempt to draw attention to the XKC's perceived likeness with the car on which it was based, Sayer's approach was to smooth out the familiar lines of the gorgeous 120, creating a superb flowing and streamlined shape with a much reduced coefficient of drag. Although the frontal area of the newly designed race car was not much smaller than the XK 120, the combination of smooth body surfacing and lightweight construction ensured that the XKC was a potent performer.

A limiting factor for Malcolm Sayer in the creation of the XKC shape was the upright grille of the XK 120 which had to be retained in order to continue the family resemblance, while at the same time ensuring that the race car was as streamlined and efficient as possible. This tall grille dictated the basic style of the car and also pretty much set the height for the rest of the body, something which no doubt frustrated Sayer, but a feature which he rectified on later models, as we shall see in due course.

The C-type, as it became universally known, was a race car created solely for the purpose of winning the Le Mans

↓ The bare chassis, engine and frame of C-type XKC051, the 1953 Le Mans-winning car driven by Duncan Hamilton.

← Jubilation as car number 20, the Jaguar C-type (XKC003) driven by Peters Walker and Whitehead, wins the 1951 Le Mans 24-Hour race on its debut.

24-Hour race. To Sir William Lyons, no other race event really mattered. Le Mans was to him the race which most of the British motoring public were interested in and certainly the rest of the motoring world were equally absorbed by the tales of endurance and stamina of both man and machine which this great race demanded. For Jaguar to win at Le Mans meant that their name got mentioned in all the international press and the prestige gained by such a victory was worth its weight in gold.

That moment was to come sooner than many expected, as the 1951 Sarthe race was to prove decisive for the Coventry manufacturer, demonstrating the value of Malcolm Sayer's vehicle aerodynamics and design methods after just twelve months in the job. Even though only one of the three official works cars finished, the Peter Walker/Peter Whitehead car took the most important spot, first place. In addition to this crown, the Stirling Moss/Jack Fairman car clipped a massive six seconds off the lap time, setting a new record for the circuit. For the Coventry manufacturer, the 1951 event was perhaps

↓ This is the C-type that kick-started Jaguar's success in motorsport. The vertical orientation of the C-type grille was retained in order to show the link with the XK 120 road cars.

153 FW

their most important race and the one which put them on the international motorsport map. John Maries, a senior marketing manager at Jaguar (from 1981) confirms this: 'Because Le Mans to this day is probably the only motor race in Europe that is still recognised by the Americans.'

Even though this was impressive stuff, it was only the beginning of Sayer's magic, as he soon began work on the successor to the 'C'. However, for Malcolm Sayer, the C-type was still just a modification of an existing model and the satisfaction of designing and building his own creation was still to come. In the words of Keith Helfet, a Jaguar designer (1978–2002): 'Although the C-type was quite beautiful, it was still a modified XK. The C-type was a special racing-bodied 120, it really was.'

However, such was the potential and brilliance of the XK power unit that this engine continued in service in both Jaguar's road and racing cars simultaneously. In 1953, a prototype emerged that with hindsight was the evolutionary link between the C and what eventually became the D-type. Although it was sometimes (but only later) called the C/D, for obvious reasons as it was this car that linked these two great racers, Malcolm Sayer preferred to call this halfway model the XK 120C Mark II. Lowering the central nose-line made the wheel humps more pronounced, a feature that became the hallmark of the later D-type, but it also had the added advantage of making the bodywork even more streamlined.

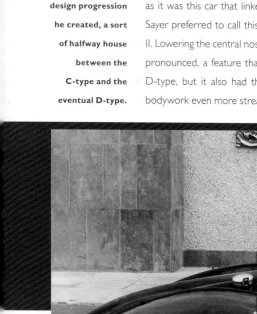

↓ **This XK 120C MKII prototype by Malcolm Sayer clearly shows the design progression he created, a sort of halfway house between the C-type and the eventual D-type.**

The all-conquering D-type

To say that the Jaguar XKD, or D-type as it was more widely known, was a development of the C-type is to skew the picture somewhat. In reality, the D-type only really shared its engine and running gear with its predecessor, but the C-type was without doubt the spiritual father to a whole generation of Jaguar racing cars which followed.

Once again, the D-type was produced explicitly for racing, being designed and created to spearhead the company's onslaught at Le Mans. It was intended to beat the Mercedes, Ferraris, Aston Martins and Cunninghams of the racing world and to bring glory and, of course, that all-important publicity to Jaguar. More significantly for Jaguar, the D-type represented a major step forward in the company's sports-car development programme, thanks to the aero-industry training and experience of Malcolm Sayer. In the process of the D-type's development, one of the typical methods of aircraft manufacture, that of riveting and bonding aluminium panels together, was clearly evident. Its unique and tremendously strong central tub, or monocoque, formed the basis of Jaguar's sports-car construction that followed, and signalled a move away from space frame to monocoque sports-car construction.

Brian Martin explains: 'The D was the first inroad into monocoque construction and that, without any doubt, was Malcolm Sayer's real contribution to the D because he

brought the methods of aircraft fabrication into motor-car manufacture.'

However, in Jaguar's own world of styling and design, and through no fault of his own, Malcolm Sayer was unfortunately trespassing on the very hallowed ground that had been the personal realm of the company's founder. In the words of Keith Helfet: 'I have enormous admiration for the "Old Man", but I think what had happened was that Malcolm Sayer had started to tread on Sir William's design toes here because that was his domain, and he loved designing. Unfortunately for Malcolm Sayer, Sir William was always the public figure of Jaguar design and he never really received the recognition he deserved for the cars he designed.'

One of the most significant steps taken by Malcolm Sayer was to turn the 'mouth' of the Jaguar from a vertical orientation (as in the XK 120 and XKC), to a horizontal orientation (as in the D-type), a design cue that has continued in Jaguar's sports-car design to this day. This move allowed him to sculpt a lower nose line and frontal section, thus creating a more streamlined

body which also had a smaller frontal area offering less wind resistance. Such was Sayer's attention to streamlining that the back end of the D-type was fashioned into a more tapered edge, thereby reducing the amount of air turbulence created at speed by the stubby end of the C-type. This entirely new style, created by Sayer, was to set the pattern for future sports-car design at Jaguar, right up to the end of the E-type era (1975).

As indicated above, one of Sayer's hallmarks was the use of advanced aircraft-construction methods in his cars. This is clearly visible in the C-type's successor, the D-type, with its central monocoque of riveted aluminium. The body's stiffness was enhanced with the use of internal sills that ran from the front to the rear, which were then strengthened by cross-bulkheads fore and aft. The car's separate body panels were then riveted to this central monocoque, making it not only very light but also extremely strong. The vertical fin installed behind the head of the driver significantly improved stability at speed, 'because it put the centre of pressure further back', explained Jim Randle, product engineering director at Jaguar from 1978 to 1991.

↑ In this close-up shot of the D-type, one can clearly see the rivet construction of the body panels as introduced by Malcolm Sayer.

← This contemporary press shot of the legendary D-type shows how the horizontal mouth of the car created by Malcolm Sayer effectively lowered the bonnet line, allowing a far more streamlined body shape.

As with the C-type, the D-type was created as a car with one aim: to win the Le Mans 24-Hour race. Although Jaguar had fielded a full works team on many occasions, some of their most notable victories were achieved by the Scottish Ecurie Ecosse team under David Murray's leadership. The D-type first appeared at Le Mans in 1954 as a Jaguar works car where it retired, but 1955 proved more successful as Jaguar took their only victory in a D-type as a full works team. Ecurie Ecosse were victorious at the famous Sarthe circuit in 1956, the event which signalled Jaguar's last appearance as a full works team for many years. Following the activities of the 1956 season, Bill Heynes and his engineers felt that the D-type had run its course and that a new race car would be needed if the company was to continue in motor sport.

How wrong they were, as the best was yet to come. 1957 was arguably the company's finest hour, as the Scottish Ecurie Ecosse team swept to victory in the most convincing fashion, with Jaguar D-types taking five of the top six places. The D-type's final appearance in Ecurie Ecosse team colours at Le Mans was in 1960, ending a remarkable run of six years, which is almost unheard of with modern race cars which are seldom used for more than one season.

However, one of the major constraints facing Bill Heynes and his team following the 1956 season was that the factory was running at full capacity with their production car programme, and the experience gained by the racing personnel through

motorsport was now required on the shop floor. Valuable lessons learned on the racing circuits of the world now had to be applied to their road cars, and there were no additional resources or spare capacity with which to develop a new race car. Even in the D-type's last days, suspension tests were being conducted that would shape the next generation of Jaguar sports cars. Brian Martin explains: 'We did run two D-types with independent suspension, one with a huge de Dion tube across it and one with a very rudimentary independent suspension, which is similar to the one that eventually went into E2A and then into the steel E-type.'

Although the factory's withdrawal from racing was seen as only a temporary measure, perhaps a year or so as Lofty England saw it, it would be almost another three decades before Jaguar would re-enter the world of motorsport with a full factory team. The main purpose of the factory's efforts on the race track was to gain publicity. To say that they had done well would be a massive understatement. Prior to the success of the C-type, Jaguar had enjoyed reasonably good sales worldwide, but following their racing achievements throughout the 1950s their sales were significantly boosted.

In the words of Keith Helfet, arguably one of Jaguar's most successful designers since the Sayer era: 'With the D-type, he [Malcolm Sayer] did his own thing; that was his first complete car, it wasn't just a modification. The D was just a piece of sculpture, it was gorgeous.'

↓ Ivor Bueb, this time partnered by Ron Flockhart, won the 1957 Le Mans 24-Hour race in the Ecurie Ecosse-liveried D-type. This year saw D-types taking 1st, 2nd, 3rd, 4th and 6th places, an unprecedented achievement.

← ← Two assembly workers riveting a D-type body in the Browns Lane competition shop.

← Jaguar D-type works victory at Le Mans driven by Mike Hawthorn and Ivor Bueb at a record-breaking average speed of 107.07mph, 1955.

Introduced in 1957, the XKSS, which was not a planned model in any way, came about as a result of the factory's attempts to use up the competition department's unsold D-type monocoques. It is not Keith Helfet's favourite Jaguar design: 'It's ugly actually. One can see the chronology of it, but I think it happened really by chance.'

These rather hairy-chested cars were basically converted from the excess short-nose production D-types and, in order to comply with road-going regulations in America, they were fitted with small doors, a full wrap-around windscreen and slim quarter bumpers. Any luggage had to be carried on a rear-mounted rack as there was no boot or other storage capacity.

As Tom Jones recalls: 'As a matter of fact, the idea really came from Duncan Hamilton. He had a D-type and he converted it into the SS and then he showed us what he had done. But that is where it came from, and we converted it in our service department. There was nothing major done really, there was no design, it was just done on the floor.'

One of the first attempts at this was the XKSS, a thinly disguised D-Type fitted with just enough equipment to make it street legal. Equipped with a 3.4-litre version of the XK engine essentially in race tune, it offered 250bhp at 5,750rpm. The Midland editor summed up in the 3 May, 1957 issue of *Autocar*: 'The Jaguar XKSS is a true-blue sports car in so much as it has racing characteristics with touring equipment.'

But on the other side of the coin, the XKSS, available only for export, set one back $5,600 in 1957 while a fuel-injected Corvette of the same year cost a little more than half as much. Further, the Corvette was a far more civilised automobile. By 1957 it had roll-up windows and a decent convertible top, while the XKSS was in most ways rudimentary. And because its engine was essentially ready for the track, it proved to be a handful to drive well on public roads.

Only 62 D-types had been produced between 1954 and 1956. In February 1957, and with a total of only 16 XKSS cars converted (a further two D-types were converted later, making the total of 18), a huge fire destroyed much of the factory at Browns Lane. Unfortunately, much valuable equipment and tooling in the competitions department was completely destroyed, putting paid to any hope of a quick return to the sport.

Although regarded by some as a rather crude road-going D-type, the XKSS did help to soak up some of the excess stock in the competition department, but following the fire of 1957 the XKSS with its quirky, dumpy looks passed without ceremony into the history books. While these cars may not be the prettiest Jaguars ever created, the XKSS nevertheless showed the design direction of Jaguar's next generation of sports car.

Aluminium prototype E-types

In the early 1950s, Tom Jones was the prototype designer at Jaguar responsible to Bill Heynes, and following a trip to the States to research the automatic transmissions for the saloon-car range, Heynes told Jones, 'I want you to run the competition car section'. In 1953, Jones took over the C-type chassis development and then went on to become chief chassis designer for the D-type and thereafter the first E-type.

Early in 1956, however, Tom Jones was given the instruction to prepare a competition successor to the D-type. This new car would follow in the racing footsteps of the D and was to be a natural evolution of its forerunner. 'Yes, what it was, was a bit of a hybrid of the D-type. The view was that Lyons wanted to

produce a sports car, but it had to be one that created an image that went with Jaguar's image and it had to be a very fast sports car. So this first one was just a very, very low key prototype following the D-type', recalled Norman Dewis.

Heynes intended to have this 'experimental' race car ready for the 1956 Le Mans 24-Hour, as Tom Jones remembers: 'The E-type was going to be the 1956 race car, definitely, because I was responsible to Bill Heynes for the chassis design.'

This first experimental E-type race car had an all-aluminium, unpainted body, and ran with a 2.4-litre engine. Although no photos of this car exist, Norman Dewis remembers that it was dimensionally very similar to the E1A which came a short while later. Fitted with an early version of Jaguar's independent rear suspension, this experimental D/E-type was intended for racing only, but as Dewis again recalls, there were a lot of experimental cars which had very short lives at Jaguar, and this one, sadly, did not survive. The car was developed into a running vehicle and even underwent testing, but, as Jones had not been given sufficient time to further develop the car properly, it was not ready in time for the 1956 Le Mans 24-Hour, and so the trusty D-types were brought back into service for that race.

Following the disappointing competition results by the factory team in 1956, Bill Heynes and his team felt that the bar in international sports car racing had once again been raised, and that the D-type had now run its course. It was time for a new car, but with the factory running at full capacity with

EIA has an unmistakable D-type shape and profile even though it is still very plain and unfinished at this stage.

their passenger-car programme, there was neither time nor spare resources to allocate to a new race-car project. With the factory racing programme now on hold, the D-types were sold to the Ecurie Ecosse team for £1,000 each and raced under the blue and white Scottish team colours in 1957 and 1958. As Tom Jones recalls: 'The launch of the Mark I [saloon car] was a bit of a disaster and it meant that all the workforce was spent on racing cars and not on the production cars, so it was decided then that we would pack up racing and that's what put the E-type on one side.' The experimental racing E-type prototype was subsequently destroyed in early 1957 after it was decided to discontinue with the racing programme. 'Phil Weaver was the superintendent in charge of the competition shop and he rang me to say that Bill Heynes informed him to scrap it', recalled Jones.

In its very early development stages, the E-prototype racer was clearly intended as a successor to the D-type, but as Jaguar had abandoned racing the concept of the E-type began to develop more along the lines of a road-going sports car. From all the success and experience gained on the track through innovative body streamlining and construction methods, there was no doubt that racing had improved the breed immeasurably.

Had this experimental E-prototype race car existed today, it would have been an incredibly valuable historical link in the story of the evolution of the final production E-type, but

despite getting the car running, the project didn't progress much further at that stage. Not to confuse this vehicle with the E1A which came a little later: 'It was just called the Experimental E-prototype. We certainly moved onto E1A which was the official one that we started to test. As I say, this was only basically put up as a styling exercise; we did make it into a runner, but we didn't do anything with it really', added Dewis.

Following that first experimental E-prototype, Malcolm Sayer came up with a slightly changed body style and that car became known as the E1A. Once Bill Heynes and Malcolm Sayer had agreed in principle to proceed with the next generation of Jaguar sports car, things began to develop more positively in this area. It is, however, interesting to note that Jaguar used very few prototype cars throughout the period of testing and development of the legendary E-type. We shall see in the next section that all the prototypes developed were quite different from each other, but with each one bequeathing some design or construction elements towards the final production E-type.

The prototype's designation of E1A referred basically to the first in a series of E-type production prototypes, while the 'A' indicated an aluminium body. This early running prototype (registered VKV 752) featured a combined forward-hinging bonnet and wing section, which followed in the C- and D-type tradition. The body lines were very clean and simple and, with hindsight, one could already see the early resemblance between this car and the final production model. In structure,

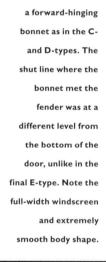

↓ **E1A was fitted with a forward-hinging bonnet as in the C- and D-types. The shut line where the bonnet met the fender was at a different level from the bottom of the door, unlike in the final E-type. Note the full-width windscreen and extremely smooth body shape.**

it was very similar to the D, with a front sub-assembly frame carrying the suspension and motor, and a monocoque tub and rear section. The monocoque rear section already hinted at the production-oriented design, replacing the D-type frame structure which was not practical for mainstream production and far too costly to manufacture.

It was clear at this stage that Malcolm Sayer and Bill Heynes wanted to continue down the design route of a new sports car that followed in the style of the D-type and XKSS, and to make a clean break from the now outdated XK 150 styling. Brian Martin recalls: 'Well you've got more progression there you see, because the first E1A was a follow-on from that [D-type].' Modern auto-body construction methods began favouring an all-steel monocoque anyway, so Heynes and Sayer pressed ahead at that stage without the blessing of Sir William Lyons, who was initially known not to be very enthusiastic about the proposed style of the new prototype sports car. This was perhaps partly because he was not driving this development himself, and it therefore wasn't really 'his' design. His only real input was with certain styling details later.

In the late-1950s, from a purely developmental perspective, the era of the separate body and chassis construction was in its death throes. When one considers the old style of construction of positioning an engine on top of a heavy chassis, and then placing a welded body on top of that, it was inevitable that the resulting structure was going to be fairly tall. Taking the D-type

Mark I saloon engine production line. Despite this low-specification motor, the E1A was surprisingly swift and agile with a 130mph top speed, but this was achieved after more than just a little testing by Norman Dewis. The E1A could accelerate from 0–60mph in 10.5 seconds and could pull away in top gear from as little as 10mph. The sleek and smooth body was devoid of any bonnet bulge as seen on the D-type and XKSS, because the shorter ('shorter' referred to the stroke which was 76.5mm on the smaller power plant and 106mm stroke on the bigger 3.4 and 3.8-litre motors – the engines were dimensionally very similar except for the reduced height of the actual motor) 2.4-litre engine sat lower in the body and did not require the high bonnet clearance of the bigger XK unit.

Jaguar test driver Norman Dewis had his work cut out with testing and retesting, changing wheel castor and camber, brakes, cooling, wind deflection and all the other aspects of new model assessment. The E1A was later fitted with attractive tapering side screens, but always remained an open car with no hood being made for it.

Suspension man Bob Knight, worked on the E-type chassis and was also responsible for the development of the independent rear suspension which started life in the E1A. Brian Martin recalls: 'It was very similar to the production E-type but with different bottom links and single-coil spring damper units instead of twins each side, and it had in-board disc brakes. The basic design was very similar as was E2A, but not the same. And

The prototype's designation of E1A referred basically to the first in a series of E-type production prototypes, while the 'A' indicated an aluminium body. This early running prototype (registered VKV 752) featured a combined forward-hinging bonnet and wing section, which followed in the C- and D-type tradition.

construction method forward as the basis for a new sports-car range allowed the new production body styling to become more sleek and streamlined, lighter and lower to the ground.

The E1A, which began its test life in 1958, was devoid of headlamps at first, and, contrary to popular perception, it was longer than the D-type but slightly shorter than the eventual production E-type. Being therefore a fairly small car with a lightweight aluminium body, it was powered by a standard 2,483cc twin-carburettor engine taken from the 2.4-litre

the biggest thing of course was that on E1A, the suspension was built into the car, assembled into the car rather than being built as a totally separate sub-frame which then could be fitted in its entirety into the car.'

Norman Dewis's job was to test the E1A, and to improve its ride and handling. 'So E1A was the forerunner, the first viewing of an E-type style, not with the correct engine. It started off with a small 2.4 engine, but it also got introduced with the independent rear suspension. So a lot

of work was done on E1A, I really got it into a nice motor car.' he remarked.

If the factory had abandoned its recent successful motorsport programme because they were running at full steam on passenger-car production, one might reasonably ask how and under whose authority did the E1A sports-car project progress.

Norman Dewis explains: 'It was started by Bill Heynes; he was the director of engineering. He basically looked at it as a follow-on to the D-type in conjunction with Sayer, of course. It was looked at as a competition car, as a starter, but again we were looking at a smaller car.' The rationale behind the whole project was that, being a smaller car, it could conceivably have gone into production later on if it had proved successful in competition first.

Once again, the E1A prototype provided many excellent opportunities for engineering and design development and after the lessons and experience had been accumulated, those developments were built into the next prototype and the E1A prototype was broken up. Dewis again: 'It was broken up just

after we got E2A, because once we had got E2A, E1A became redundant really, and all that you have learned from E1A was transferred to E2A, so you are progressing all the time.'

In true fashion, Malcolm Sayer was always working at improving what he had already designed, and in late 1958, he and Bill Heynes began with the next prototype in the sequence, E2A. During the development of the production E-type (E1A), it had conceptually been the intention to include a competition car (E2A) in the mix and so the appearance of a race car did not take long to materialise.

However, this small, light-green prototype had a hard test life of about two years, eventually being cut up and sent as scrap to the company's contracted Kensington scrap merchants. Now relegated to the history books, the E1A was seen by only a tiny handful of people outside the factory development department, but what that car would have meant to the company's museum today, had it been preserved, can only be imagined.

While the E1A experimental car was steadily racking up the test miles, Jaguar engineers were hard at work on the E2A, a

car which many hoped would bring Jaguar back to the starting grid at Le Mans. With a vast amount of development work having been carried out on the E1A, the technology and styling improvements were simply transferred to this new test bed.

With racing rather than volume production in mind, the E2A was a sophisticated machine for its day, so what was the justification behind the expense of preparing a single car if the company had no real intention of re-entering the racing world with a works team? Jim Randle explains: 'They were thinking about the XJ13 around that time and where they were going to go for the next car and sort of trying to work out how the rules were going to change. And I guess that was sort of staying in touch as much as anything else.'

The feeling among several of the senior engineering staff at the time was that Jaguar would have built another two or three E2A-type cars and entered them as a works team, but looking beyond just the motorsport possibilities, the E2A also hinted at Sayer's future sports-car styling. Although there were no production plans for E2A, as the car had been developed

purely as a race car, it was nevertheless an indication of how keen Jaguar was to go racing again.

Dewis continued to carry out testing and development work on the E2A until one day Sir William Lyons got a phone call from Briggs Cunningham who wanted to compete in the Le Mans 24-Hour, and he asked Lyons if they had a car he could buy for this purpose. A meeting was called to discuss the request and Bill Heynes suggested to Sir William that Cunningham could use E2A, but Dewis pointed out that they would need to comply with the new regulations which limited engine capacity to just 3.0 litres. Up to that stage, the E2A prototype had undergone testing fitted with the standard 3.4-litre engine, but fortunately, according to Norman Dewis, a 3.0-litre engine was in the pipeline, no doubt the product of some competition planning by Wally Hassan which had taken place behind the scenes in the event of this being required.

Sir William agreed to the proposal with certain strict conditions, recalls Dewis with a smile: 'Briggs Cunningham

↑ The rear view of E2A shows a smoother although heavier line than that of the D-type.

↑ **E2A in the pits during the Le Mans 24-Hour race, 1960.**

must not say it was a works car, it was his car, and that I, Dewis would have to be with the car at Le Mans. Again: "You've requested Dewis, we haven't sent him"'. In other words, what Sir William was trying to do was keep the Jaguar company out of the picture, but at the same time supply the car from the company and provide factory know-how in the form of Norman Dewis to observe and advise where necessary.

This didn't give Norman Dewis much time in which to get the E2A ready for the 1960 24-hour race, but all the stops were pulled out and Dewis was able to work his magic. The only exposure that E2A got outside of the factory was at the 1960 Le Mans 24-Hour, but in many ways this prototype race

car is an interesting one and shows how advanced Jaguar was in streamlining and lightweight body construction. It had an all-aluminium body and was fitted with a 3.0-litre version of the XK engine with a racing-type dry sump system, aluminium block and triple carburettors to start with, but these were later replaced with mechanical fuel injection.

Unfortunately, the E2A bowed out with mechanical failure in the sixth hour but despite this unsuccessful outing, it nevertheless provided an additional and valuable platform on which to analyse the car's aerodynamic and handling performance. The car was then brought back to the factory and fitted with a larger 3.8-litre motor after which Cunningham took it over to the States where it enjoyed some limited competition success.

The E2A is clearly another important link in the evolutionary chain of the production E-type, as it resembled the finned, long-nose D-type but was perhaps closer in appearance to the production E because it was narrower and longer than the D-type. Similar in style at the front to the production E, its wing lines run straight back without any sweeping curves to a rather hunched rear end. Now sporting a full-width windscreen in accordance with race regulations, the E2A at this stage showed a very strong resemblance to the final production E-type. The E2A is perhaps not the prettiest sports car to look at as the body had to comply with sporting regulations which required a certain amount of 'luggage' space at the back while the rear

Taken ten years after its Le Mans debut, E2A is piloted around Gaydon Airfield by owner Penny Graham with Ted Eves (Autocar journalist) riding as passenger (1970).

COMPARATIVE DATA AND SPECIFICATIONS FOR D-TYPE, XKSS AND E-SERIES PROTOTYPES

	1955	1957	1958	1958	1960	1961
	D-type	XKSS	E1A	Prototype	E2A	Production
Details	Racer	Sports car	Prototype	Red No. 1	Racer	E-type Roadster
Engine	3,442cc	3,442cc	2,483cc	3,442cc	2,997cc	3,781cc
Output	250bhp	250bhp	112bhp	250bhp	295bhp	265bhp
Length	12' 10"	13' 10"	14' 1³/₄"	***	14' 2"	14' 7¹/₂"
Width	5' 5³/₈"	5' 5³/₈"	5' 2³/₄"	***	5' 2³/₄"	5' 4¹/₄"
Height	2' 7¹/₂"*	2' 7¹/₂"*	32"*	***	3' 8³/₄"**	3'11" (with hood)
Weight	1,904lbs	2,016lbs	1,766lbs	1,925lbs	1,925lbs	2,688lbs

*Scuttle height   **Windscreen height   ***Close to final production dimensions

flanks featured flared air ducts which fed air to the inboard disc brakes. The bonnet of the E2A had the familiar central power bulge to accommodate the original 3.4-litre engine and this was left unchanged for the 3.0-litre power unit.

Anders Clausager, chief archivist at the Jaguar Daimler Heritage Trust commented: 'E2A was intended for racing, but development along these lines was given up when the car was found to be uncompetitive. Indeed at the time, prototype cars which raced at Le Mans were restricted to a max engine size of 3.0 litres and the Jaguar XK engine in 3.0-litre form probably was not competitive against Ferraris of similar engine size.'

In production timescales, the E2A was very close to the E-type that was launched at the Geneva Motor Show in March

1961, as only nine months separated the 1960 Le Mans 24-Hour race and the E-type's Swiss launch. In fact, the preparation of E2A for the Cunningham onslaught at Le Mans set back the development of the production E-type by several months at a crucial time in the programme. As a model, E2A had a very short lifespan at the factory and it spent much of its time in America following its unsuccessful attempt at the 1960 Le Mans 24-Hour.

Brian Martin remembers: 'E2A was probably laid down first, but certainly there was a steel E-type running around at the time that E2A was running around, so there wasn't a progression that "right we've built E2A now we're going to build a steel one". It was being done at the same time.'

← Penny Graham with Ted Eves in E2A again at Gaydon Airfield. This side profile clearly shows the higher rear end which incorporated air scoops for cooling the rear brakes (1970).

Steel-body prototypes

'The next one was the production steel car; E2A came after that. E2A and the early steel E-types were in time scales very close together.' recalls Brian Martin.

At this time the factory began to look more seriously at the E-type from a production point of view, and how it could be made into a sports car that would sell. Norman Dewis remembers that Sir William Lyons's policy was that, 'it hadn't got to cost a lot of money', and so for development and testing purposes, the experimental steel-bodied E-types were fitted with standard 3.4-litre engines.

There were not many prototypes used in the development of the E-type, but each of them played an extremely important role and as such, each one had a definite place in the E-type story. It was decided fairly early on in this process that aluminium was not the route to go with the production cars, and so the first steel-bodied E was developed in the experimental shop. This first car, which was started in early 1958, was never intended to be anything other than a static model in the experimental shop and was only brought to life following an instruction from Bill Heynes, in order for Norman Dewis to assess it as a runner. However, with the 'car' still only a static model, its body shaped over a wooden former and secured to the floor of the experimental shop, the engineers had to work around the clock to lift the body panels off the wooden buck and to form them together into a whole car and make it into a runner.

This prototype, which Dewis ran for about four months, was very hastily put together for testing purposes, became known as the 'pop rivet special', because its panels were assembled and fastened together with pop rivets. Dimensionally, this vehicle more closely resembled the final production E-type than its predecessor, the E1A. Finished in pearl grey, this was the second E-type in the development of the eventual production road car and this car's preparation from static model to a running prototype took just a week. According to Tom Jones, the panel-beaters working in the experimental shop were actually seconded from Abbey Panels, because Sir William had vowed never to hire any panel-beaters again after the strike at Jaguar a few years earlier. There were five panel-beaters from Abbey Panels who were responsible for knocking out the first E-types on the wooden bucks in the experimental shop.

Comparing the bonnet shape of the E1A and E2A prototypes, one can see that there is a similarity of smoothness across the bonnet, but also a definite progression in styling between the two cars. According to Norman Dewis, Sayer then took this bonnet style and working further with the design developed the more-shapely E-type bonnet with more pronounced wing lines and an altogether more shapely finish. Following further extensive tests with the E1A and the 'pop rivet special',

→ Called 'Red No. 1' by Norman Dewis, this roadster served as a faithful test car for around 18 months. Still in test trim, it is missing the chrome headlamp surrounds, windscreen stiffener bar (note rear-view mirror mounted on the dash), and horizontal bonnet-mouth motif bar. This car still has the external bonnet handles and, although not visible in this picture, the rear lights were like those on the D-type/XKSS.

'As you can imagine, a lot of today's testing is done theoretically, but there was very little theory to go on in those days – you built a motor car, and all you could do was take it out there and drive it. It was a very, very hard and tiring job, routinely driving for hours and hours and hours.'

Brian Martin – Jaguar Cars (1949–67 and 1972–78).

WORKING EXPERIMENTAL PROTOTYPES IN THE DEVELOPMENT OF THE E-TYPE

Car description	Production date	Engine	Colour	Application
E1A	December 1957	2,483cc	Light green	First experimental prototype
Pop rivet special	February 1958	3,442cc	Pearl grey	Second experimental prototype
E2A	Late 1959	2,997cc	Blue & cream	Racing car
Production style	September 1959	3,442cc	Cotswold Blue	Third experimental prototype

two further cars were made in the experimental shop which showed for the first time a prototype much closer to the finished production E-type, a Carmen red roadster and a metallic-grey fixed-head coupé (see Chapter 3).

'The first E-type I had was painted red, it was very basic. I always call that one 'Red E-type number 1', that was the first prototype, an open car. We had got it with a 3.4 engine, independent rear suspension and I had just been working on improving the disc brakes; we had made some changes on the disc thickness. I would say that was the beginning of '59, when I first started with the first one, because I went nearly eighteen months on that car', recalled Dewis. This car was the first production-style E-type with which Norman Dewis conducted extensive testing.

Besides the normal development and testing which Dewis carried out on new models, he also had to consider legislation which was coming through from America concerning emission controls and safety factors, especially

regarding braking, and they were introducing front and rear impact tests. It wasn't being pushed hard at that stage, but these new requirements were obviously going to make an impact on future models, and with America being their most important market Lyons was keen to consider these requirements early on.

Following the fabrication of 'Red E-type No. 1', there did not seem to be a lot of E-type body development taking place, and two years later the production E-type popped out onto the world stage. With just a few styling changes, the final production E-type was actually developed in a fairly short space of time considering the amount of hands-on time spent on the vehicle. Although this is perhaps a slightly distorted picture, because the D-type had provided a large chunk of expertise and knowledge through the company's motorsport programme, not a lot of time was allocated to the development of the final production E-type because of the production demands of the saloon-car range. ■

Jaguar styling

'For those few among us who are totally committed to excellence in all things'

Jaguar sports car advertisement

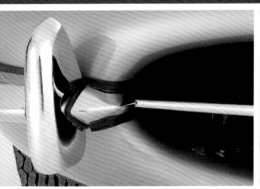

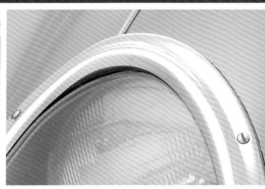

1958	1959	1960	1961
E-type car begins as a concept	Steel bodied E-type tested by Norman Dewis	E2A competes at Le Mans 24-Hour	E-type launched at Geneva Show

No designer is bigger than the car he designs. A designer is merely the custodian of the brand that he is working on, and his task must be to convey the message of that brand through modernising the model's identity created by that car's previous designers. A designer seeking fame and recognition through the cars he designs is seeking the wrong goal and in the process doing the brand a disservice. It is the car that will live on in history and it is the public, not the designer, who will pass judgement on its style. This is confirmed by Keith Helfet, designer of the awesome Jaguar XJ220: 'The people who actually decide are the public, they are incredibly astute.'

When compared with its predecessors, the E-type's styling was like that of no other production sports car Jaguar had ever made. In order to trace its design lineage, however, one must not look to its road-going forerunner, the XK 150, but to its cousin, the D-type, which was designed for the racing circuits of the world. The foregoing range of sports cars in the Jaguar stable, namely the XK 120, XK 140 and XK 150 had all been the work of Sir William Lyons and the styling heritage from the first of these models in 1948 through to its final form in 1960, is quite clear. The styling trend created by Bill Lyons for the pack of Jaguars in the 1940s and 1950s was graceful, sleek and immortal, but if one was to dare to pick a weak point, it would be that they were just a little heavy by modern, late-1950s standards. Up to that point, Sir William Lyons was Jaguar's designer-in-chief, and therefore ultimately responsible

many designers, and even fewer company executives, possessed. How then did Lyons produce the world-beating looks of Jaguar without all of the necessary qualifications? Keith Helfet explains: 'I just think he did what he thought was right and what he liked.'

Lacking any formal tertiary education, Bill Lyons would sit for hours in his special design studio instructing his 'tinnies', a specially selected band of metal workers and body craftsmen, in the design which he saw in his mind. This hand-picked group of men would beat out the lines and shapes straight into metal, full scale, without the use of any drawings or plans, and many of these initial forms would be sent to his residence, Wappenbury Hall near Leamington Spa in Warwickshire, for further viewing.

Brian Martin remembers: 'He was not a draughtsman, never had any draughting experience at all. He had a gifted eye, the ability to see the shape; his difficulty was trying to impose that thought on people who could do something with it. There would be a lot of hammering and banging and making different shapes.'

He continues: 'Now Malcolm Sayer was just the opposite and I think that is why they were successful together. Malcolm was a pure aerodynamicist, and worked very much in the early age of computers, but with his engineering and draughtsmanship background, he could draw a complete motor car. I have seen him do it, a whole full-sized car on the wall and from his mind's

for all of Jaguar's saloon and sports-car design and styling, a task over which he had firm control, and his own very definite set of ideas.

It is well known that Sir William Lyons had no real ability to draw, at least not as would normally be expected in a world-class automobile designer working for a motor manufacturer of the likes of Jaguar. However, being born with a natural eye for style and being able to see a finished three-dimensional image in one's mind with uncanny accuracy was a gift that not

eye he could generate the dimensions; now Sir William could never do that in a million years.'

William Lyons's way was no less effective; his was just a slower process than drawing a line and saying ,'I want it like this'. To compound matters slightly, Sir William was not known by his contemporaries as a good communicator, which made his method of verbal instruction to his metal workers all the more critical. Seen in this light, his achievements appear even more remarkable. This approach, though far from being scientific,

Design – the way it used to be

When considering the development of a new model in the early days, somebody would say first and foremost, 'We want to build a motor car'. The question was then more likely, how do you build it, and the construction and assembly, even the finishing, was down to the engineers. There might be some liaison between Engineering and Marketing during the process, but only in so far as the final car's market potential was concerned and usually only towards the end of the vehicle's development phase.

'Marketing, Advertising and Sales were part and parcel of the same department', according to Brian Martin, and there was no PR department as we know it today. As Engineering and Design were also part of one department, it became the responsibility of the Sales department to sell the cars that the Engineering department produced.

A new model was generally developed on the back of the success of the preceding model, as Brian Martin explains, 'And only then, somebody went to Advertising and Marketing and said, well here is the car, it's your job to go out and sell it, thank you very much. And very often, the first thing that Advertising and Marketing would know about it, would be when it was a finished car, basically'.

enabled Sir William, in his own way, to create some of the most stunning designs the automotive world has ever seen. For Sir William, this was a work style which he had developed and honed over many years, right from the very first car he designed. Free of the constraints of corporate accountability or fashion influences, Sir William was interested only in creating designs which reflected a style that people aspired to, rather than one which followed a trend dictated by others. Allied to this skill, was his ability to interpret where the market was heading and to produce designs to meet those requirements at the right time.

He was certainly very innovative in his pursuit of the perfect style, using a wide variety of methods to achieve his final design. According to John Maries, 'Bill Lyons was well known for getting a mock-up of the car and shining lights on it and seeing where the highlights were. Bill Lyons was doing styling by shining lights. But also he had this ability to actually look at a car and to just make minor tweaks so that he was happy with it.'

Keith Helfet, who worked with Sir William in his final years, explains: 'The thing that struck me about Sir William was that here was a guy in his 80s who was firstly incredibly open to new ideas. He loved new ideas, he wasn't conservative. And of course when you look at the stuff he did, nothing was ever conservative about Jaguar; it was all sort of mould-breaking stuff.'

Motor-car design up until the mid-1950s was all about presence and making a big statement with graceful, sweeping lines. Certain constraints like technology and materials played a part in influencing vehicle size in Britain and Europe, while across the Atlantic, a belief in endless supplies of steel and oil meant that size and fuel efficiency never really entered the equation in America in any meaningful way. In the style of the day, cars were constructed on a large, heavy chassis which meant that the engine and body sat 'on top' of the chassis, resulting in a relatively high structure. For Jaguar, as with most other motor manufacturers at the time, fitting the straight-six XK engine into the chassis and body of a sports car inevitably resulted in design challenges, which saw most sports cars featuring high engine compartments. In order to accommodate this inevitability, a tall radiator and grille adorned the front of most cars and to achieve a sleek flowing body behind this structure was a constant challenge for most designers. Sir William Lyons did better than most of his competitors in reducing the car's bonnet height by sloping the radiator of the XK 120 backwards, thus creating a sleeker body style.

John Maries, Jaguar marketing manager in the 1980s, expands: 'There was a reaction to wartime poverty, if you like, austerity, and so the 1950s were very much about elegance and style.'

Indeed, an analysis of Jaguar's styling up until the late 1950s will show that the sweeping lines of the cars' flanks followed

➤An XK 120 engine and chassis showing the substantial strength of the separate-chassis construction.

those of the cycle fenders style of earlier automobiles – up over the front wheels, down towards the door and up over the rear wheels again. Nothing innovative about that, it's just that Sir William made it look so sensuous and graceful. The SS100 was a good example of this, but after the War, the XK 120 went a step further with its enclosed fenders, known within the industry as the envelope style, so named because the fenders 'enveloped' the wheels. This styling accentuated the muscular character of the sports car but at the same time created a very graceful and elegant look which appealed to the sporty nature of its driver. The Americans later called it 'Coke bottle' styling when Bill Mitchell introduced the Chevrolet Camaro, but back in 1948, it was the natural flair of William Lyons that successfully captured this design feature.

John Maries again: 'It actually provides that "Jaguar" look, side-on. The rear haunches of the car look very much like the animal, and you can actually see that the rear wheel arch is like the rear legs of an animal as it leaps forward. And the wonderful thing about a Jaguar is, when you look at it, you don't confuse it with anything else. That is a Jaguar.'

Julian Thomson, current chief designer in Jaguar's advanced studio sums it up this way: 'If you look at William Lyons and when he did his groundbreaking cars, they certainly weren't influenced particularly strongly by the model that had gone before them. He was very much trying to create the best he could at that point in time, and so he went forward with great

technical innovation and great aesthetic innovation and great segment innovation.'

Most pre-war motor vehicles were constructed according to the engineering constraints or material limitations of the day, not by parameters set down by market demand, so vehicles tended to be larger because therein lay the strength of the body. It is therefore fair to say that the design of the cars in this era was engineering led, and the market expected this, as they were, by and large, not used to anything different. In those early days, the sales department sold whatever the engineering and production departments could produce; that was how motor manufacturers developed and produced cars, and customers didn't expect the process to be any different so there was no great need for the manufacturers to change things.

Over-engineering was quite normal in many cars right up until the time of the E-type's introduction, because it provided the manufacturer with the satisfaction that the car's occupants would be better protected. The result was that most cars were extremely heavy and many a car could fell a reasonably sized tree with little damage to itself, which gave the driver and occupants of the vehicle a certain sense of safety. That this perception of safety was quite false due to the lack of seatbelt usage did not enter their minds. Despite this overkill in engineering and body strength, there were some incredibly beautiful motor car designs produced during this period.

↓ **Visible in the National Motor Museum at Beaulieu are the distinctly different lines along the flanks of the XK 150 on the left, and the XK 120 on the right.**

To understand the dynamics of sports-car styling in the post-war automotive world, one needs to take a step back to the time when sports cars were not a common sight. Brian Martin explains: 'Sports cars were only for the rich; they were very expensive; they weren't regarded as the thing you normally drove around in as a means of conveyance: they were very much a rich man's toy.'

This then brings into focus the risk taken by Jaguar in producing 'volume' motor vehicles for a market which did not have much money to spend on a luxury such as a motor car. Martin again: 'If you think about it, a company like Jaguar sets out in 1948/49 to build luxury cars in a depressed market immediately after a major World War where there aren't any buyers, no money. It's a pretty brave enterprise isn't it? And I think it is fortunate that they were able to identify and successfully penetrate the American market, otherwise I don't think Jaguar would have lived at all, wouldn't have survived.'

As surely as economic growth follows a period of conflict, so do the aspirations of people grow as they plan a new life in the stability of the aftermath of war. William Lyons knew this, and so he set out to provide cars for aspirational buyers. This is one of the main reasons why the American market so enthusiastically embraced the XK 120 when it hit the showrooms in 1948/49.

Today's Jaguar stylists refer to the 'shock factor' which Lyons created so successfully with each new model he launched, and this does not refer only to the car's low price; it was the sheer beauty and elegance of the vehicle which caused this reaction. This was certainly true with the SS100, the XK 120 and the E-type, all of which represented a new era in sports-car design at Jaguar. The shock factor, as described by Julian Thomson is, 'Not caring about what went before', and moving boldly forward with innovation.

With hindsight we can see that many people have bought Jaguar cars because they felt they were buying a little bit of England, or to the real diehards it even meant owning a little slice of Coventry. But William Lyons wasn't so much worried about establishing a great British tradition; he was preoccupied with creating great cars that people would buy. He succeeded in doing just that, as John Maries explains: 'Jaguar had a little trace of niche about it, certainly for many a long year, our customers would buy nothing else. I would meet people who had had 17 Jaguars, one after another, you know, wouldn't dream of buying anything else.'

Understanding the 1960s Jaguar customer

In the time which led up to the introduction of the E-type Jaguar, it was the changing profile of the traditional sports car buyer and indeed the usage of the sports car itself, which had altered so radically. Where previously a sports car was principally a competition vehicle with little or no thought given to comfort, or was perhaps a highly tuned version of a road car stripped out for increased performance, the sports car genre was beginning to undergo a transformation by the late 1950s.

Higher performance potential in sports cars gave rise to increased competition on the tracks, and this development gradually began to separate the enthusiasts from the more professional drivers as competition cars became more specialised. This meant that where previously an enthusiast would use his car for both competition and private purposes, now, in order to remain competitive as an amateur racing driver, he would need to upgrade to a more dedicated race car, keeping a second car for business or family use. This development began to separate the men from the boys as it required an increasing commitment of time and financial investment to purchase and maintain a competitive racing car, and an amateur XK 120 driver would now have to consider the expense of running a C-type or D-type.

Were sports car enthusiasts able to continue to afford two or more cars, one of which was a dedicated sports car, then there would have been no need for any compromise on comfort in the high-performance dual-personality sports-car genre. However, as car manufacturers realised this, sports cars began to take on features that allowed an enthusiast to consider making such a sports car his daily transport while still providing that element of sportiness. No longer did owners want to tinker with the tuning of their car's sophisticated high-performance engine just for a trip down to the local shops, they preferred to 'get in and go'. Increasingly, therefore, sports cars developed more as grand tourers leaving the specialist sports machines to the more dedicated competitor who did not mind the lack of comfort and a harsh ride.

This change in the characteristics of the sports car during the post-war years was driven by several factors, namely, a different set of criteria demanded by the customers themselves, and the very fact that improved technology meant that more and more cars than ever before could reach the magic 'ton'. So speed was no longer the only factor to be

considered when selecting which sports car to buy; it had also to do with style, comfort and ride. Through the 1950s and 1960s, the sports car was increasingly used for Continental travel, and it therefore needed to have a boot of sufficient size to carry luggage for two. The days of whizzing off to an exotic European destination in your fast two-seater, only to send your luggage on ahead by rail because there was insufficient space in the sports car, were long gone.

The Americans, too, it seems had changed their minds about what constituted a sports car. *Autocar* (1962) stated: 'It seems that to Americans, a sporty car is something small, fast and foreign.' This development came about following the return of servicemen from Europe who possessed a newly found appreciation of what performance machinery was available across the Atlantic and of the lack of comparable cars for them back home.

Features such as wind-up side windows, reclining seats and occasional seats in the back for children, better wind and weather protection and even the option of air-conditioning became regular features in sports cars. Softer suspension was introduced; better sound insulation kept excessive exhaust noise at bay, while a detachable hard top still gave the owner of a grand tourer the option of wind-in-the-hair driving. However, all of this added weight to the car and this is where the concept of the original sports car was

compromised – lightweight, swift and nimble versus powerful, heavier and more comfortable. It's what is known as the evolution of the sports car, and the E-type Jaguar developed and survived in the market by successfully adapting to the demands of a more exacting sports car buyer.

But what was it that drove people to buy a Jaguar, specifically? This is indeed a question that is as valid today as it was back in the 1950s and 1960s, when the E-type Jaguar was being developed. However, as we have seen, the market has changed dramatically in the past 50 years and while the rationale for buying a Jaguar today may well be quite different from what it used to be, the emotional demand nevertheless still exists.

When Jaguar introduced the XK8 in 1996, they sought to reduce the average buying age of the car by about ten years, which meant that where previously most Jaguar sports cars had been bought by 55-year-olds, they were now aiming at the younger, 40-something age group. This had several advantages, the first being that Jaguar would sell more cars, and secondly that they could secure buyer loyalty at an earlier age, thereby ensuring continued customer loyalty as those buyers matured into their saloon-car years. This required a different marketing approach that appealed to the new, younger group, but at the same time it could not afford to alienate those stalwarts who were already established Jaguar sports-car drivers.

➔ **The XK 150 was a popular car in the States with both male and female drivers.**

This type of market research was not carried out back in the 1950s because it wasn't considered necessary, as the typical Jaguar customer was easily identifiable and nowhere near as demanding and sophisticated as he or she may be today. Present-day motor cars and associated advertising campaigns target very specific age groups and even sexes, whereas in the days of old, if your father or uncle drove a Jaguar, that was more than enough reason for you to do the same when the time came. Only through market and customer research carried out recently have the motor manufacturers come to identify which buttons to push in order to get a customer to buy their product.

Keith Helfet remembers how enlightening this was: 'We knew from the market research we were doing at the time that Egan took over Jaguar (1980), every sale was researched, three months and nine months after purchase, so they had data as to why people bought the cars – and basically it was emotion.'

Jaguar survived through those early days because of that

emotion, although this was not known at the time. Helfet continues: 'People bought Mercedes and BMWs for rational reasons; they bought Jaguars for emotional reasons, because they wanted one. And they had to find reasons to justify the buy because the resale value was poor and their reliability at one stage was very poor.'

Usually, when a buyer is contemplating the purchase of a new vehicle, there will be one name on the shortlist which sticks up head and shoulders above the others, whether this preference is due to brand loyalty or for emotional reasons. Even when the decision is a foregone conclusion, the buyer may often consider, albeit briefly, an alternative vehicle or vehicles even if it serves only to justify his preferred choice. Finding out what creates that preference is what marketers do, and today they do it very well and very thoroughly. Research has shown that one's formative years in this process of preference creation are between the ages of 11 and 14 and for any young car enthusiast who was around that age when the E-type was introduced, just seeing the sleek new

↑ The XK 150 looks stunning in this country scene. The left-hand drive and white-wall tyres combination would suggest that this was taken in an American setting.

Some day, some day.

JAGUAR

→ **Although depicting a more modern XJ6 in this advertisement, the 'Some day, some day' strap line illustrates the power of the emotional purchase decision being taken at a young age.**

Jaguar's marketers knew this when the XK8 was introduced and they were confident that they would be able to attract a significant number of those youngsters from the 1960s who could now afford to buy a Jaguar sports car. As an example, an 11-year-old youngster in 1961 would have been 46 years of age by 1996 when the XK8 was launched, placing this potential new Jaguar buyer in the middle of the age group being targeted by the company 35 years after the launch of the E-type. John Maries confirms this: 'When I used to go out promoting Jaguars in the 1980s, guys in their 50s, our typical customer, would come up to me and they would say, "I've done it, I've bought my Jaguar, and do you know I made my mind up when I was 11".'

This phenomenon was pounced on by a number of manufacturers, as well as Jaguar. In the 1970s, Jaguar ran a print ad showing a little schoolboy with his satchel, wearing his short trousers and a cap, looking into a dealer's showroom with the strap line, 'Some day, some day'. That message was so evocative that when Jaguar started to do television advertising years later, they ran an ad which referred back to the early years of preference creation, just as they had with that schoolboy.

Creating a lasting demand for a product cannot be the result of a clever marketing campaign alone, and so producing the right mixture of emotion, desire and function is the result of manufacturing the right product to satisfy your customers'

sports car on the showroom floor would have left a lasting impression.

The purchase decision would have done a full circle by the time those youngsters reached the age of being able to afford a Jaguar, as many of them would return to the car of their dreams, represented now by Jaguar's current sports car.

↓ **The purposeful sports car – this stylish photo of an American-spec Series I E-type shows a model with a detachable hard top.**

aspirations. It sounds simple, but finding out what makes a great sports car is no simple matter, especially if it has to carry Jaguar's torch.

Julian Thomson, a Jaguar designer suggests that '…sports cars should trigger different emotional responses to normal cars. They should be much more exciting, they should reflect a sort of adrenalin in the character of the owner. A sports car is about being purposeful. So they have just got to combine all those passionate responses, and they've got to look great. Jaguars have got to be very beautiful cars, but they have also got to look very fast.'

The attraction of a good sports car is in its visual appeal, its performance and its supreme roadability, as the Americans term it. In order for a good sports car to achieve all of this, it must stand out from any of its competitors and indeed its own stable mates, providing a halo effect for the other models produced by the same manufacturer. As Julian Thomson explains: 'They mustn't be overly adorned with details and fussiness, and very, very important is the purity. They've got to reflect a high quality of engineering underneath.'

Producing a legendary sports car is not something that you set out to try and achieve. It is the result of long-term attention to detail, experimentation, refining, sporting achievements, quality of engineering and finish. Beauty and form come from the successful marriage of art and engineering, and a car that expresses this over a long period of time will earn the respect of those who appreciate such workmanship. In the field of true sports cars, it is often through the achievements of racing drivers who have tested the car in competition that its place in the history books as a great sports car is confirmed.

The process by which a Jaguar sports car is designed and the parameters and requirements around which it is shaped and finished are quite different from those of other sports cars. There is no doubt that the design of a Porsche 911 is realised by means of a very different process from the way in which a Lamborghini Diablo is designed. Julian Thomson confirms this: 'How you do that, and how important style is versus the function, that is just down to the choice of product [for the customer].'

Very little market research, if any, was carried out by British manufacturers in the 1950s and 1960s, but it is a certainty that people felt the same emotions back then when seeing the car of their dreams as they do today. The real difference for the customer is that, nowadays, the manufacturer knows more about the interpretations of those emotions than does the average customer himself, and as a result they know how to appeal more effectively to the modern-day buyer. In the 1950s and 1960s, customers would not have interpreted or understood the emotions they were feeling as well as they can today, and this has been brought about by the exposure of marketing methods through the various forms of media. ■

↓ The E-type was a practical sports car in its day with an easy-to-fit and attractive soft top for all-weather travel.

The E-type gestation period

'The influence of racing cars lends
the E-type its most striking
feature, its styling'

Museum of Modern Art, New York
Refining the Sports Car – Jaguar's E-type

1957	1958	1959	1960	1961
XK 150 launched in May – the final model in the XK sports car line	E-type car begins as a concept	3.8-litre engine available in XK 150 in October	E2A competes at Le Mans 24-Hour	E-type launched at Geneva Show

D-type design link to the E-type

Malcolm Sayer was an aerodynamicist and he was employed by Jaguar to design fast and efficient race cars. The XK 120, 140 and 150 sports cars were all made during his tenure, yet his brief at that time was only to improve upon Jaguar's race cars, and his styling influence was not evident in the company's road-going sports-car range until much later. Fuel consumption was not such a priority for the Jaguar buyer in those days, so there was no real call from the market for aerodynamic improvements to the saloon car range; besides, saloon-car design was very much the domain of William Lyons. Sayer's work, therefore, did not impinge directly on the territory of others in the factory, as the C-type, which was Jaguar's first purpose-built race car, and the D-type which followed it did not really draw on the heritage of any previous model, nor did the C-type influence the design thinking of any other current models. But once the success of the D-type had been demonstrated in competition, Heynes and Sayer sought to put all the development work that had been done on that vehicle to good use, in a new project.

Keith Helfet explains: 'It was obviously decided to replace the XK 150 at that point and in a sense that style statement [D-type] had been made, and Malcolm Sayer got the job of doing it.' The important observation here is that with hindsight, one can see that the D-type/XKSS clearly showed the development path of Jaguar's production sports cars that followed. Through this progression, Malcolm Sayer had created a body style that would allow Jaguar to develop and improve their sports car platform for decades to come. In some ways, these were uncharted waters for Sayer as he had never previously designed a fully-fledged production car, because within Jaguar that had only ever been down to Sir William Lyons. Looking at the D-type and E-type family lines, you can see a very clear chronology, but these are Malcolm Sayer's cars and not Sir William's. Malcolm Sayer was ushering in a fresh, new style, but Sir William must have been confident that he would have the ability to retain the quality of lines and the graceful style for which Jaguar had become renowned.

It must have been very tough for Sir William to hand over the design reins on the sports cars to Malcolm Sayer, a function which he had regarded as his own since the inception of the company. The style of each of these two masters was

Malcolm Sayer (far left) with Bill Heynes (hand on car) and other workshop colleagues attending an early D-type racer. Norman Dewis is at the wheel.

ROAD CARS: XK 120/140/150

E-type (combining features from both lines of heritage)

RACE CARS: C-type/D-type

unique to themselves, and their method of arriving at the final product could not have been more different.

The challenge for Jaguar, and Malcolm Sayer in particular, was to ensure a seamless transition between the outgoing XK 150 and the new E-type, while incorporating the new technology and construction methods of the racing D-type. Brian Martin worked on the early development bucks for the E-type: 'That is why the E is closely allied to the D-type because the method of assembly is very similar. The materials

are different obviously and the method of adjoining the materials is different, but the principle is exactly the same.'

This smooth changeover to the new model came about because the construction of the E-type and its close association in design with the D-type naturally created a strong family likeness. Leveraging the success of the C and the D in competition, the Jaguar publicity department would have wanted to capitalise on that and the logical alphabetical progression to the 'E'-type was simply begging to be exploited.

↑ The strong, muscular lines of the D-type are clearly shown in this side-profile shot.

And, in a roundabout way, just as the C-type was derived from the XK 120 (which formed the basis of the XK 140/150 line), so too was the E-type derived from the D-type, which in turn had been a development of the C-type. While there is clearly no direct styling progression between the XK 150 and the E-type, there is undoubtedly a family bloodline which can be traced back to the earlier XK-series sports cars.

Jaguar Journal, the respected in-house magazine of Jaguar Cars Ltd, was the responsibility of Ernest W. Rankin, advertising manager at Jaguar for 31 years, from 1933 to 1964. As managing editor of this publication, 'Bill' Rankin, expounded the virtues of Jaguar's new sports car in the most complimentary way, as one might expect. The article, which appeared in the March 1961 issue of the publication, went on to explain that 'the general concept of the car has been kept as closely as possible to the D-type car, and in fact all the main construction features of the D-type have been incorporated in this new design'.

Amongst the more important features being referred to was the method of body construction. This was based on the monocoque principles, where the stressed-skin structure forms the main body shell. 'There is no chassis, all loads being taken by the body and sub-frame assemblies. The body shell is produced almost entirely of 20-gauge steel sheet and the rounded form of the panels – resulting from the streamlined shape of the car – makes a major contribution to the immense stiffness of the structure. In addition, the whole shell is welded up to form a single unit and thus all panels – including the outer panels – are load carrying', the article went on to say.

To the average car enthusiast, the E-type which followed was the sports car that replaced the ageing XK 150, which was true enough, but the E-type had its roots in competition, born out of the lessons learned with the D-type. Jim Randle explains: 'Well, the whole basic body structure [D-type] was the same. It was a monocoque passenger cell with a space-frame front end, which is exactly the same as on the E-type. I mean it was very much D-type and SS. It was actually quite predictable.'

Early E-type development (1957–1961)

With the development of the E-type, the factory had to switch from the traditional production process used in a chassised car to a unitary construction process, as the XK 150 represented the last separate body/chassis Jaguar ever made – it was the end of an era. Moving away from the top-mounted body method, the unitary assembly method then allowed assembly line workers to attach components to what was referred to as the central tub. No longer were they lifting parts onto the body or installing anything underneath the vehicle, as all the suspension and drive-train components would be attached at the same level as the base of the passenger tub as the workers looked at it on the assembly line.

Analysing the construction method of the E-type through the eyes of a different industry, namely, the aircraft industry, it is clear where Malcolm Sayer got his inspiration. It is evident from as early on as E1A and E2A that Sayer employed similar construction methods to those used in the fabrication of early single-seater aeroplanes when he worked at Bristol. Starting with an aircraft tub, the aero engine was mounted in a sub-frame system of tubes and cross members which was then bolted to the front of the aircraft body just ahead of the cockpit, so that it became easily detachable from the body should the need arise. In the same way, the engine and

front suspension of the E-type were mounted in a sub-frame which was then bolted onto the bulkhead of the central body tub, forming an extremely strong and rigid structure. This construction method also gave the new sports car a much lower roofline when compared with the XK 150, which essentially had a tall body sitting on top of a substantial chassis.

The E-type construction method consisted, therefore, of three basic components: the central tub, the front engine-and-suspension sub-frame, and the rear suspension unit, which was also just bolted into place as a complete unit. This new assembly system consisting of three basic but complete units replaced a system of two basic units in the old chassised car, those being the complete chassis and the complete body which was lowered onto the rolling chassis. The system of assembling complete units all in one plane, or the same horizon, enabled the production line workers to carry out the task of assembling the vehicles in a much more efficient manner.

This construction method also allowed easy repair to racing E-types, where front-end damage was quickly repaired by simply unbolting the damaged section and bolting on a completely new one. Running the completely different assembly lines alongside each other, the monocoque saloons on the one side and the E-type assembly on the other, did not pose any assembly problems in the factory. E-type assembly

← **Early E-type Series I production at Browns Lane, Coventry.**

was far easier and was actually preferred by the workers because getting at the engine or suspension without leaning over bulky wheel arches into a tight engine bay was much simpler.

In many ways, Malcolm Sayer was a remarkable man. Not only did he introduce groundbreaking new design and aerodynamic principles, but he was able to do so in a fairly short space of time and to communicate this revolutionary new production car design and construction method to his colleagues in different departments without too much difficulty. Sayer worked almost entirely on his own and without any direct help, as nobody else in the company could really get to grips with how he produced his designs and drawings. Sir William Lyons was usually the man seen posing in the press photos with the E-type, but in reality he had very little to do with the design of the car, his only real input being on the styling of the bumpers and some other small finishes.

Norman Dewis recalls how Malcolm Sayer worked: 'He worked on his own to the point where he would do the whole schematic drawing on the wall in his office, all along the wall. And on there would be all these curves in different colours – red, green, blue – and they were just curves all the way across this paper and then every two or three inches, vertical lines all the way, hundreds and hundreds of these lines, and every line had got a number, a different number, and from that, he worked out his curvatures. I used to work with him quite

frequently because in the winter I wasn't doing testing physically on the road, I would sit there and say to Malcolm, "What's all these lines?" you know, and he would say, "Well that's the car", and I would say, "Hang on, where is the bonnet?", and he would say, "Follow the line of the blue", and I would say, "Well where is the wing line?" and he said, "Well there it is, the red." You couldn't see a car in this, but from all those curves, there was this shape and so what he used to do was translate off that onto other drawings which he would then take down to Harry Rogers in the body shop, and he would say, "Right can you make that up", and slowly Rogers would start doing the panel bits and slowly you would see it coming together. When Malcolm died, he died very suddenly and it was a shock to us all, really, he was only 54, people went into his office, clever people who thought they knew all about figures and curves and all that, and not one person could decipher how he did it; nobody knew.'

With the benefit of hindsight, we can see that the E-type was to the D-type what the C-type was to the XK 120, that is, in hereditary terms, each new model took its predecessor to the next level of technical development and aerodynamic sophistication. However, even following on from the competition success of the D-type, it was necessary to modify many components and assembly processes for the E-type to become a higher-volume production sports car. During the period 1957–1961, the factory created very few prototype

↓ A line drawing of the E-type Series I monocoque and engine subframe. This Sayers creation was an immensely light and strong structure.

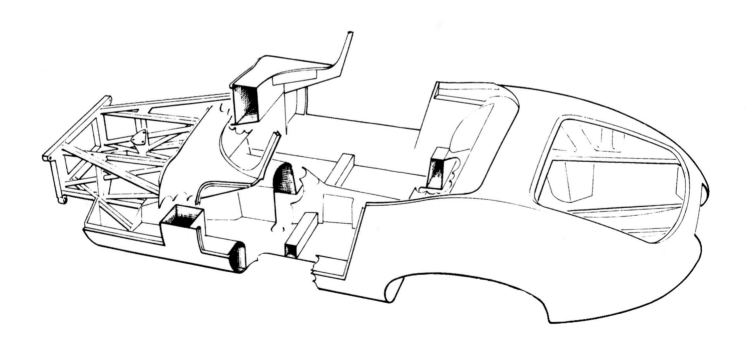

vehicles in the run-up to the final production version of the E-type; however, there was a lot of development activity going on behind the scenes. There was even talk of producing a smaller-engined sports car, one which used the 2.4-litre XK engine from the Mark I saloon, but advice from his American distributors showed Lyons that the name Jaguar was synonymous with power and performance, and a small-engined sports car was not the way to go.

Although the D-type and XKSS cars had both run with a live rear-axle set-up, there were two D-types that were fitted with early versions of the new independent rear-suspension units. These early independent rear-suspension units were the forerunner of what was used in the developmental prototypes EIA, E2 and E2A, although they also differed slightly from the final production units found in the E-type. On the surface there doesn't appear to have been much happening during the development time-gap between the EIA in 1957 and the Geneva Show car in 1961, but this four-year period was packed with the testing and evaluating of components and assembly processes.

Tom Jones explains the background to the legendary Jaguar suspension: 'The production IRS was a follow on. Actually, I did the design for the Mark X and they shortened it for the E-type and then I lengthened it again in between for the small saloons, so it was all the same design, it was just a question of the lengths of the half shafts. That became universally used right across the range of cars.'

Brian Martin remembers: 'EIA was not so much a development car, although lots of development was done on it. It was very much a "foot-in-the-water" investigation.' This confirms that the engineers were still not yet convinced as to the correct componentry required for the car or the best construction method for the E-type, as EIA was fabricated along the same lines as the D-type. As this was very much a hand-built process, the E-type concept would certainly still have to evolve a long way.

It was realised quite early on that Jaguar could not build the production car out of aluminium, and so the development switched to steel. The next hurdle was to secure a source for the pressed panels, as the production car could not be made in the same way as the D-type and XKSS, which were all hand built in-house. Construction methods conducive to easy assembly-line processes had to be devised, tested and put in place. Finally, there was the development of the independent rear suspension, which although it had started in principle, still had to be proven on the road. Its development was a major factor in the smooth ride of the production car, because in the EIA it had been built into the car rather than being made as a totally separate sub-frame and then fitted to the car as a complete unit.

Brian Martin was lucky enough to have been there at the start: 'We were working on the hand-built lower halves of the

↓ A cutaway drawing as shown in *Motor* magazine at the time of the car's launch.

↑ Malcolm Sayer's handiwork is evident in the car's sensuous waistline, the gentle curvature of the rear fender line and the gradual tapering cabin line down towards the back of the car. This side profile shows the strength of the E-type's silhouette.

first E-type, not the first car but the first mock-ups, in around '58. And that was purely and simply to work out what would go where, how things would fit, what needed to be fitted, what space was available, that sort of thing.'

In a very real way, it is fair to say that the E-type as we know it started with chassis-development engineer, Tom Jones. In an interview with the author, he explained: 'That's what Malcolm started with, the track and the wheelbase, and that was the only thing that I gave him; also the height of the engine and its position, you see, and he would work around that.' Very basically, the procedure was that Tom Jones gave Malcolm Sayer the dimensions of the E-type to work from and he got on with designing the body around those parameters. This is a relatively modern example of an iconic engineering-led design and not a car devised by the marketing department, which is more the practice today.

Julian Thomson, Jaguar chief designer confirms this: 'I guess you are right; that is a pure engineering design statement about how the car should be. I am sure they didn't go to

marketing and ask them what they wanted, because they would have said, well they wanted a [XK] 120 with another ashtray and bigger windows and a larger trunk.'

However, it is important to acknowledge that design departments did not exist back then in the same way that they do today, and much of the design work was left to the engineers. Observing the fantastic designs that these engineers produced places a quite different emphasis on the role that they traditionally played in the development of a new model. There was still a very important line to be walked which required careful balancing of the engineering versus the aesthetic aspects of a car, as engineers in those days had to understand both elements very well, and how these two worked together.

Thomson continues: 'So, to say that that was just engineering making a statement about the future is wrong, because it is a noble vision of those cars from the people who understood how everything worked together that made those cars.'

66

Understanding the E-type design language

Automotive designers are ordinary people, and as such, are influenced by similar factors which might inspire others in the creative world, such as certain art forms, period styling, structural forms, nature or even other forms of transport such as aviation or nautical themes. However, the art of styling is a very emotive and expressive function while designing is somewhat more scientific, yet it must also show traits of the former in order to successfully convey a message of power or speed in a sports car.

Keith Helfet explains further: 'Malcolm Sayer was an aerodynamicist, a designer and an artist; he used to do watercolours. What he didn't realise, probably, is that like Sir William he was an unbelievable sculptor. He had that talent and he had that aptitude and he had that passion, and there is no way that those cars could be as beautiful without that. You cannot specify that, people either have it or they don't.'

As outlined in the *Jaguar Journal* of March, 1961, 'The Jaguar

E-type car is not just another sports car in the conventional sense of the word. It is an entirely new concept of high-speed motoring'. The article went on to say that the company had set out to produce a car having a performance equal to that of the most specialised sports cars available at that time, while combining the renowned comfort, safety and smooth ride of the Jaguar saloon car range.

Before even getting into the beauty of the E-type design and its underlying secrets, it is important to analyse how the basic shape of the E-type came about. From an engineering perspective, without a conventional chassis as in the XK 150 or a floor pan as in the monocoque saloon range, there were several key factors to be considered when laying out the E-type.

It's all in the package, as Jim Randle explained; 'First of all, the thing that matters is where you put the engine, and the E-type was a very logical use of the positioning of the engine. You put the engine centre of gravity (CoG) well behind the front-axle centre line, and that drives the passenger space; the

67

↓ From this low angle, one can see that all aspects of the front-end design were intended to accentuate the speed of the E-type. From the faired-in headlights and smooth bonnet and fender curves to the evocative central power bulge in the bonnet – it all shouted 'speed'. Even the small indicator/parking lamp clusters were streamlined in shape. The relatively small mouth opening and the radius of the 'lips' were designed by Sayer to maximise the airflow through the radiator and to keep the powerful XK engine cool.

passenger space then determines where the rear axle is. But that doesn't determine the styling; well, I mean some things determine the styling. The position of the A-pillar is determined by the bulkhead structure, which is a key driver in the styling, and engine height is another one which determines its form. And then to a large degree it depends on how much luggage you want to carry.'

In designing the E-type, Malcolm Sayer regarded the silhouette as paramount to the car's performance and therefore attached the highest priority to this element of its shape. By way of his mathematical formulas, Sayer used variations on the theme of the ellipse to calculate the car's classic outline and to define the bumpers, lights, windows and other exterior elements. This attention to detail produced fluid, uninterrupted lines that maximised aerodynamic motion over the body. With no projections from the solid form of the basic body to disrupt this flow, the continuous, sensuous lines of this perfect shape were a feast for the eye.

In trying to unravel the thinking and methodology of the designers and stylists responsible for creating the E-type shape, it is necessary to delve a little deeper into the complex art of this profession. Although William Lyons and Malcolm Sayer both produced some of the most admired car designs of the twentieth century, they arrived at their objective via two very different approaches. Being essentially self-taught, Lyons could hardly draw at all and worked with full-scale

models created by his body-shop staff in the metal, whereas Sayer would rely on full-size drawings using the design studio wall or even the floor. In other tests he would attach small bits of wool, or 'telltales', to the car's body then drive along beside the car as it was being taken around the circuit at MIRA, just north of Coventry, and actually observe the effect of the wind on the wool tufts. Malcolm Sayer just had an altogether different approach to creating an efficient sports-car design.

One cannot hope to do justice to the intriguing world of styling and design in a short paragraph, but some understanding of line and form in design language is necessary in order to appreciate just how evocative the E-type body shape is.

Keith Helfet explains: 'This was a little bit of a revelation to me. When you start off life as an engineer, you begin to look at beautiful shapes. Many of the most beautiful shapes start with a woman's body, or parts of a woman's body, because actually, form or line can have movement. A point is still. A straight line has direction. A curve, if you have a constant radius, your eye sees a constant speed in that curve. But if a curve tightens up, it actually has acceleration, so that certain shapes look kind of dumpy or pumped up and other shapes look lean and have tension to them. So if you look at the [XK] 120 and you just look at the line, you can see that the 120 has got incredible movement in those lines. The E-type looks like it is moving when it is standing still because the shapes look dynamic. Whereas other shapes look more static or less

'Although the E-type's revolutionary appearance was based on functionalism and Sayer's desire to best minimise the amount of drag, its styling is not an anomaly among Jaguars. The cars are fluid, reflecting Sir William's preference for curvilinear forms. They imply movement and presuppose a relationship between the automobile and the elements of wind and ground.'

Museum of Modern Art, New York
Refining the Sports Car – Jaguar's E-type **April, 1996.**

This angle clearly shows how the slats on either side of the bonnet combined with the vent at the rear of the central power bulge to allow the hot under-bonnet air to escape while at speed.

dynamic. And of course that can be a line or form. You can "feel" movement, and I design a lot by feel.'

Although it was derived principally from the D-type, the E-type was an altogether much longer vehicle which added to its sense of streamlining and sleek shape. History has shown us through cars like the Bentleys, Mercedes SSK, Renaults and Napiers of the early twentieth century that large, extended bonnets had long created the perception of speed and power. A long bonnet undoubtedly hid a large engine, or so it seemed,

and so the E-type benefited from this perception when in actual fact it was entirely necessary in creating the right proportions. The length of the bonnet was further accentuated by the narrow form of the car as well as the way in which the bodywork below the doors and along the sides of the car folded underneath as opposed to other sports cars where the bodywork appeared to go straight to ground. This feature helped to create an almost elongated cigar look, giving the E-type a real sense of speed.

Malcolm Sayer knew this, and proceeded to make the E-type bonnet even longer than that of the car on which it was based, the D-type, despite there being already sufficient under-bonnet space for the engine in that highly respected race car. Sayer wanted to convey this message to the market, and in particular the American market, where this type of sporting body language did not go amiss. American car buyers, many of whom were hooked on muscle cars and power, simply drank in the sensuous designs of many imported cars and so the powerful language of the long bonnet was a feature well worth exploiting.

The E-type's bonnet is in fact a remarkable piece of work in itself and despite its overall size, adds no strength to the car at all. The bonnet is not a stressed part of the bodywork and is a completely free unit, hinging forward on a bracket attached to the forward sub-frame. This was made possible because the front suspension was attached to the front sub-frame which carried the engine, and was thus not attached to any chassis or inner bodywork as in the monocoque saloons. This is an unusual solution to the problem of overall strength and possible body twisting in a production sports car, which by its very nature, requires extraordinary rigidity to deliver its power to the road while maintaining excellent cornering and ride qualities in the process.

Staying with the bonnet theme, the strong image of the central power bulge was not just for aesthetic purposes. The low front end of the bonnet needed the additional 'bump' to clear the leading edge of the engine, and so the power bulge feature was carried right through to the rear edge of the bonnet, thereby also providing longitudinal strength to this huge structure. Despite the tall configuration of the XK engine unit with its double-overhead-camshaft configuration, it was actually only the leading edge of the engine rocker covers which presented a clearance problem, as the engine was canted down towards the rear by three degrees, allowing even greater engine clearance towards the bulkhead. Jim Randle explains: 'I think it was more of a styling issue because you've got to have the height at the front end to clear the engine and if you had taken it straight back, it would have looked rather strange, I think that the "Old Chap" decided that he would carry the feature through.'

Purely from a design perspective, the central power bulge of the bonnet complemented the sensuous wheel-arch curves perfectly, but this was just further evidence of the brilliance of the Lyons and Sayer teamwork. The E-type bonnet indeed attracted the attention of the design office for several reasons. The forward-opening bonnet derived from the C-type and D-type models provided superb engine access, despite the challenges presented in clearing the engine, but the engineers also had to ensure that hot air was able to escape from the engine compartment. This was achieved in two ways: firstly through the narrow air outlet at the back end of the central

→ The up-slope of the E-type's rear underbody combined with the gentle angle of the upper bodywork is designed to allow the air to flow off the back of the car, thereby creating a slippery shape and preventing the air from 'hanging on' at the rear of the car.

power bulge, thus providing a neat and stylish solution to the problem, secondly via two sets of rear-facing air vents located either side of the central power bulge, which allowed fast-moving air over the bonnet surface to draw out the hot air generated in the engine bay.

Although these air vents were necessary in allowing hot air to escape, they also gave the added perception of a powerful engine in a high-performance car. However, because of the front-end shape of the E-type, it wasn't the best place to position the vents. Jim Randle explains: 'The slots were there to let the air out because you have got high-velocity air passing over them, so you can draw air out from under the bonnet, but it's not a good place to let air out because you've got a depression there.'

The shape of the D-type front-end and air intake was the result of a combination of styling and aerodynamic efficiency. Thanks to the extensive testing and race track experience gained with the D-type, the 'mouth' of the E-type was also kept attractively small when compared with other performance

cars of the day. As a result, the E-type did not require a grille to cover this relatively small opening; a slim badge bar was sufficient, thereby also saving valuable weight, especially when one considers the heavy chrome grille on the earlier Jaguar XK sports cars.

As a result of the particular positioning of the E-type's passenger compartment, as explained above, the long bonnet was further accentuated by the shortness of the car's tail. Again, there are good design reasons for this as Malcolm Sayer wanted to create a sharp, pointed tail end to the car for improved aerodynamic purposes, as this allowed the air to slip off the back rather than create a vortex of swirling air that clings onto the body.

In fact, the positioning of the car's axles allowed Malcolm Sayer to maximise the effect of the front and rear body overhangs of the E-type which had quite a lot to do with the car's aerodynamic efficiency. Keith Helfet explains the concept: 'The overhangs really allow the streamlining of the car, whereas with blunt ends, streamlining is more difficult.' The

↑ The production E-type was two inches wider than the original prototype 'E' of 1956.

↑ **For a sports car with the performance potential that the E-type possessed, it had a remarkably light and roomy interior. The side-glass profile was reminiscent of the wing shape of the WWII Spitfire fighter plane, a classic British design.**

front overhang is in fact fairly short; it's the rear overhang that gives the perception of the car's slippery shape. 'You can see it is a real bullet-shaped car, with the leading entry and exit angles for the air.' Helfet continued.

Tom Jones remembers with a smile: 'Well of course, the aerodynamics of the E-type was secret to Malcolm Sayer. He never divulged what his method was and he wouldn't even divulge it to Bill Heynes. So nobody knew really, because what

I gave him was the wheelbase and the position of the axle, but the overhang, that was him.'

Perhaps with a view to a future design which Sayer already had in mind, he lengthened the nose of the D-type for the 1955 Le Mans 24-Hour. Dubbed the 'long-nose' D-type, this experiment with the race car's aerodynamic properties was detrimental to the car's cooling in the 24-hour race and it retired from the event with overheating problems. Tom Jones

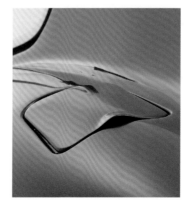

recalls: 'Nobody else knew. The only thing I knew from Malcolm was that I didn't have to reduce the aperture of the intake of the nose, and the radius didn't have to be reduced from one inch, a one-inch radius on that lip.'

Clearly, the radius of the front lip of the D-type air intake was crucial to the race car's engine cooling capabilities, airflow over the bonnet and overall aerodynamic efficiency of the front end of the car, and that was not to be altered by order of Mr. Sayer. 'I could do other things, but not that.' Tom Jones laughed at the recollection.

In keeping with its race-car heritage, the E-type was free of unnecessary trimmings, so adornments and excessive chrome, the custom on many American cars of the time, were avoided. Sayer was content to let the styling do the talking, the simplicity of style and lack of adornments on the E-type allowed the strength of the body lines to draw attention. Small, slim bumpers front and rear further emphasised the lines of the E-type's sinuous silhouette, enhancing its sense of speed, even when stationary.

'Sir William had a bit of a say in the bumpers.' recalled Tom Jones with some amusement. This comment just illustrates how little Sir William Lyons was involved in the basic E-type design process, allowing Malcolm Sayer and his team an almost free hand in the car's development; all this despite the boss not being very enthusiastic about the car's initial design direction.

Studying early copies of the *Jaguar Journal* shows clearly that the company was leaving no stone unturned in ensuring that they had thought of the needs of the sports-car driver more than ever before. Although boot space was somewhat restricted in the roadster, the owner of the coupé could really travel in style and comfort on long journeys, sure of being able to carry a good deal of personal luggage. Not only did the owner have excellent access to the storage area via a large sideways-swinging rear door, but the boot floor was fitted with parallel rubbing strips that protected personal belongings or luggage. Should the owner wish to carry more luggage, the top half of the rear-seat backrests could be folded forward,

↑ **The Series I E-type had a larger than expected luggage area and certainly in comparison with other more exotic and expensive sports cars, the Jaguar was in a league of its own.**

thus further enlarging the boot floor. This, of course, eliminated any space behind the driver and passenger seat that was normally available for carrying small parcels.

It is a testament to Malcolm Sayer that the design of the E-type changed little from the early prototypes that were fabricated in the experimental shop and subsequently tested by Norman Dewis. From the early E1A to the production model, the car grew a little in length and width but the proportions remained almost the same. Tom Jones remembers: 'The only difference in the body shape for the first E-type in '56 to the production one was that I put two inches in the track, and the body engineer, Cyril Crouch, he altered what we called the "ten" lines, you sort of split the body from the middle outwards you know, and you mark it ten inches, twenty inches etc.; so I put two inches down the middle of the car and we put the "zero" as "plus 1", "plus 11", "plus 21". I can tell you the E-type is 48-inch track, the first one and then I put it up to 50 inches for the production car.'

Even though the E-type was the work of the genius of Malcolm Sayer, it was Bob Blake who styled the coupé. When Lyons saw the crude mock-up of a coupé body in the experimental department, he immediately told Sayer to create the design in the drawing office. It stands to reason that the roadster was the first body style produced as this had been modelled off the D-type, an open-top race car. The bonnet, fender lines and general body shape of the D-type

can all be seen in the E-type roadster, and had the D-type been a closed race car, then undoubtedly the E-type would have started life as a coupé as well.

As we have seen at the beginning of this section, designers, too, must derive their inspiration from somewhere, and it is known that Malcolm Sayer drew some of his inspiration from the little Alfa Romeo concept car, the 1952 Disco Volante, or 'Flying Saucer'. Equally, the rear section of a Porsche 356 (first launched in 1948) is not very dissimilar from the styling of the rear quarters on the E-type fixed-head coupé. Sayer had already used the styling of the tensed rear haunches in the D-type and the well-developed wheel-arch curves of the E-type emulate the flowing lines of the early XK 120, with more than a little hint of 'Coke bottle' styling, as it was later called by the Americans.

The clean, sloping tail allowed Sayer to develop a sideways-opening door which allowed easy access to the rear luggage area. This style, the forerunner of today's hatchback, was later used extensively by the American manufacturers and indeed the rest of the world. The narrowing of the rear section of the E-type combined with the sloping rear-boot door accentuates the smooth, muscular rear fenders. In harmony with the E-type's short tail and up-sloping under-boot panel, this helps by allowing the smooth flow of air over the car, thereby enhancing the aerodynamic stability of the vehicle.

Although the E-type's starting point was with the roadster,

↓ Looking down the length of the rear fender, the E-type had one of the most curvaceous, simple and yet sophisticated styles in its class. It was undeniably a winning design in the 1960s and still is today.

← The E-type
underwent extensive
testing for all aspects
of safety and
passenger comfort.
Here it is seen
undergoing a water-
sealing test.

it was the fixed-head coupé that many regard as having the more graceful and flowing body style of the two. From the Spitfire-wing shape of the side glass to the sleek fastback shape of the rear bodywork, the coupé was both an aesthetically pleasing as well as an aerodynamically efficient overall style. Complex, yet simple, is how one could describe the E-type. Admired the world over, it was a winner right from the outset and it all started on the race track with the D-type.

Aerodynamics and Testing

Before he came to Jaguar, Malcolm Sayer had worked for the Bristol Aircraft Company as an aerodynamicist, and he arrived at Browns Lane just at the time Bill Lyons wanted to go to Le Mans. John Maries continues: 'There he learned, as part of his training, the mathematics of streamlining and the mathematics of airflows. And he had done all of this, not by eye, but actually by calculation, and remember this was before computers.'

Within the space of just a few years, the world of automobile design had all of a sudden become a much more scientific environment, and the days of the self-made, self-taught industrialist holding all aspects of new car design and development in the palm of his hand were fast drawing to a close. The demands of overall vehicle design had moved on from being largely stylistically focused, to include aspects such as vehicle functionality and safety as well as having to satisfy the increasingly sophisticated customer's requirements for comfort and convenience in a sports car. Malcolm Sayer was able to combine Jaguar's traditional design elements with functionality in a more modern way, while still ensuring jaw-dropping good looks. As John Maries explains: 'He would actually draw up a car using mathematics, and therefore what you are getting are cars that looked more like aerofoils.'

Jim Randle confirms this: 'Malcolm actually created his own formulation formulas, because he was an aero man, and he was able to compute the performance of the car from the general curvatures of the vehicle and so forth, in effect working out the drag coefficients.'

It is interesting to note that even as late as 1959, it was internally acknowledged by Jaguar, and no doubt other motor manufacturers too, that sports cars were in fact called sports racing cars or prototypes. This just confirms the point made earlier that a 'sports car' was a car that was used for the sport of motoring, made possible through the removal of certain body panels and usually also the windscreen. Saloon cars were referred to as 'touring cars', no doubt for the pastime of taking longer trips, while the term 'grand touring' was given to cars that were suitable for touring at a faster pace and in grand style. It is only through the efforts of the marketing departments within the auto industry that the initials 'GT' later came to be attached to many sporty versions of normal saloon cars, or touring cars. Models such as the Cortina GT, Viva GT and many others of that era were no more 'GT' than the standard sedan versions on which they were based, and were certainly not in the same league as a grand touring Jaguar E-type, Maserati or Ferrari. The grand touring vehicle segment during the 1950s and 1960s was the embodiment of fast, comfortable touring on a grand scale, in a vehicle that was, by virtue of its low production and higher price, a car of special and distinctive design. With their fast touring capability, these cars were lower, more sleek, had powerful engines and only two doors, and were therefore generally of aerodynamic- and performance-oriented design.

Perhaps the best way of explaining the complexities of developing a car's shape that is both beautiful and efficient is to cite a short section from an article prepared for the company publication, *Jaguar Journal*. The following extract is taken from the issue which accompanied the launch of the

Jaguar Journal

When setting out to design the E-type body, Jaguar naturally took as a basis, the D-type and the XKSS bodies which had been used so successfully for racing. The shape of the body is, of course, governed to quite a large extent by the disposition of the main units and, although during the original design work an unconventional position of the engine was considered, it was decided that for general handling, combined with an efficient shape for the body and correct weight distribution the conventional engine position gave the most satisfactory results in a car designed mainly for use on the road in the hands of both experts and general drivers.

First of all, the position of the power unit, the driver and the passenger, the seating, the steering, were determined together with the minimum wheel base that would give the correct weight distribution and, around these, a streamlined shape was developed that would enclose them all with the lowest drag that could be devised. As soon as this basic body form was arrived at, a one tenth size model was built for wind tunnel tests.

This model is then tested in the wind tunnel. The forward resistance is measured and any modifications which appear to reduce the drag are incorporated in the model until a minimum drag figure is achieved. The model is then

E-type in 1961, and explains the advanced steps taken to ensure a clean, streamlined shape for the new sports car.

Malcolm Sayer's aerodynamic work on the D-type had already been proven through its success on the race track, and as the E-type was modelled on that race car, the drag coefficient on the new sports car would have been at the very least, good for the day. Tom Jones confirms this: 'Well of course the issue was really, as far as aerodynamics was concerned, it was designed as a racer, so that was already part of it you see.'

The aerodynamic efficiency of the Jaguar E-type was a well-calculated and tested concept, having had the performance characteristics of the D-type to work from as a starting point. Satisfied with the upper body design of the E-type, Sayer then turned his attentions to the underside of the car. As Jim Randle recalls: 'He was trying to get some down force out of the E-type by using venturi effect under the car.'

The E-type has often been unfairly cited as possessing poor aerodynamic properties, but as Jim Randle points out: 'You have to say it on the day don't you? Yes it didn't have a

← In the Jaguar Daimler Heritage Trust Museum, Tom Jones stands alongside the very first D-type Jaguar OVC 501 (chassis XKD401), a car which he helped to develop.

checked for the effect produced by a side wind. To do this, the body is placed in the air stream at varying angles and pivoted at the point of the centre of gravity over the complete car. This has already been assessed by calculation and, from this, the centre of pressure of the body is obtained. The effects of cross winds from different directions and intensities are studied by varying the angle at which the car is set. In addition to these figures, which are taken in a horizontal plane, it is also necessary to check the shape of the body for forces produced by the air in a vertical plane. It is most important that the vertical forces so produced should not tend to lift the tail or depress the front of the car unduly, as this would make the car unstable at high speed, since the alteration in attitude of the body to the air stream can increase the drag by a very considerable amount. The upswept underside of the body at the rear is functional in this respect and, in fact, the general streamlining of the body has been carried to an extent where it is believed that any further alterations would impair the suitability of the car for the purpose for which it is intended – that is the fast, safe and comfortable transportation of two people and their luggage.

March, 1961

particularly good drag coefficient, but you have to compare it with whatever else was around on the day.' Taking into consideration the efficient lines of the Jaguar D-type and how successful that sports car was, it is hard to imagine that Malcolm Sayer would have designed anything that wasn't as aerodynamic as he could possibly make it. If the D-type was a super-smooth shape, then it stands to reason that the E-type which was based on it would have been good too in its day. With Sayer's background at Bristol Aircraft, he was able to gain access to the massive wind tunnel at Farnborough for aerodynamic tests on the E-type.

Jim Randle again: 'In fact if anything, the E-type would be better because the open cockpit on a D-type is quite a bit of a drag. I tell you what would have been better on the D-type, and that would have been its stability because it had that fin built behind the driver which put the centre of pressure further back.'

Norman Dewis remembers that the coefficient of drag on the Series I E-type was excellent, but admitted that when

the factory modified the body with the introduction of the Series 2 and later the Series 3, the coefficient of drag did worsen somewhat.

Looking at the work that Sayer did on the race cars, one might be forgiven for thinking that he worked only on the C and D-types before turning his attention to the production E-type. After all, his styling work was not evident on any of the XK sports cars that were produced during his time with the company and nor could his influence be easily seen on the saloon car range. However, his aerodynamic techniques were applied across the model range, and he worked very closely with Sir William on many cars.

Norman Dewis remembers: 'You see, one thing that Lyons couldn't do was work out the coefficient of drag or what the aerodynamics were; all he saw was a shape, a style. I mean, every car that we made was wind-tunnel tested by Sayer and he controlled it [the aerodynamics] from there. He would make some alterations to the models in conjunction with Lyons; he worked very closely with Lyons.'

For Sir William, the advantage of having Sayer involved was that before he made the body, Sayer could calculate what the coefficient of drag was going to be. First, Sayer would make a model which was wind-tunnel tested in the scale model wind tunnel, then he would make the first prototype which was a running vehicle. The full scale prototype was then tested in the wind tunnel and he would record the necessary co-efficient of drag figures and perhaps make slight changes on the prototype based on those readings. After the wind-tunnel tests were completed, Sayer would then take the vehicle out to the test track and conduct the wool-tuft test. At this time, one of the few other performance car manufacturers carrying out the wool-tuft test was Porsche in Stuttgart, Germany.

The wool-tuft test, a simple but effective method of fixing woollen 'telltales' to the car's bodywork, involved running the car on the road through the air and observing the turbulence and airflow over the car as indicated by the behaviour of the woollen tufts. When he did the wool-tuft tests and compared his observations with his wind-tunnel readings, Sayer always found that running the car through the air was slightly worse than in the controlled environment of the wind tunnel. Norman Dewis explains: 'In other words, you're pushing air over the car; the car is stationary, the air is being pushed. When you're driving the car through the air that is, you get a slight difference.'

At the time, Dewis remembers that the other car manufacturers were only using their coefficient of drag figures as per their wind-tunnel tests. In order to keep the findings of their test methods confidential, Jaguar would hire the MIRA test facility over the weekends and run their secret

SELECTED SPORTS CAR SPECIFICATIONS:

Vehicles	Year	CD	Capacity	Engine type	Speed	Price**
Jaguar E-type Roadster	1961	0.5*	3,781cc	Straight 6	150mph	$5,825
Mercedes 300SL Roadster	1957	n/a	2,996cc	Straight 6	156mph	$8,125
Porsche 911	1963	0.363	1,991cc	Flat 6	131mph	$5,475
Ferrari 250GTO	1962	n/a	2,953cc	V12	185mph	$17,970
Chevrolet Corvette	1961	n/a	4,639cc	V8	128mph	$3,934
Aston Martin DB4	1961	n/a	3,671cc	Straight 6	140mph	$11,344

*Estimate   **Conversion to US$ based on average 1961/62 exchange rates

↓ Increasing pressure from safety groups in the USA meant that even the E-type had to undergo crash tests. Here an early model is seen in action at the MIRA test facility in Warwickshire, England.

wool-tuft tests on Saturdays and Sundays when no-one else was there. Dewis was convinced that the other manufacturers didn't know about this method, as they always took their wind-tunnel figures as the true and final aerodynamic efficiency figures.

Dewis did more testing than anyone else at Jaguar, and remembers the situation with a smile on his face: 'We used to have a cup of tea at the drivers' rest room at MIRA, and we were talking amongst ourselves when they were testing the Ford GT, and the guys there were saying to me, "It's funny, we don't know if there is something wrong with our test road or what", I said, "Why?", and they said, "Well, we calculate we should

be getting that top speed and we don't see it, and yet according to the wind-tunnel figures we should". And I used to say, "Well, probably something to do with the wind tunnel". We'd never tell them that there would be a difference, you see.' It wasn't until after Jaguar ceased racing that the stories and photographs started to come out about the wool-tuft tests.

Contrary to popular belief, road testing is far from the glamorous activity it is sometimes perceived to be, irrespective of the vehicle being tested. Around the time of the E-type's

↓ **The classic E-type shape is stunning from any angle, but this frontal three-quarter shot emphasises the long, sleek bonnet and the sporty stance of the car.**

development, safety legislation requirements began to filter through from the States, and this added both time and test elements to the schedule created by Norman Dewis for all Jaguar models. One of the tests he remembers carrying out was the pavé test, a bone-jarring 1,000-mile test run at MIRA on a surface made up of Belgian cobblestones, with a pattern of deep potholes and raised mounds exactly like the roads in Brugge, Belgium. The driver could only manage 30 minutes at a time behind the wheel on this torturous suspension test which was carried out at 30mph. This 1,000-mile test run at 30mph was the equivalent of a 100,000-mile test on normal roads but Dewis had the advantage of being able to carry this test out in a relatively short space of time as it shook the car so badly, exposing almost any defects, especially body-panel alignment. The idea was to improve the vehicle where they had achieved a failure, modify it and

retest until they had completed 1,000 miles on the old pavé road surface.

Dewis recalls those days: 'So the first production E-type went through all that. What we hadn't done was put E1A or E2A through that rigorous testing, but with the first prototype E-type, I said, "Now we've got to start to do the full test schedules".'

Prior to Norman's arrival at Jaguar in 1952, there were no laid-down test procedures at all; he had brought his test schedules with him from Lea Francis where he had worked before. The first E-type to be put through the torturous test programme by Dewis, was the 'red roadster', a car he called 'Red Number 1'. This prototype was fabricated in the experimental shop and was sufficiently far advanced to start to develop it as a production project. However, despite a rather less than illustrious start for this red car, for the next eighteen months it played a vital role in the development of the final production E-type.

Following the 'red roadster number 1', Dewis had another experimental prototype, a metallic grey car that was also made in the body shop. It is important to note that these two vehicles were made in the experimental body shop, and not on the production line, but they obviously related closely to the production models.

Dewis then set aside the two of the earliest production cars to come off the E-type assembly line, those being the famous 9600 HP, the very first left-hand-drive production coupé to be manufactured and 77 RW, a roadster. 'We again put those two production cars through the same test procedures that we put the two prototypes through. It was 9600 HP, a fixed head and 77 RW was the open one, those were the two and those two did a whole lot of work as well, you know, lots and lots of miles. 9600 HP was the one I took to Europe when I went out there to devise a road circuit for the Mark X, putting the car under Continental conditions.' recalls Norman Dewis.

Jaguar Experimental Shop

The 'experimental' department of any motor manufacturer is as expected, one which is shrouded in secrecy, and admission is allowed only on a strictly controlled basis. Back in the late 1950s at Jaguar, it was no different, as it was a self-sustaining department and operated in a corner of the general factory.

Norman Dewis is a man renowned for his tireless attention to detail and would spend hours at his desk after a hard day's testing, writing up his log for the day, right down to what he had had for lunch at the MIRA canteen, and even how much it had cost him. It was when he was busy recording these findings that Sir William Lyons would often stop by his office late in the evening, and invite him to view some progress on a project that was being worked on in the experimental body shop. Dewis might pass some comment that a piece of trim should be chromed or some small change would look better if altered slightly in some way. Sir William

E-TYPE PROTOTYPES AND PRODUCTION TEST MODELS:					
Car description	Body type	Produced	Colour	Engine	Registration
Experimental	Prototype roadster	Experimental Shop	Red	3.4-litre	-
Experimental	Prototype roadster	Experimental Shop	Metallic Grey	3.4-litre	-
Test & press car	Fixed Head Coupé	Assembly line	Metallic Grey	3.8-litre	9600 HP
Test & press car	Roadster	Assembly line	BRG	3.8-litre	77 RW

↓ The radius of the 'lips' of the E-type mouth was critical to the car's overall aerodynamics, but Malcolm Sayer never disclosed these findings to his colleagues. The thin leading edge of the half-bumpers, the streamlined shape of the indicator lenses and the covered-in headlamp fairings all contributed to the car's sleekness.

would always take note of what was said, but would not record the suggestion or draw an image to remind himself, and frequently he would call Dewis in a few days later or stop him in the factory and thank him for the suggestion that he had now implemented. It was all done by eye, with no notes or drawings, and it was normally Harry Rogers, superintendent of the experimental body shop, who would have to carry out the changes required by Sir William.

The experimental shop, as it was usually called, consisted of an engine department, chassis shop and the body shop. Obviously, the engine department prepared all the engines and gearboxes for any experimental projects which then passed to the chassis shop where they were married to the chassis and the vehicle prepared for testing. The body shop, up at the top end of the experimental shop was run by Harry Rogers, and in a corner sectioned off in this area, he would have two styling guys working on body panels or changes for experimental projects.

Harry Rogers would then make up a wooden body buck from which full-size panels were fabricated. They could only make about half a dozen bodies from those bucks before they had to be replaced, but it was enough to get the project going, a method that worked well as changes could be made quickly and cheaply. Harry Rogers was responsible for building the first one-off bodies from these, or if Dewis found any faults on the bodies that he was testing, Rogers was the

man to cure them. Harry's team would make the modifications or changes and Dewis would test these again, so it was a well-equipped, totally independent facility whose parts worked effectively together.

The experimental shop was a self-contained manufacturing unit in that they could start a project as drawings came down from the drawing office. Special parts and panels were made in the experimental shop from those drawings. 'We could make anything we wanted.' added Dewis.

It was more than just good design that made the Jaguar E-type such a styling success: its appearance expressed a sense of understated power and performance. Julian Thomson explains: 'They constructed a very mathematical function and the beauty of it comes from the form that is made from this function and that is what those cars are all about.'

It is interesting to note that while the E-type had a sleek and efficient shape, Sayer's work in this area was concerned mainly with airflow over the body surfaces which resulted in an extremely smooth overall shape. The rear section was tapered both vertically and horizontally and with the car in motion, this allowed air to slip off the body with a minimum of hindrance or turbulence. While the main thrust of aerodynamics in the 1960s was to do with airflow, today's aerodynamic efforts are concentrated mostly around the issue of down force. ■

The E-type birth

'Sports car – a low-built fast car'.

Oxford English Dictionary

1958	1959	1960	1961
E-type prototype testing begins with E1A	Dewis tests the first roadster, 'Red No. 1'	E2A competes at Le Mans 24-Hour	E-type launched at Geneva Show in March
		XK 150 ceases production in October	

Geneva Motor Show (16–26 March, 1961)

Revealed to a stunned audience at the 1961 Geneva Motor Show, the Jaguar E-type fixed-head coupé attracted crowds that even Sir William Lyons could not possibly have anticipated. The star of the show was undoubtedly the gleaming new gunmetal-grey Jaguar sports car, which took its place on the show stand amongst the company's other products.

Announced in the company newsletter, *Jaguar Journal,* in March, 1961, Bill Rankin's headline referred to the newcomer as 'The New "E" Type Grand Touring Car'. The E-type's tense rear haunches, a much modernised interpretation of the voluptuous XK sports car, must have conjured up thoughts of a real jaguar cat, the *Panthera onca,* to give it the correct species name, ready to pounce at any moment. In its natural habitat, the jaguar relies on the element of surprise, combined with stealth and speed, in its quest to conquer its prey. Captured in the language of automotive designers, the fast styling lines and the tight, muscular curves of the E-type's rear

haunches conveyed a message of power and speed, while the short, sharp tail reduced the effects of the airflow 'hanging on' to the car and slowing it down. In a subtle way, the E-type's long bonnet gave the unmistakable message of power and drive, symbolising the long powerful legs of the animal as it leapt forward with speed in pursuit of its prey.

The interesting thing about the E-type is that Jaguar had made around 54 C-types and 78 D-types (including XKSS), and by early accounts, Sir William attended the Geneva thinking that he was going to make only 250 of the E-types. John Maries again: 'He gets down there and finds that he has got an amazing success on his hands. The thing was, at Geneva, the crowds in 1961 were ten deep around the car.'

If Sir William Lyons had originally intended making only 250 E-types, it may seem odd that he would then go to the trouble of launching it at Geneva if he didn't anticipate a longer production run. Although this initial build estimate had grown consistently during the car's development, first to 500 and then 1,000, it is possible, as Mercedes Benz and Ferrari

→ The Jaguar E-type proudly on display in Geneva.

↑ The promotional poster from the 1961 Salon International de l'Automobile Genève at which the E-type was launched.

were his closest competitors at Le Mans, that by going to Geneva Sir William was hoping to steal the thunder away from his two rivals in their own backyard.

As ever the perfect publicist, Sir William Lyons launched the E-type on 15 March, the day before the official opening of the Geneva Motor Show at the Parc des Eaux Vives, an exclusive hotel overlooking the beautiful Lake Geneva. Set in a large restored 19th-century house less than two kilometres from the centre of Geneva, the Parc des Eaux Vives was the perfect setting for this media introduction.

It is interesting to note that Sir William decided to launch the new E-type in Geneva, when all of Jaguar's previous new sports cars had been launched at Earls Court, London. Sir William Lyons did not have a history of parting with his money very readily, but there were nevertheless several good reasons for going to Geneva for the launch of the E-type. It was an important car for Jaguar and had to make the right impression from the start, and for the company's first all-new sports car to be launched overseas, the Geneva Motor Show was chosen as the most suitable event. John Maries explains: 'It was an important show. It is also a very fashionable place to be.'

Switzerland was in itself an important market for Jaguar, and by the early 1960s, Geneva had already become one of the most important European motor shows, attracting an international audience with many journalists from all over Europe. In addition, held early in the spring, the Geneva Show was the first motor show of the year in Europe, being followed by the Turin Show, which at that time was not so important internationally and tended to be a showcase for Italian manufacturers and coachbuilders. But more importantly, the New York Show was held very soon afterwards, and by launching at Geneva, followed by New York, Jaguar achieved invaluable exposure for the new car at two of the biggest international motor shows and in two very important markets, in quick succession.

'The time was right; we couldn't wait for the Turin Show and New York was going to take too long. I think it was Geneva that just came in at the right time when we wanted to launch it and get it off the ground and let people see it, that was the nearest, quickest way to do it.' Norman Dewis recalls.

← Displayed on a simple carpet, the E-type was one of the main attractions of the motor show.

The Geneva Motor Show therefore offered an ideal opportunity for the European market to view the car, and with the advent of jet airliners, travel was at that time becoming easier thus giving the public and the international media greater access to the new vehicle. For the same reasons, the New York Motor Show also offered a golden opportunity for Jaguar to showcase its new sports car there too. Looking at the potential global appeal of the E-type, a high-profile launch on the international stages at Geneva and

New York was certainly going to give the car the impressive start it needed.

On the stand at the Geneva Show was a single gunmetal-grey E-type coupé. The car had been transported there by road as it was not a running car. 'It wasn't really a runner actually; we would have driven it probably if it had been a runner.' remembers Dewis.

The only running car that the company had taken to Geneva for press and customer demonstrations was the famous fixed-head coupé, 9600 HP, the first fixed-head off the production line. Jaguar publicity boss, Bob Berry, was himself responsible for driving the demonstration car, which offered the opportunity of taking only one person per run. Berry would collect his passenger from the show, and head out along the lake and towards the designated demonstration route which was being used by Ferrari, Mercedes, Alfa Romeo, Jaguar and other sports car manufacturers represented at the show. The route followed a hill-climb course up a hill, round a series of snaking corners to the top and then along a straight section on top of the hill, down the other side and back to the show to fetch the next person, a distance of around two-and-half miles.

When Berry saw the length of the queue of people waiting for a demonstration run, he mentioned to Sir William that he would not be able to keep up that rate for the whole week, to which the boss responded, 'Well, the only thing we can do is get Dewis out here with the other car.' An urgent call was hastily put through to the factory by Sir William, instructing factory test driver, Norman Dewis, to drop everything and make his way to Geneva in the spare test car, as fast as possible. Sir William Lyons could not have anticipated the enthusiastic response to the car's launch and he had no idea at that point that the E-type was going to be on a 70,000-plus production run.

The only problem was that Norman Dewis was out at the MIRA testing ground conducting brake tests in the other E-type when the call from Sir William came through. The track manager

at MIRA, Ozzie Dolby, drove out in his Land Rover to where Dewis was testing, and said, 'Norman, you'd better get back to Jaguar, they want you back urgently.'

Norman headed back to the experimental shop where he was received by Bill Heynes, Bob Knight, the shop foreman Bill Cassidy and about three or four fitters who were all standing in a group waiting for him. As he got out of the car, Bill Heynes said to him, 'Ah Norman, good. You've got to take this car to Geneva for demonstration runs.' Stunned, Dewis replied, 'I can't, it's got all the brake stuff in it.'

It was already about 15.00 and Heynes quickly got the fitters to dismantle the gauges and other testing equipment, while another group set to cleaning and polishing the car. Dewis was just about to dash home to get his passport and a suitcase of clothing for the trip, when Heynes said, 'Oh that's already done; it's in your office.' Dewis laughed, 'They had done this before on me you see, the guys went up and told my wife that I'll be going straight from here to Geneva.'

With just enough time for a cup of tea and a sandwich before he had to leave, Dewis departed the factory gates at around 20.00 that evening giving him just enough time to make the 21.45 boarding time for the ferry passage that Heynes had booked, which sailed from Dover at 22.00. He 'screamed' down to the port, arriving just as they were closing the gates for vehicle boarding, and it was only because the gate attendant noticed the gleaming E-type and asked what it

← Jaguar's well-travelled press car, 9600HP, poses for a PR photo.

← Jaguar E-type Series I caused more than a stir when it was introduced to the media at the Parc des Eaux Vives, a hotel alongside Lake Geneva.

was, that Dewis said he would show him around the car if he let him onto the ferry because he had to make it to Geneva.

Arriving at Ostend the next morning while it was still dark, he disembarked with the gleaming new E-type. Heading for Brussels, Dewis took the road down through the Black Forest towards Geneva, driving non-stop all the way, arriving at the show entrance at 09.45 having averaged 67mph for the whole trip. Expected only 15 minutes later for 10.00, Dewis was welcomed by a more-than-relieved Sir William Lyons and Lofty England. Laughing, Norman recounts the moment he arrived: 'And when I got there, he was so casual, the Old Man, "Oh good show Dewis, you made it all right", you know, as though I had driven 20 miles up the road.'

Understandably Dewis was more than a little tired having been testing the E-type all day at MIRA, driven straight back to Coventry then down to Dover and without much sleep on the ferry; he had then driven flat out to Geneva. So when he asked Bob Berry where he could check into the hotel that had been booked for him, Berry laughed that idea off and told him that he would be doing demonstration runs for the rest of the day because they had told the press contingent that they would now have two cars for the demo runs. Berry was understandably eager to pacify the expectant throng of journalists who had been promised the second car.

Dewis quickly fell into the routine of collecting journalists from the show and taking them out on demonstration runs,

but after a while he suggested to Bob Berry that they should get one of the other lads to bring a batch of four journalists out from the show in a Jaguar saloon as they could get more demo runs in that way. On the second day, Norman had just collected another eager passenger when he was approached by a Swiss spectator sporting a couple of stop watches around his neck, and who said to him, 'Mr Dewis, I would just like to tell you are the fastest up the hill.'

Dewis replied, 'Oh I didn't know.' The Swiss spectator was used to doing the timing for the regular hill-climb events held there and had been timing all of the cars just for his own enjoyment. 'That E-type must shift quick.' he smiled at Dewis. Some of the drivers from the other manufacturers overheard this conversation and decided to try to 'improve' on their times, and so they all started going faster and faster up the hill and as a result, the rest of the week turned into an impromptu hill-climb race.

Recalling the incident today, Norman laughs, 'Those poor customers, the people we were demonstrating to, it was terrible really; you forgot they were there.' At the end of the week, the two E-types were still the quickest. But it was all good-natured rivalry as Dewis recalls: '…because the Ferrari chaps came over and said, "Well that E-type is a fantastic car and you've been going quicker than any of us all week, do you think we could have a ride in it?" and we said yes, so it was all good fun you know. You wouldn't have that today, but it's a story that goes with the E-type really.' he laughed again.

↓ **The media could not get enough of Jaguar's new sports car (Parc des Eaux Vives).**

Engineering and manufacturing the E-type way

When the decision was made to put the E-type into production, chief chassis engineer Tom Jones remembers the instruction from Bill Heynes was, 'No expensive tooling'. Apart from the suspension parts, which were forgings, the body panels had to be 'cut and guillotined and folded', and in order to save on cost Jones was not allowed to use aluminium panels as they had done for racing.

Tom Jones recalls: 'And the sanction was for 250, so I started off the design on planning for 250 and actually before it had gone into production, the sanction had increased to 500 then to 1,000. Their confidence was building up as they could see the development of the car coming along, and then of course, consequently there was something like 80,000-odd.'

But was this combination of a monocoque body and sub-frame assembly for the engine going to be robust enough for a production sports car? 'Oh yes definitely', replied Tom Jones.

'And of course when we started off, it was in aluminium, the body and the frame. As far as I recollect, we had already made the decision to productionise it with steel panels, and as I said, the tooling had to be kept to a minimum.' he added.

It may surprise some readers to know that the E-type manufacturing process was a very labour-intensive one, which normally means a high manufacturing cost, and subsequently a high showroom price. In fact, for a volume producer like Jaguar, the E-type could almost be considered a hand-built car. From the outside, Jaguar truly appeared to employ a variety of manufacturing and assembly methods towards the end of the 1950s. The 1955–59 2.4/3.4-litre (Mark I) saloon-car range became Jaguar's first full monocoque construction vehicle, then there was the XK 150 (although production was just coming to an end) which still comprised a separate chassis and body construction while at the same time, the D-type and XKSS sports and racing machines which were a combination of advanced lightweight monocoque and sub-frame assembly. When the final XK 150 was made in 1960, the assembly line

↑ Ten days before the official launch of the E-type in Geneva, Dewis's test car (77 RW) was given a shakedown in a 3,000 mile run across France by Motor magazine, bringing nothing but praise from the journalist crew.

→ The E-type body shell underwent a lot of welding and fettling on the production line. Here two workers are assembling components on the bulkhead.

← Factory assembly hall with unpainted E-type bodyshells.

workers had to then switch to a 'volume' sports-car manufacturing process which up to that stage had been employed only on racing cars in the competition department, and not on the normal assembly line.

The move from a traditional separate chassis and body construction method to that of a fully welded stressed body or monocoque, was based on significant industry developments in automobile assembly. The technology of motor car construction and assembly had moved on from the long-established separate chassis and body structure, relegating that construction process to the history books as being far too heavy and costly. This was due in part to the advances made in welding and assembly methods on the

production line which made monocoque construction much cheaper than the traditional technique.

Brian Martin explains: 'Jaguar wasn't the first company to produce monocoque-constructed motor cars, and it was pretty obvious that sooner or later everybody was going to go down that route. The cost of producing a separate chassis with all its running gear attached to it and then dropping a body onto it must have been prohibitive against having a chassis/body unit already built and just attaching things to it; simple as that.'

It must be remembered that very few manufacturers up to that point had taken this step, and it was as much of a change in the mindset of the assembly worker as it was in a technical sense. Martin continues: 'I think the problem up to then had

→ The bare shell of the Series 1 shows just how sleek and streamlined the E-type was.

Quality means good workmanship

← After the panels were pressed by Abbey Panels, body assembly of the E-type took place at Browns Lane, Coventry.

always been: how do you replace this enormous structure which was self-supporting and carried all the running gear and transmission and engine, with a body virtually just suspended on it? And that was probably the technical innovation.'

By comparison, in the 2.4 saloon (and later the Mark II) saloon cars, the engineers built up an imitation chassis that served as a mobile jig which held the suspension units, engine, gearbox and drive-train, over which the body was then dropped. In that respect, for the assembly line workers it was very similar to having a chassis ready made and dropping the body onto it which then only required the suspension systems to be bolted up into it.

However, as Brian Martin explains: 'The E-type was different because you didn't have the ability to build this separate system and drop the body over it. It happened with the rear suspension because that could be built as a complete unit and then the body could be dropped over it, but then you had to come along with the engine, gearbox and front frame as a unit and bolt it directly onto the front of the car.'

This system of fixing the front sub-frame to the bulkhead of the E-type was extremely strong and rigid, and in principle is not very different from the way in which the engine and suspension fixtures are fitted to the monocoque of a modern-day Formula 1 car. But wasn't the E-type assembly process, which was a combination of steel monocoque and lightweight engine and suspension sub-frame, an expensive way to manufacture even a small-volume sports car? Jim Randle explains: 'In tooling terms it was very cheap. The piece cost would be higher, yes, because there is quite a lot of manual content in that, but [it was] a perfectly rational and logical way of doing it and it comes straight from aircraft practice.'

The strength of the E-type monocoque body and sub-frame combination was already proven in the D-type in competition, so there was little doubt about its application in the new sports-car assembly process. Due to the anticipated smaller volume of production E-types, the cost of setting up a complete body-panel pressing facility would have been prohibitive.

Tom Jones explains how they used a process called 'stretcher pressing' to form the panels: 'Cyril Crouch was my body engineer who worked with me on the E-type then, and we had this method of pressing which was called "stretcher pressing". You made up a very thick panel, like 16-gauge, polished it, shaped it, then filled it with concrete and then you stretched a panel over the top of it. So that is the way you did the pressings, and then you trimmed it all off.'

Later, the factory decided to adopt the Kirksite method of panel production. The Kirksite method of panel pressing was in Jim Randle's words, 'A fairly cheap and cheerful way of doing it. Kirksite is a moulding process using not particularly hard material, and if you just have Kirksite tools then the edges where the metal is drawn over the edge get worn away. But if you put hard steel edges onto it, then you can avoid that and the tool will last quite a long time.'

The Kirksite method allowed for a much quicker method of panel production and the presses were good for about 5,000 pressings, but the advantage of this method was that you could change models and reshape panels much more quickly if necessary. Body panels were fabricated by Abbey Panels and transported over to the Jaguar body shop where they were assembled; it was only much later that Abbey assembled the bonnets at their works and delivered them as fully made-up units. Following this labour-intensive method of body assembly, one would expect Jaguar to have had a

fairly large body shop, 'No, just the one line.' Tom Jones replied, laughing.

Geoff Turner, who started his apprenticeship in August 1959 with Daimler Motor Company, was transferred to Jaguar when that company bought Daimler in 1960. He continued with Jaguar and upon completion of his apprenticeship in 1964, was offered a job in manufacturing engineering, but when he and his ex-Daimler colleagues saw the production methods applied to the assembly of the E-type, they couldn't believe it.

Geoff explains: 'When I saw them welding these bodies together over in the old body shop, I thought, "What is this? You know, this is a 150mph sports car", there were no major body pressings, it was all small panels and bits, it looked like a jigsaw.' Coming from Daimler, Geoff had been used to high-quality work there and had expected to see the same at Jaguar. The body assembly process involved loading several panels into a jig and welding them up, then lead loading the finished item to get all the fit and shut lines straight. 'It all seemed to go together okay, none of them ever split in half, but you used to wonder.' he laughed.

This made the assembly process extremely labour intensive, but as Anders Clausager explains: 'It is a fact that the E-type body as designed was not tooled up for true mass production. Jaguar therefore avoided a high tooling cost, and each body required much work by hand, in welding up individual small panels, lead loading and fettling.'

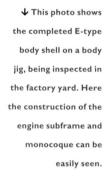

↓ **This photo shows the completed E-type body shell on a body jig, being inspected in the factory yard. Here the construction of the engine subframe and monocoque can be easily seen.**

← A Jaguar factory
worker welds up
component panels to
form the bulkhead.

Few cars look their best in a bare metal state on the production line, and yet just the body-in-white shell of the E-type already looks like a supercar even at this early stage of the assembly process.

Even as late as 1964, Jaguar did not have a formal manufacturing engineering department. Up until that time, it had been the responsibility of a small group of clerks, who would write up the assembly process of a new model, which was typically being carried out by a group of only two or three fitters in a small workshop. The first few cars of a new model run were built up on static trestles, and the clerks simply wrote down what they observed the fitters to be doing, literally as they bolted together the new car. 'Not much sophistication about it', as Geoff Turner recalled, as there was no detail reference to the use of hand tools, air tools or electric tools, and once this process had been recorded, the new car would be deemed ready for manufacture.

At that stage (1964) Jaguar was still manufacturing the Series I E-type, which called for numerous small day-to-day modifications. 'They introduced changes and modifications by the day but in latter years we managed to convince the board to do model-year changes because the workload was such that I almost couldn't cope with it all the time.' recalls Turner.

With the introduction of a more-formal manufacturing engineering department in 1967, the quantity of problems or changes being made on the assembly line began to diminish. Turner recalls: 'You didn't suddenly find you couldn't make something or build something, which used to happen sometimes in the early days, because you didn't see a design until the design department handed it over to you. So, if they had got something wrong, you didn't find out until you actually tried bolting the car together.' The manufacturing engineers were then able to assess changes in their own fully equipped workshop before applying the modifications to the actual cars on the assembly line.

Gradually, as the Daimler SP250 sports car and Majestic Major production lines were shut down at the old Radford factory, the remaining Majestic Major production was

transferred to the Browns Lane plant. Amazingly, much of the assembly of Jaguar cars was still being done with hand tools in those areas where no power tools were available, as Sir William was not one to spend his money without good reason. Geoff Turner remembers: 'But as the last car moved up the track at Radford, we were literally taking the tools out of the hands of the guys on the track at Radford and putting them into cars and bringing them up here and giving them to the fitters on the track at Browns Lane.'

The E-type was assembled on a separate assembly line from the Jaguar saloons, due mainly to the very different process required for the new sports car. The engine and front-suspension assembly was built up as a complete and separate unit and then mated to the bulkhead of the monocoque. The rear suspension, too, was built up as a complete unit and the body lowered onto it, and so the E-type and saloon assembly processes could not be carried out on the same assembly line. As demand for the E-type was high right from the outset, it soon became apparent that additional capacity would be needed, so an extra assembly line was installed at Browns Lane in 1968. Extra space was provided by moving the E-type body assembly area which allowed not only for the much-needed second assembly line, but both assembly tracks could be extended in length at the same time. In this way, the assembly process was speeded up and as a result, a higher volume of output was maintained.

To further highlight the extent of manual input in the whole E-type assembly process, car bodies obtained their first coat of paint at the Castle Bromwich plant and were then sent over to Browns Lane for assembly. Because fitters and assembly workers inflicted some unavoidable minor damage to the paintwork by leaning on the body, the cars were only given their final coat after the assembly process was completed. Geoff Turner again: 'We used to finish the cars totally, with everything on them, and then take the bumpers and stuff off and mask it up and give them a second coat. All cars had a second coat in those days, which reduced all the assembly line build damage and scratches. Yes, that's how we used to build the cars in those days.'

It was often a source of wonder how Sir William Lyons was able to produce the most stunningly beautiful cars, both saloons and sports cars, at such low prices. Even more surprising for the motoring press and public alike, was the fact that the E-type, when it was announced, cost almost the same as the outgoing XK150, which it was about to replace. Indeed, a key factor in the success of the E-type was the car's affordability for what it delivered. Tom Jones sums it up: 'It was the old "cut and shut" business you know. There was no expensive body tooling at all, you see, and Abbey Panels made the bonnets and shipped them in. All I can say is that my brief from Bill Heynes was "no expensive tooling", so that ruled out body tooling.'

Series 1 production E-type (1961–67)

There can be few cars more sensuous, more stylistically inspiring than the Jaguar E-type: sleek and simple, yet elegant to the point of sophistication. Fast, yet it does not have to travel fast to be appreciated and admired. The E-type is indeed a testament to the professionalism and commitment of its designer, Malcolm Sayer.

As Stephen Bayley later wrote in *The Daily Telegraph* (1996), 'No question, the E-type Jaguar was one of the most beautiful and remarkable cars ever made: the resolution of technical demands and artistic desire was achieved with such perfect balance.'

You could do the old car park test – if you walked into a car park full of cars, you could pick out the E-type from almost any distance, and it wasn't just the E-type, you could do it with most cars in the 1960s, they just all had such individual styles. Keith Helfet agrees: 'They had something special and that actually is about emotion and desire. So

there is some very good design that is not desirable or emotional but is in other ways influential. But that is what was special about Jaguar.'

In the March, 1961 issue of *Jaguar Journal*, under an article headed, 'The New E-type Grand Touring Car', Bill Rankin praised the new car and appealed to those involved with its manufacture, to work at keeping the costs of this newcomer as low as possible, as it was the most expensive model in the Jaguar range.

Even in the 1960s, the company went to great lengths to ensure that the car was well suited to drivers who were accustomed to high-speed cars. 'Large windows combine with the wide wrap-round windscreen and thin screen pillars to provide superb all-round visibility. Bucket seats, adjustable for reach and a steering wheel adjustable for both height and reach, enable a driver to select his own ideal driving position – an important safety factor', explained the *Jaguar Journal*.

In one of the first reviews of the E-type in America, Jesse Alexander wrote in the well-known motoring journal, *Car* and Driver (May 1961) that the new Jaguar was the most exciting sports car news of the year. He went on to say that the Coventry company was in the enviable position of being one of the few manufacturers in the UK enjoying full production at that time. Throughout the article Alexander scarcely paused long enough to draw breath, so full of praise was he for the new E-type. 'One might conveniently call the XK-E a "production D", but this oversimplification doesn't really do the new Jaguar justice.' he wrote. Actually, the E-type was 21 inches (525mm, or over half a metre) longer than the D-type.

The fixed-head coupé version of the E-type was an entirely new type of car for Jaguar as the fast-back coupé with its large rear door offered generous amounts of room for both passengers and luggage. This euphoria for the new fixed-head coupé was not out of place either, as the E-type's styling was indeed cutting new ground for the company. Never before had Jaguar produced a car in this mould, with its closed hatchback shape and large opening rear door. The sleek Sayer design with its revolutionary independent rear suspension had shaved some 500lb off the weight of the XK 150S, a remarkable feat by any standard.

COMPARATIVE TABLE OF JAGUAR SPORTS CAR DIMENSIONS:

Model	Introduced	Length**	Width**	Height**	Weight
C-type	June '51	157	64½	42½	2,240lb
D-type	June '54	154	65⅜	31½	1,904lb
XKSS	March '51	173	62	53½	3,024lb
XK 120 FHC	March '51	173	62	53½	3,024lb
XK 140 FHC	October '54	176	64½	52½	3,136lb
XK 150 FHC	May '57	177	64½	55	3,220lb
E1A	1956	169¾	62¾	32 (scuttle)	1,766lb
E2 (Red No.1)	1958	-	-	-	1,925lb
E2A	1960	170	62¾	44¾ (screen)	1,925lb
E-type FHC Ser.1	March '61	175⅓	65⅖	48	2,700lb

*These dimensions were very close to the final production E-type   **Length, width and height dimensions measured in inches

↓ This early public relations shot of the Series I E-type accentuates the long bonnet and the seating position just ahead of the rear wheels. Note also the bonnet locks, which appeared only on very early cars.

Car and Driver's Jesse Alexander again: 'How fast is the new Jag? The speedo reads to 160mph and test driver Norman Dewis has lapped the banked MIRA track at 150. Under the right conditions it would seem that it wouldn't be too difficult to get the needle close to its 160mph maximum. From the aerodynamic standpoint, in fact, the car should be capable of no less than 180mph, with 265bhp and the right gearing, which would pretty effectively make it the world's fastest series production car today, as the XK 120 was in its time.' Perhaps a rather ambitious account of what might have been, yet the new E-type was certainly up there with the best of the sports cars of the day, most of which cost several times the price of the E-type.

Competition for the E-type in the market was substantial with the Mercedes Benz 300SL Roadster (1957), Aston Martin DB4 (1958), Maserati 5000GT (1959), Ferrari 410 Superamerica (1960) and several others. With the possible exception of the Chev Corvette in the States, these cars and others which competed with the E-type were generally much more expensive, even three and four times more costly; maintenance costs were prohibitive and they were usually only made in extremely small quantities. When the E-type arrived with its claimed 150mph top speed, this shook the sports-car establishment to its core, and all this for around £2,000.

When comparing the E-type with its earlier stable mate, the XK 150, it is interesting to note that the newer sports car offered far better performance, greater comfort with a stunningly modern style, at almost the same cost. A factory cost analysis showed that the E-type was actually cheaper to build than the XK 150, in such respects as body, trim, hood and transmission (for instance the XK 150S had an overdrive which the E-type did not).

Geoff Turner, an apprentice with Jaguar in 1961, was transferred from the Daimler factory at Radford to the road test department at Browns Lane after the Daimler company was bought in 1960. He remembers one of his first jobs with the Jaguar: 'We drove them [the E-types] off the end of the track literally, checked them over and then took them out on the road.'

It was about the time that Jaguar took over the GEC block (a General Electric Research and Development building) that Geoff began his apprenticeship with the company. He remembers his first assignment with a smile: 'My first transfer from Radford to Browns Lane, I went into the road-test department, that's when I used to road test E-types as a 19-year-old apprentice, a brilliant job.'

Following a well-worn 15-mile test route through the outskirts of Coventry, the new E-types were driven down one of the lanes past a farm with a farmhouse on one side of the road and the farmyard on the other side. Geoff picks up the story: 'And you never took much notice of it, I used to flash through at about 80mph or 90mph. Then one morning I went

→ The low angle on this photo strongly emphasises the strength and muscular appearance of the rear 'haunches' while also showing how well the rear of the cabin and roofline is integrated into the overall design. The slim bumpers also serve to heighten the perception of speed of the E-type.

through there, and there was this load of chickens running across the road and one of them didn't get out of the way fast enough. The wire wheels almost totally de-feathered this chicken, you'd never seen anything like it, there were feathers everywhere, they were all up in the air and floating about and they were all in the engine bay, what a mess. It was almost as if you had put it through a machine and plucked it. I offered the farmer a few pence and took it home', he added laughing.

The early Series 1 E-types had an aluminium fascia panel in the centre and aluminium trim around the gear stick between the seats. These early cars are referred to as the 'ally dash' or 'flat floor' models, and are regarded today as the most collectable of all the E-types. The aluminium finish was a departure from earlier Jaguar sports cars, although the XK 150 had also recently gone this route, and was distinctly different from the 'wood-and-leather club room' feel of the

↑ **Despite being such a streamlined sports car with phenomenal performance, the E-type was not constrained by a low roof and small windows – it was indeed blessed with excellent all-round vision.**

SELECTED JAGUAR SALOONS, XK 150 AND E-TYPE MODEL PRICE COMPARISON:

Model	Produced	Engine	Price**
Mark IX saloon*	September 1961	3,781cc	£1,994
Mark X saloon	December 1961	3,781cc	£2,392
XK 150S OTS*	October 1960	3,781cc	£2,176
XK 150S FHC*	October 1961	3,781cc	£2,175
E-type 3.8-litre OTS	March 1961	3,781cc	£2,097
E-type 3.8-litre FHC	March 1961	3,781cc	£2,196

*Last produced.   **Prices include British purchase tax.

saloons. There was also a sound financial reason for this, as Jim Randle explains: 'It was just a piece of thin formed aluminium that was all, cheap and cheerful stuff.'

Of course, it was cheaper to fabricate than the more complex wooden fascia, but Tom Jones adds an interesting point of view: 'It actually goes back to the racing days you see. We had aluminium fascias [in the race cars], and it was thought that really it was a good thing.' This is actually a very logical explanation seeing as the E-type was first intended as a D-type replacement and it shows the racing heritage of the E-type very well.

Later, E-types were subject to a wave of new safety regulations emanating from the US, when road safety campaigner Ralph Nader brought pressure to bear on the large vehicle manufacturers. The fascia underwent a change with the traditional Jaguar toggle switches being replaced with

rocker switches and the E-type gained a collapsible steering column. The American motoring press then proceeded to slam the new layout saying that the switches all looked the same and they were difficult to tell apart. What they had failed to realise was that this style was reminiscent of the British fighter planes of the Second World War, and evoked images of an engaging drive with the pilot in control of his sleek speed machine. It was a very British thing, and Jaguar drivers were quite happy to wallow in the atmosphere.

The sleek style of the E-type had resulted in a rather shallow windscreen height on the roadster which required an unusual triple windscreen-wiper arrangement, as the engineers could not achieve the necessary sweep with just two wipers. Although this may

↓ **Undoubtedly, Malcolm Sayer created one of the most desirable sports cars of the century. This rear three-quarter shot of a Series I roadster illustrates how brilliantly Malcolm Sayer crafted the E-type body.**

← Unique to the Jaguar E-type was the fitting of triple wipers. This was necessary due to twin wipers not providing sufficient sweep of the windscreen. One can see the central windscreen stiffener bar required to add rigidity to the windshield frame.

have been more costly to produce, it became a unique feature on the car as the E-type must have been one of the only cars on the road at the time to have had this. What may have started out as a bit of a headache for the Jaguar stylists turned into a feature which made the car a bit different in the market, and Jaguar was all about being different.

Explaining this, the *Jaguar Journal* noted: 'For adverse weather conditions, triple-blade two-speed wipers and electrically operated windscreen washers are provided.'

Also unique to the E-type roadster (right up to and including the Series 3 roadster) was the chrome stiffener bar which supported the windscreen. This bar, which may have harked back to the old days of open-top motoring in British sports cars, was necessary as Norman Dewis found out during his MIRA testing sessions. When subjecting the roadster to the *pavé* test for structural stiffness and rigidity at the MIRA test track, as well as revealing weaknesses in the suspension and body, the torturous testing programme would cause the windscreen frame to twist and distort, a problem that obviously did not occur in the fixed-head. When trying to fit the soft hood later, he found that the windscreen frame was often distorted in the centre and the hood would not align and seal properly.

The stiffener bar was therefore fitted in the centre of the windscreen frame and bolted onto the scuttle top, creating a much stronger frame and in the process created a uniquely

British feature which was not seen on any American convertible sports cars. It also doubled as a convenient locator for the rear-view mirror which could be moved up or down the stiffener bar to suit the driver's needs, but that was purely a secondary use for the chrome bar.

The story of the development of the E-type as a model is not a simple one. Designed by Malcolm Sayer, the roadster was the first derivative to be fabricated both in the experimental body shop and on the assembly line. Before the fixed-head coupé became a reality, the roadster was running around the factory with a detachable fibreglass hardtop fabricated by the same department responsible for the manufacture of the fibreglass Daimler SP250. The idea was that the detachable hardtop would be available as an optional extra with the roadster to be used in the winter months, and stored away during the summer. Norman Dewis used such a hardtop on his early test cars extensively before a coupé became available for him to test. 'And I ran that quite a bit with this top on you know. But then we went from that to a full sloping back with the boot lid opening from the back of it.'

Although Malcolm Sayer drew the E-type fixed-head coupé and tweaked it a bit on paper, it was Bob Blake who turned it into metal. Norman Dewis recalls: 'Yes, I saw his drawing of it, you know, because he [Malcolm Sayer] said, "That's what we're going to do next". So, Sayer designed it and Bob Blake

↓ The 'office' – a pilot's view of the controls in a WWII Spitfire. The typical British sports car had long been equipped with numerous gauges and switches, giving the driver an unmistakable sense of control and speed.

made the first one, but in conjunction with Sayer, yes.' In motoring terms this coupé version was rather unflatteringly referred to as a hatchback, a name which does not do the sleek lines of the E-type any justice.

Once again out at the MIRA testing ground, Dewis put the fixed-head through its paces. Apart from going through the *pavé* test, he took it on an additional test course which had an extended pitch sequence, covering this test track repeatedly at different speeds. He recalls doing this test at 30mph and the first two pitches were all right but the third pitch would always undo the catch on the rear door. It was the frequency and length of pitching and rolling sequence that would always undo the catch and it took ages to get it fixed. Norman adds: 'Oh it was a terror. It used to be just a certain slight movement that just released it every time. We finished up having to redesign the catch in the end.' These are

↑ 'Room with a view' – the well equipped interior of an early Series I E-type.

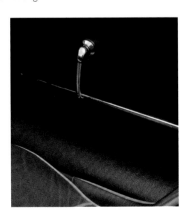

↓ Norman Dewis had a lot of trouble with the early rear door catch which kept opening during testing. A redesigned catch solved the problem. The E-type's luggage area was surprisingly spacious.

just a few of the tests that the driver had to endure endlessly, just so that the E-type owner could have a car that satisfied his or her expectations.

First shown at the 1961 Geneva Show, the E-type was introduced officially to the home market in July that year. Those early E-type roadsters and fixed-head coupés produced until June 1962, are now referred to as 'flat-floor' models, a feature that turned out to be quite awkward for the occupants, and subsequent models featured recessed foot wells to provide greater comfort for taller drivers.

In October 1964 Jaguar introduced the 4.2 E-type, which eliminated most of the earlier 3.8's short-comings. The bigger engine gave even better flexibility and low-range pulling power and the all-synchro box that went with it was judged to be a vast improvement over the 'agricultural' Moss four-speeder, fitted previously. The brakes were improved too as were the seats, and overall, the 4.2 was regarded as a vastly improved vehicle, especially as performance remained the same and the car was now easier to drive.

Media and celebrity reaction

In general, the success of the sports-car genre in the early 1960s was as much a product of the right socio-economic conditions as it was about appealing designs and sleek styling. The early 1950s had still been under the influence of war time austerity and its resultant limitations on styling and design. At that time it was thought that styling and design had to be economical because anything that could be vaguely construed as flashy was considered extravagant. But with the dawning of the 1960s came a different mindset, as the Baby Boomer generation became aware of the positive economic prospects in the market. The 1960s was a very expressive decade, and all of a sudden the sky really seemed to be the limit for personal achievement. This decade brought with it a greater personal disposable income and with the advent of the jet age, international travel and other similar previously unthinkable endeavours became a reality. As a result of this dramatic social and economic revival, car buyers became

↑ **This 1965 Series I fixed-head coupé is finished in midnight blue. The Series I fixed head is probably one of the most pleasing automotive shapes ever to be produced.**

much more sophisticated and demanding people, and their purchasing power now gave them a much greater influence in the market.

This period saw an increase in the awareness of styling, and with it a greater emphasis on conscious, practical and stylish design on a broad scale. For instance, around the home one began to see the emergence of Italian design and style, signalling a change in people's thinking, as well as an appreciation of visual presentation. These social conditions were not created by a single manufacturer or government, but emerged directly from the people, creating their own momentum. The E-type was part of this environment, and its success was not the product of an opportune marketing campaign; it was just a car absolutely right for the time.

In the early 1960s, it seemed as though opportunities in the music, fashion, movies, sports and entertainment industries could launch the career of anyone who was prepared to tackle this brave new world into the commercial stratosphere. It was cool to drive a Mini around London or a Volkswagen bus with a flower stuck in your hair, but this period ushered in the era of that most outrageous of characters, the denim-clad Rolls-Royce driver. Gone were the pinstripe suits and chauffeurs, this was all about your image and being seen in the right places by the right people. The new opportunities for wealth creation through entertainment and sport in the 1960s changed the social landscape of the

↓ A native Texan, Roy Orbison is probably best known for his hit single *Oh! Pretty Woman* in the early 1960s, released just a few years before he acquired this Series 1½ E-type roadster. He was inducted into the Rock and Roll Hall of Fame in 1987.

world forever, and the E-type was right at the centre of this revolution.

The early 1960s was a period in which many freshly styled products were exploding onto the social scene, while the automotive market saw some dynamic new entrants as well. This was a period when the horsepower wars were contested on all fronts: Italian, German, British and American. On the Continental side of the Atlantic divide, it was all about style and high-performance machinery while on the American side it was muscle and brute force that ruled the day, topped off with loud exhausts.

While the general post-war population willingly abandoned their previously conservative approach to life and grasped the fruits of this new-found freedom with both hands, the automotive designers and stylists were also influenced by these same liberating factors. It is generally acknowledged by many engineers and designers in the motor industry that the 1950s and 1960s saw some of the most outstanding automotive shapes and styles ever to grace our roads. It was during this period that the Italian designers such as Pininfarina, Bertone, Michelotti, Frua, Gandini, Giugiaro and many others, fashioned some of their most daringly creative styles. Similarly, Bill Mitchell, William Lyons, Alec Issigonis, Ferdinand Porsche and other international automotive designers produced advanced designs which were all undoubtedly the product of this creative freedom.

← Tony Curtis poses with his new Series 1½ roadster. Curtis was well known as a film actor, but who could forget him in the series *The Persuaders* alongside Roger Moore. Tony Curtis is also an accomplished artist.

The entertainment industry

February 1962 saw Cliff Richard at the top of the UK charts with *The Young Ones*, while Chubby Checker filled the second spot with the ever-popular *Let's Twist Again*.

In August that year, Marilyn Monroe died, allegedly from an overdose of sleeping tablets, at the age of 36.

Pop star Adam Faith burst onto the UK music scene in 1959 and was regarded as second only to Cliff Richard at the time. His 1962 hits included *Lonesome*, *As You Like It*, *Don't That Beat All* and *What Now*.

Other well-known E-type drivers included Sid James from the Carry On series, The Beatles' George Harrison as well as footballer George Best.

This period saw the development of the sports car as an important component of a complete model range for the motor manufacturer, as the sports car was seen as a closely linked by-product of prosperity and having a very definite halo effect on the rest of the model range. To have your sports car linked with popular film and sports stars was certainly the way to get your brand noticed.

Jaguar sales in America unarguably benefited from the popularity of all things British during the 1960s. Fashion model Twiggy, James Bond movies, television's *Avengers* and the music of the Beatles and Rolling Stones, to name but a few, propelled interest in British motorcars among US Anglophiles; in the inimitable words of Austin Powers, 'Yeah, Baby!'

With the high demand for the E-type in America, a small number of right-hand-drive press cars accounted for most of the E-types in Britain in 1961 and the media were envied for their ability to gain access to them, or for the lucky few, to even drive them. Michael Kemp was the deputy motoring

→ This elevated view of the Series 1 E-type shows its true sports car proportions. Thin chrome trim along the fender tops, slatted bonnet vents and the dominant power bulge all contributed to the car's performance and appeal.

correspondent of the *Daily Sketch* (London, England) from 1960, but it was only the editor who got his hands on the E-type at launch. It was only later in the year, after the Geneva launch that Michael got to drive the car. 'It was the car that everybody wanted to possess. It was a dream, it was a topic of conversation, to see one was a sensation, to be able to actually sit in one was an enormous privilege, to drive one was a gift from heaven and they couldn't make enough of them. There was a tremendous waiting list for the things.'

The manner in which a car is launched in the 2000s is a far cry from the way it was done in the 1960s. Today, the media do much of the work of launching a new model through the pages of magazines, newspapers and on television, but 45 years ago, the anticipation of seeing a new model for the first time at a motor show or on the dealer's showroom floor was almost a tangible thing. 'It was known that a sensational car was coming but when the veil was lifted at the Motor Show, there was a gasp and, I mean, it just swept everybody off

their feet. Mind you, everybody thought it was sensational, so it was easy to believe it was sensational.' Michael Kemp recalled from those early days.

There was even a different approach to the way in which a new model was reported on and covered in the media back then as Michael Kemp explains: 'The writing about cars was "bumper to bumper" as it were, it was about the car, the car was the focus whereas now it is not only the car that is in focus within motoring, it is all that surrounds the car that is also interesting.' ▪

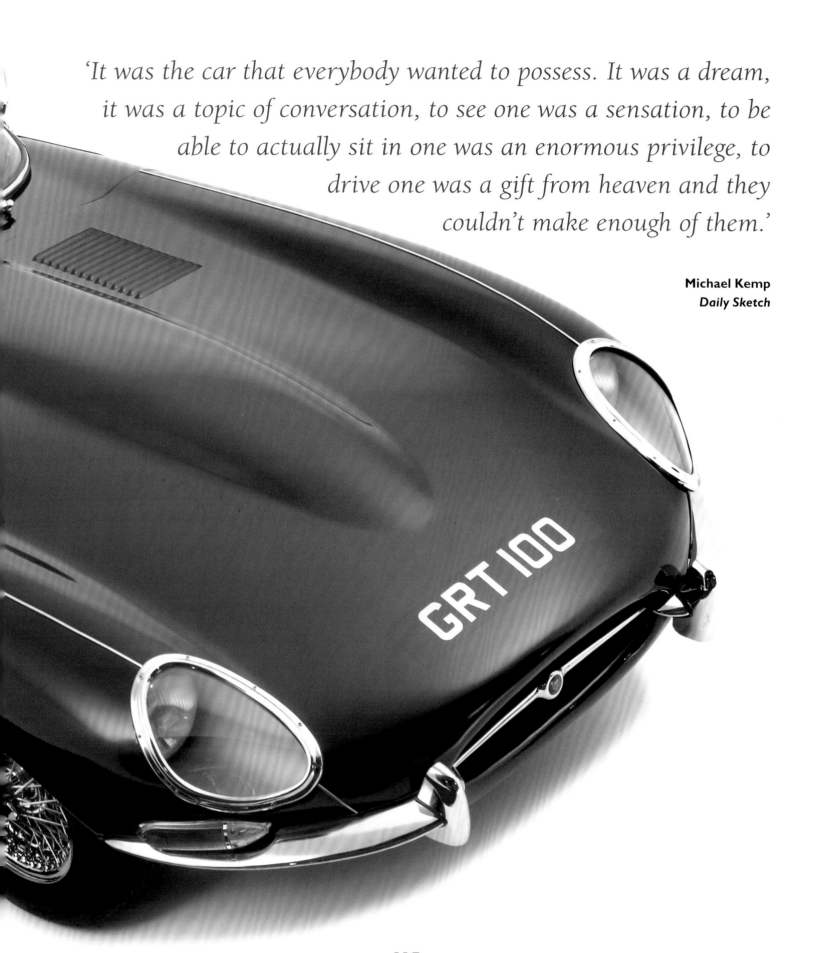

'It was the car that everybody wanted to possess. It was a dream, it was a topic of conversation, to see one was a sensation, to be able to actually sit in one was an enormous privilege, to drive one was a gift from heaven and they couldn't make enough of them.'

Michael Kemp
Daily Sketch

The E-type grows up

'I think the car is famous not for its aerodynamics, but its looks. Its sculpture and its design, you know, the guy was just a genius.'

Keith Helfet, Jaguar designer (1978–2002)

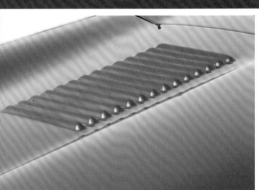  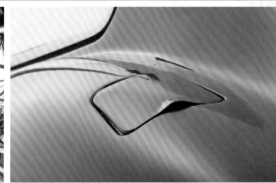

1961	1962	1964	1966	1968
E-type launched in Geneva in March	E-types finish in 4th and 5th places at Le Mans 24-Hour	Larger 4,235cc XK engine introduced in E-type	Series 1 2+2 FHC introduced	Series 1 E-type production ceases in September

JAGUAR'S ALL-NEW PRODUCTION XKE

All early production bound for USA

It was in late January, 1961 that Sir William gave the green light to plans that would see the new XK-E launched at New York's International Automobile Show, right in the heart of the company's biggest market. The American launch in that April was only a month after the car's highly successful international debut at the Geneva Motor Show, but within 30 minutes of the show opening in New York, six cars had already been sold.

Autocar reported that reaction from the Coliseum, where America's fifth International Motor Show was held, was indeed 'encouraging' and as the report went on to say, 'The new E-type Jaguar may justifiably be claimed to have "stolen the show".' In fact, Jaguar was riding high in the popularity stakes in America, and the president of Jaguar Cars of New York, Johannes Eerdmans, placed an order of over $30-million with the factory in Coventry, which had undoubtedly been boosted in no small measure by the E-type's overwhelming reception.

Mike Cook, who is today in charge of Jaguar's American archive in California, was at the show although working for Triumph Cars at the time. He remembers the event clearly: 'I can confirm that the E-type launch was a mob scene and there was a crowd around the car most of the time for the entire ten days of the show.'

For the event, Sir William, wearing his publicist hat, hired the model Marilyn Hanold to be present on the Jaguar E-type turntable for the duration of the show, and as she was *Playboy*'s Playmate of the Month (June, 1959), there was some speculation as to whom the crowds had come to see.

At first glance, it seems odd that most of the E-type's production was destined for delivery across the Atlantic. Here was a sports car that was quintessentially English in every respect, with a racing heritage based almost solely on European and British circuits, and yet potentially its biggest market was on a different continent. Initial design and styling had been for the home market and it cost a good deal more than anything the Americans had to offer, even if there was not much to compare with it on the US market. However, combined with this and the fact that it cost a lot less than any Italian or German exotica, the E-type was well positioned for the US market with the performance and looks of far more expensive machinery.

Sir William Lyons knew this well enough, and drove the point home repeatedly with his engineers and staff. Norman Dewis recalls this well: 'That was Lyons's requirement all the time, America comes first; always top of the list.'

Geoff Turner also remembers the strong demand for the E-type from across the Atlantic: 'The majority were American

orders. It was quite restricted in this country and on the Continent. I mean the sales were just fantastic in America, it was amazing. Everybody wanted one.'

Given the importance of the American market, it is perhaps surprising that the car was designed without the option of automatic transmission. The XK 140 and XK 150 had both been offered with auto 'boxes from as early as 1956, which had proved to be quite popular in the States. Tom Jones commented that it was because the E-type was considered as a 'sports car', but it was probably more for reasons of being constructed along the lines of the D-type that no provision was made for an automatic transmission at launch. Within the set wheelbase of the E-type, there was just insufficient space in which to fit an auto 'box.

'They just designed a car. Obviously they considered the American market but it was not aimed specifically at that market, it was more a Ferrari basher.' observed Keith Helfet.

The E-type could never have been an American-only style of car, as that would not have had the same impact, even in

↑ The view that most motorists would see briefly in the mirror of the new bigger engined 4.2-litre E-type Series 1.

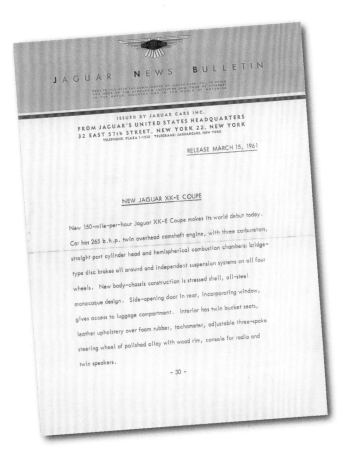

COMPARATIVE SPORTS CAR PRICES IN AMERICA 1961:

Vehicle	Price
Alfa Romeo Giulietta Spider	$3,520
Chevrolet Corvette V8	$3,934
Porsche 356 Super 90 Roadster	$4,334
Jaguar XK 150S	$5,120
Jaguar XK-E	$5,600
Aston Martin DB4	$10,400
Mercedes-Benz 300SL	$10,950
Ferrari 250GT Cabriolet	$12,600

Source: *Car and Driver*, May 1961

Jaguar afford it) to make a dedicated American sports car. The new sports car had to be universally accepted, and for a British motor manufacturer to make a sports car that was not aimed at its home market was unthinkable. Britain in the 1950s and 1960s was regarded as the international capital of the sports-car world, as they manufactured more sports cars than any other country at that time. However, Lyons knew just how to position his new grand tourer so that it suited the American buyer, who inhabited a distinct market that had a different set of buying and driving criteria, in a land with a climate that was quite different from that of the UK and one in which the Californian lifestyle played a big role.

↓ **Malcolm Sayer got the proportions of the fixed head coupé just right – it looks good from any angle.**

the USA. It needed to appear as an exotic or foreign sports car, and to possess those typically British qualities, in order to appeal to American buyers. In general, customer expectations were far more flexible around the time of the E-type's launch, and as a result, it wasn't considered necessary (and nor could

Marketing and advertising

Historically, at least up until the 1960s, motor manufacturers used two main avenues when promoting new vehicles to the public, namely, the print media and the motor shows. In former years, visual communication would be have been through cinema news reels, but today there are several other ways of communicating with the customer such as the internet and television, so the actual delivery mechanism has understandably changed quite dramatically.

However, during the decades from 1930 to 1960, one of the prime ways of communicating with customers was through the Motor Show, and each year Sir William Lyons would launch a new model at Earls Court in London. John Maries, a senior marketing manager at Jaguar (from 1981) confirms this: 'For many a long year that was the way that you communicated with your customer, largely because there was little else.'

On the print media side, specialist motor magazines in the UK were printed in standard black ink, with only the front cover being printed in colour. As colour printing was so expensive and rarely seen, the magazines would use the front cover not to promote what was inside the magazine, but rather to sell this space to the motor manufacturers who jumped at the opportunity of having a colour ad on the cover. Special issues, which covered the London Motor Show, might carry some two-tone advertising within the body of the magazine, but it wasn't until the 1980s that colour began to appear more regularly throughout. This meant that colour advertising became a regular fixture in magazines only quite recently and motor manufacturers would have had to make do with black-and-white illustrations only in their advertisements, as high-quality photographic reproductions were still a fairly

→ This advertisement which appeared in several American car magazines conveys several very strong messages: firstly, it promotes Jaguar's efforts as an exporter by highlighting that the sports cars are being despatched from Coventry (postmark), while the simplicity of the advertisement ensures that the reader has little else to focus on.

This is the new Jaguar XK-E!

Jaguar Cars Inc., 32 East 57th Street, New York 22, N. Y.

costly option. A further example of the use of print media by the motor manufacturers in the 1960s was the advent of car supplements published in the weekend broadsheet newspapers, which became very popular and were widely read by most motoring enthusiasts.

It was, however, the big international motor shows that were used by the motor manufacturers to launch their new models, and so the media coverage of these events was quite extensive. Apart from these shows, manufacturers, and Jaguar in particular, would use motor sport to promote their products, which is one of the reasons why the Le Mans 24-Hour is still so highly respected internationally. Very few Americans would ever have heard of Snetterton, Brands Hatch or even Silverstone, but they would have known about Le Mans as many prominent US teams and drivers competed there, because not only was it a good test of the vehicle but the event was internationally known. To this day it remains one of the few motor races in Europe that is still recognised by the Americans.

John Maries explains: 'Bill Lyons used motor sport as a way of promoting his company; that is why he went to Le Mans; that is why we did rallying as well. Bill Lyons was always looking for an angle to get his cars into the specialist press, and you would see Bill Lyons going motor racing purely for publicity. So if you won Le Mans, your name was made.'

You could argue that from an engineering perspective, racing improved the breed, but the overwhelming purpose for Sir William Lyons was to get on the front pages of the newspapers. Not only did he use motor sport for this purpose, but he used endurance, reliability and performance tests to promote his cars as demonstrated by the XK 120 at Jabbeke in Belgium, and the Montlhéry tests in France, involving seven days and nights running at an average speed of over 100mph. He would demonstrate that his cars could actually achieve the performance levels claimed by the company, and these were then screened by Pathé News and Movietone News for the public to view at the cinemas. This is the way that motor manufacturers created their publicity campaigns back in the

→ In this simple monotone advertisement in a well-known British magazine, Lodge seek to promote their product through the success of the E-type's first motorsport win. There is no mistaking which car won the race, but there is little reference to spark plugs.

↓ The E-type cabin offered a high degree of comfort compared with many of its high-speed rivals. Note: the gear knob in this photo is not original.

1960s; it was all about proving your product in a world which admired such engineering progress because not only was the car the star, but the medium of cinema and movies was itself a sought-after privilege for many at that time. The public hungered for it because it was all done in the name of entertainment.

Unfortunately for Jaguar, as a relatively small company with a big brand reputation, they did not have the money to advertise on television in the early days, although not that many people had television sets back then. However, in the 1950s and 1960s, the typical Jaguar buyer could be generally quite well defined as a 55-year-old male, and at that time this group was reached through advertising in the specialist motoring magazines or in the newspaper motoring supplements. It was only later when Jaguar was seeking a far wider audience that television became a more economical and effective way of reaching them because no longer did the public visit the cinemas nor did they read the motoring magazines in quite the same numbers that they used to.

John Maries again 'I don't think anybody knows what Jaguar spent on advertising in the 1950/60/70/80s, but let me tell you it was not much. But when they were doing so much on the track and when your car was in the headlines, why do you need to advertise?'

In the UK around the time of the Earls Court Motor Shows, this was a little different as Jaguar publicity would kick

into top gear, making good use of outdoor advertising. They would billboard all the major roads leading into London announcing the car that was going to be at Earls Court so the billboards were actually telling the public to 'come and see' their latest models.

With Jaguar's two prime markets being so far apart geographically and the typical buying groups in each market having very different expectations of their cars, it can be appreciated that separate marketing campaigns would be inevitable. In the early days, Jaguar UK would go to Nevada for their advertising shoots because of the advantageous light, while the American ad agencies would come to the UK to get their ad shots because the US market liked to see thatched cottages. 'That was a nonsense that existed for many years, but we've found a way around that these days.' John Maries adds laughing.

Jaguar sports cars did not enjoy a continuous flow of marketing attention, and with the two main product lines being saloons and sports cars, it usually worked out that the launch of new models alternated between these two different lines. As a result, fresh advertising resources would only really be allocated when a new model or upgrade was being introduced on a biennial basis, and the company therefore alternated its ad budget accordingly.

Importantly, up until his retirement in 1972, Sir William Lyons was very definitely at the helm of his company and firmly in control of the spending. In fact, as John Maries recalls, the company did not even have a marketing department; it had a publicity department and a sales department, and 'the boss was the boss and he knew what he wanted.' So up until the early 1970s, the company was not run by the marketing

department as so many motor manufacturers are today. More accurately, Jaguar up until that time was predominantly an engineering-driven company and new models were more likely to be introduced as a result of technical improvements made possible by the discoveries and innovations of their engineers. Marketing was not a word used in British motor manufacturing until well into the 1960s, as anything that had to do with the customer, would be dealt with by the publicity department.

John Maries recalls: 'The publicity department would produce the brochures and the posters and even the advertising, as it was, so marketing and marketing research were probably much later phenomena here than in the USA.'

US reaction to the XK-E

Within the confines of the Jaguar works, reference to the sports car range followed the normal corporate naming protocol, where 'X' referred to 'experimental' and 'K' indicated which engine was in that model. The 'K' engine was the familiar twin-overhead-cam, six-cylinder unit which started life in the XK 120 sports car and ran for some four decades through several generations and models.

One of Malcolm Sayer's first projects at Jaguar, as we have already seen, was the development of the XK 120C racing car where the 'C' stood for 'competition', and this eventually took on the nomenclature of XKC. It was thus not surprising that the race car which followed the XKC would be called the XKD,

↓ **With the bonnet raised, access to the E-type's engine was exceptionally good.**

but these were internal references for those particular projects, so when referred to in the outside world, they became known in the UK as the C-type and the D-type respectively. However, in the States, they tended to stick with the factory names of XKC and XKD.

When Sayer began work on the car to follow in the footsteps of the XKD, the project was given the internal factory reference of XK-E which also stuck when the model appeared Stateside, but it continued to be referred to as the E-type in Britain, in the same manner as its predecessors.

It was perhaps inevitable in 1961 that the XK-E would be compared with the only local, home-grown sports car on the American domestic market, the Chevrolet Corvette. Two more different animals one couldn't wish to meet, but nevertheless the comparison was made. Seen side by side, it is astonishing just how much smaller the Jaguar sports car appears than its rival, but this is due partly to the more-rounded shapes and contours which Malcolm Sayer gave the XK-E, as opposed to the more upright and straight-sided

Corvette. The Corvette was a good deal heavier despite being made from fibreglass, and it had the advantage of a head start of eight years of development in the market. However, in the looks race, the silky-smooth E-type won hands down with its elegant style and long bonnet. The Corvette was the product of the attentions of Harley Earl, GM's design guru, who is regarded as the first auto designer to utilise design dynamics as an instrument of brand leadership. This is reflected in his approach to grab the media's attention through the creation of extravagant show cars with deliberately elaborate designs and large fins. Earl was strongly influenced by contemporary aircraft design which showed in his rounded styling and curved surfaces on the 1953 Corvette, although in American design, 'curved surface' was a relative term.

In the comparison above, it should be noted that the base Corvette listed was fitted with a 3-speed manual gearbox as standard, no heater (extra $102.25) and solid steel wheels. If specified, the 4-speed manual gearbox would set you back an extra $188.30. The more powerful 270bhp engine would cost

↑ Towards the end of 1964, the Series 1 E-type received the new 4,235cc XK engine, pictured here in a 1965 model. The sub-frame holding the engine unit can be clearly seen here.

the owner another $182.95. Still, GM made 10,939 Corvettes in 1961 (which for them was hardly worth the effort), while slightly more then 1,800 E-types were exported by Jaguar to the United States during the period March to December 1961.

Three years after its launch in America, the XK-E was voted 'Best Grand Touring/Sports Car $3,000–$6,000' by the readers of the well-known motoring journal, *Car and Driver* (May 1964). Not only did the XK-E win that accolade,

but it was also voted the best 'All-Round Car', edging out several Mercedes saloon cars, the Ford Fairlane, Ferrari, Aston Martin, Porsche 356C, Buick Riviera, Corvette Sting Ray and many other top models which even included Rolls-Royce, Bentley and various Jaguar saloons. This was the first such survey held by that magazine, which certainly illustrates how well the XK-E was received and perceived in the USA. This reader survey proved so popular that it went on to become a regular annual feature in the magazine.

↑ **This gorgeous primrose-yellow E-type is an American-spec Series 1½ Roadster, with its exposed headlamps but still carrying the Series 1 indicator and bumper arrangements.**

COMPARATIVE TABLE SHOWING JAGUAR E-TYPE ROADSTER AND CORVETTE SPORTS CAR DIMENSIONS AND SPECIFICATIONS (1961):

Vehicles	Length	Width	Height	Weight	Engine	Power Output	Base Price
Jaguar E-type	175½	64¼	47*	2,810lb	3,781cc (235ci)	265bhp	$5,670
Chev Corvette	177⅓	72⅘	51½**	2,985lb	4,637cc (283ci)	230bhp	$3,934

*E-type with convertible hood up **Corvette over hardtop
Length, width and height dimensions measured in inches

Following specific market research, and in an effort to satisfy the requirements of the all-important American market, Jaguar upgraded the E-type with several unique features. Automatic transmission was hardly a feature that the manufacturers of sports cars in Britain and Europe would have considered, and in fact most would have resisted it rather strongly. However, when customer demand for this strengthened in the American market, Sir William Lyons was swift to react. Remarking on its 1966 introduction, Jim Randle said: 'The American market, yes that's what was driving it. The Americans didn't want anything else, didn't understand how to use stick shift.'

Norman Dewis remembers Sir William Lyons's words: 'Dewis, this car has got to sell in America, and you know what the Americans want, so make sure it satisfies the Americans.' Dewis had to ensure that the company's vehicle-development testing schedule included all aspects relevant to the American market.

There were several other areas in which the American-spec car differed from the European. Norman Dewis again: 'They didn't like heavy steering so you had to have a good 80% power steering; they didn't like heavy brake pedals; it had to be light and stand on its nose, you know, with a very light application and they don't like stiff suspensions. It had to have what we called the boulevard ride, so that's the way we produced the car.'

But producing the car principally for the American market inevitably led to some discontent on the European market, where some customers disliked the soft brakes. Director of servicing, Lofty England, brought this to the attention of Norman Dewis, who responded as follows: 'All you do is take the Mintex 114 pad material out and put in Ferodo DS11 race pads' I said, 'that will make it nice and heavy, giving it a wooden feel and they will have to really push hard. And that's what we did.'

Series 1 model changes

Towards the end of 1964, with the Series 1 E-type just less than four years old, Jaguar introduced an engine up-grade from 3,781cc to 4,235cc which saw a superb power unit get even better. Borrowed from the Mark X saloon car, the larger engine still produced the same maximum output, namely 265bhp, but the increased capacity provided a welcome boost in low-down torque thereby further improving the flexibility of the motor. Not long after the introduction of the new engine, Jaguar announced the arrival of the long-awaited all-synchromesh manual gearbox coupled to a new diaphragm clutch, a move also welcomed by many drivers.

Along with these two significant mechanical improvements, there were several interior upgrades which all just went to make the car altogether a bit more agreeable. Improved seats for taller drivers, colour-matched trim now covered the

↓ **This Jaguar publicity shot once again emphasised the increased accommodation that the 2+2 offered. Jaguar wanted to promote the family aspect of owning an E-type, suggesting that sporty motoring was still possible for the family man.**

↑ Jaguar were keen to promote the family, travel and leisure potential of the Series 1 2+2 when it was introduced in 1966. The publicity shot above suggests that the successful businessman, now with a young family, could still enjoy the sporting dreams of his youth, with the more spacious E-type 2+2.

centre console with a black-finished fascia panel instead of the central, shiny aluminium console and instrument panel. All these things, combined with a smoother ride, meant that the E-type now presented a much more comfortable driving package, an opinion supported by the press and customers on both sides of the Atlantic.

In March 1966, exactly five years since the launch of the E-type, Jaguar introduced its first major revision to their much-loved sports car. By inserting an additional nine inches into the wheelbase of the fixed-head coupé only, Jaguar were able to install a pair of small rear seats capable of accommodating two adults on a short journey or two small children over a longer distance. Called the Series 1 2+2, it was this latter option which actually prolonged the car's marketability to the young family man who wished to extend his 'young at heart' appearance, while still being able to take his wife and family for a drive in the E-type.

In order to achieve this, at the same time as increasing the wheelbase, Jaguar raised the roofline by two inches, which

also allowed them to increase the height of the windscreen by one and a half inches. As we have seen elsewhere in this book, a sports car is all about extremes on the one hand and some compromise on the other, and in order to allow for more passenger-carrying capacity, both the styling and looks had to suffer. The cost of this body-style change was an additional 250lb (approx 115kg) on the car's weight when compared with the 4.2-litre coupé of 1964, which, when combined with a more steeply raked windscreen, had an obvious impact on performance. Sadly, the smooth and sleek lines of the 1961 launch model had been somewhat eroded, and once again that old adage rings true in the automotive world – 'first is always best'. It's a strange but frequent phenomenon that once a good vehicle design is recognised for what it is by the car-buying public and it gains in popularity, drivers want more and more comfort features to be included and the model inevitably puts on weight, losing some of its youthful purity and good looks.

However, the 2+2, as it became known, was not a

→ The full Series I range – (from left to right): roadster with optional hard top, fixed head coupé, roadster with hood down and the 2+2 fixed-head coupé.

replacement, but rather an additional model which ran alongside the normal short-wheelbase E-type models. Importantly, the new 2+2 model allowed Jaguar to introduce an automatic transmission in the E-type, a significant feature in the American market. Although the Jaguar XK 140 and 150 sports cars fitted with automatic transmission had both been popular sellers in America, this option was not offered on the earlier short-wheelbase E-type models as there was insufficient space in which to accommodate the longer transmission unit.

Up until the time of the introduction of the E-type, there were very few sports cars in Europe available with automatic transmission. No doubt one of the contributing factors in this scenario was that sports cars in the UK and on the Continent were traditionally used for competition and, quite obviously, a manual transmission was preferable for these purposes. But as the 1960s wore on, in some circles, traditional sporting cars

began to give way to more comfortable, powerful grand touring vehicles where the driver still wanted a powerful engine but without the demanding challenges of a competition car. Consequently, by the mid-1960s, a growing demand for automatic transmission on large-engined luxury and GT cars began to emerge in the UK and Europe too, a move that signalled the first steps in the market away from a true sports car and towards a more purposeful grand touring car.

The first real production change in the E-type's life cycle came with the introduction of the Series 2 E-type, planned for 1968. As many Jaguar aficionados will remember, towards the end of the Series 1 production cycle in 1967, several model changes appeared ahead of the arrival of its expected successor. In effect, what emerged was an intermediary model, but how this occurred is just another example of how frequently E-type model changes were introduced. Just as the

↓ The E-type Series 1½ roadster combined the best of both worlds: improved engine performance and ride, as well as better lighting.

Series 1 production cycle was drawing to a close, Jaguar's suppliers began delivering components for the new Series 2 model but as it turned out, it was a bit too early, as the assembly line was not actually ready for them.

Geoff Turner recalls the moment with amusement: 'My boss came in tearing his hair out one day and waving his hands in the air and said, "We've got this Series 2 stuff coming in and we haven't got the bodies yet, and we haven't got the bonnets yet, what are we going to do?"'. Because Geoff knew every component on the car intimately, he reasoned that he could fit many of the Series 2 bits onto the Series 1 car, and so he showed the assembly-line foremen how all the new parts could be accommodated on the Series 1 cars. As a result of those Series 1 cars having Series 2 components fitted, they became known to the outside world as the Series 1½ model. It is extremely difficult to specify exactly what constitutes a Series 1½, because these changes took place over an extended period of time and not all at once, which would have made it easy to designate such an interim model.

Geoff again: 'Initially we moved the headlamps forward about three inches when the Americans made us take the covers off the lamps, and that became the Series 2 bonnet style. But all the switches and switchgear and various other things, they managed to fit all this onto a basic Series 1 and the public started to call it the Series 1½, but internally it was still officially known as the Series 1.'

The Series 1½ has become one of the most popular of the E-type range, as it incorporates many of the later improvements to the car which enhanced the ride and also gave better illumination at night with the lights positioned further forward and without the Perspex covers. American legislation inspired many of these changes, but all of these improvements when combined with the early Series 1 E-type styling, made this one of the best sports cars on the market to own. However, there were very few of these cars made as this intermediate model preceded the soon-to-be-introduced Series 2.

department as early as 1958. He watched eagerly as the E-type was developed and as the launch day approached, he was in the perfect position to acquire one of the early cars for the Equipe Endeavour outfit.

Tommy Sopwith picks up the story: 'Indeed, my principal claim to fame is that I can claim to be, with absolutely no fear of contradiction, the first person to take delivery of an E-type, because I went to Browns Lane, collected the car, drove it to Oulton Park, put Graham Hill in it; he won the race and then I went to have dinner with Bill Lyons the following day.' A truly remarkable story of a car that had been launched only a month before in Geneva.

The Tommy Sopwith E-type, ECD 400 or 'Echo Charlie Delta' as he called it, was indeed a standard production vehicle, but in the hands of a true professional like Graham Hill, it was able to beat established race cars such as the Aston Martin DB4 GT of Innes Ireland (finished second), and the Ferrari 250GT driven by Jack Sears (fourth place). Third place was filled by the E-type of Roy Salvadori in the famous John Coombs car, BUY 1. Despite the race-proven credentials of the D-type, the E-type was an entirely different car to drive due to the independent rear suspension, which had never been tested in competition in its final production form. Although Jaguar's E2A Le Mans racer had featured an early version of the independent rear suspension, it was different in many respects and the final production version on the E-type was a far better unit.

↓ Briggs Cunningham and Roy Salvadori brought this lightened E-type home (registration '1337 VC') in a creditable fourth place in the 1962 Le Mans 24-Hour event.

↑ 'BUY 1' driven by Roy Salvadori gets away ahead of race winner Graham Hill in 'ECD 400' in the E-type's debut race meeting at Oulton Park on 15 April, 1961. The Aston Martin of Innes Ireland is behind Hill with Jack Sears in the Ferrari 250GT one place further back.

Early motorsport victories

'Jaguar XK-E Wins First Race!' read the headline in *Car and Driver*. The first competitive outing for the new Jaguar sports car took place at Oulton Park, Cheshire, England, on 15 April, 1961, with drivers Graham Hill and Roy Salvadori both driving roadster versions of the new Jaguar E-type. Driving for the Equipe Endeavour stable, Hill won the event with Salvadori finishing in third while the two new Jaguars were separated by the Aston Martin DB4 GT of Innes Ireland. The main competition, in the form of a Ferrari 250GT driven by Jack Sears, was relegated to fourth place.

Equipe Endeavour ('Equipe' is the French for 'Team') team owner, Tommy Sopwith, was a Jaguar dealer in Brighton, England, and had been running his race team for around six or seven years by the time the E-type was launched. Being a Jaguar main dealer, he obviously had good connections with Coventry, and his close friendship with Phil Weaver allowed him access to a car that was still in its infancy in the experimental

Very few people thought that the E-type would win on the day, so just how standard was the newcomer? Sopwith explains: 'The theoretical answer is that it was absolutely standard; I mean, we didn't pay for any modifications at all but my guess is that those initial engines, which they knew were going to be raced, were put together very carefully.' ECD 400 became a familiar sight around the race tracks of Britain with its distinctive 'white lips' painted around the mouth. 'Well we did that on quite a lot of cars because it was just easier to see them in the days when we relied on hand timing.' Sopwith added.

'Tommy Sopwith and John Coombs were the two leading British private team owners who ran their own teams, with a lot of help from Jaguar at that time. The D-type had been and gone and most of the D-type technology was what made the E-type go so well.' recalled Graham Macbeth who worked for the BARC at the time and was responsible for organising the Oulton Park race.

Journalist David Phipps (*Car and Driver*, July 1961) drove the Graham Hill car shortly after this event and could only cite limited legroom as a possible drawback to the new sports car, while the small boot space really applied only to the roadster, the coupé offering more generous space in this area. Commenting about the steering, he said, 'A little more effort is required at parking speeds, but who wants to park this car?' On both sides of the Atlantic the media were generous in their praise for the E-type with only the odd grumble about mostly small things, but most were united in their opinion of the car's potential as a rival for other sports cars in the market, at almost any price.

In England in early 1961, the E-type was a rare sight on the roads as not even the dealers had E-types to sell in their showrooms. Tommy Sopwith again: 'I mean it was bloody marvellous. You see, in those days, one used to drive a car to the circuit, race and then drive it away again and there was a moment when there were only two privately owned E-types in the country, which was Coombs's and mine. And boy did they stop the traffic.'

One of the most significant achievements by an E-type occurred in the 1962 Le Mans 24-Hour in which three E-types were entered. The factory-prepared Briggs Cunningham/Roy Salvadori FHC was fitted with an aluminium bonnet; another FHC was driven by Charles/Coundly while Peter Lumsden and Peter Sargent drove the third car. The latter car was in fact a roadster fitted with a streamlined alloy, non-detachable hard top and aluminium bonnet. The result for Jaguar, despite the loss of the Charles/Coundly car during the early part of the race, was a creditable fourth-place finish for Cunningham and Salvadori with the Lumsden/Sargent pair in fifth place.

Advances made by Ferrari and others in the world of GT racing prompted Jaguar to once again begin to consider a

Peters Lumsden and Sargent drove this other well-known E-type, '898 BYR', to a fine fifth-place finish in the 1962 Le Mans 24-Hour event.

purpose-built racing E-Type. Following Roy Salvadori's crash with the Coombs car (BUY 1) at Goodwood during the Easter race of 1962, the factory recalled the car to be extensively rebuilt as a serious competition vehicle. It was rebuilt over the winter of 1962 as a 'lightweight' E-type and reappeared as 4 WPD, the first of 11 such roadsters which were later joined by a lightweight coupé. All were right-hand drive and had an aluminium roadster body with fitted hard top and featured a ventilated boot lid which served to dispel heat from the rear brakes. Running on Dunlop magnesium wheels, stiffer suspension and competition brakes, the lightweight E-type was powered by an alloy-block, fuel-injected 3.8-litre engine developing over 300bhp, and even as much as 344bhp. Through imposing a strict diet, Jaguar had hoped to shed 150lb but actually lost 250lb which made it a serious contender for the Ferrari 250GTO.

The first two lightweight E-Types were quickly built for the 1963 Sebring race, one to be entered by regular Jaguar combatant Briggs Cunningham and the other for Jaguar's West Coast importer, Kjell Qvale's British Motor Car Distributors dealership. The Qvale team of Ed Leslie and Frank Morrill finished the Sebring 12-hour event in seventh place overall and first in class.

Back in England, these five-speed works cars certainly delivered the goods and in early 1963, Graham Hill scored three GT wins at Snetterton, Goodwood and Silverstone. German Peter Lindner and fellow countryman Peter Nocker acquitted themselves well and surprised everyone by initially leading the Nürburgring 1,000km in a class field headed by some very powerful Ferraris. Other notable appearances during 1963 included a second at Rheims for Protheroe, a win at Avus for Peter Nocker and a Snetterton GT first for Peter Sutcliffe, but the prestigious Le Mans 24-Hour, where the Ferraris remained dominant, still eluded Jaguar.

As privateer racers began to appreciate the performance potential of the E-type in numerous events around Britain and on the Continent, more serious modifications began to emerge. Although Jaguar was reluctant at first to give

↑ 5 May, 1963, saw the 47th running of the Targa Florio, the fourth leg of the World Sports Car Championship. This was very much the domain of the Ferraris and Porsches, but Innocente Baggio and Clemente Ravetto managed 21st place in an E-type in that year's Sicilian event.

Pictured at the Goodwood Revival, the famous streamlined E-type, CUT 7, was successfully campaigned by Dick Protheroe in the 1960s (September 2006).

full factory support to these endeavours, Malcolm Sayer lent his expertise to some projects, developing some of the most tantalising and streamlined shapes for the E-types of Dick Protheroe (CUT 7) and Peters Nocker and Lindner. Although Sayer designed the streamlined E-type body that is so well known today, this was as a result of experimental work carried out by enthusiastic privateer racers including Dr. Samir Klat and Frank Costin of Cosworth fame. Together they formed the E-type's upper body and cabin profile to resemble that of a zero-lift wing.

The 1964 picture was similarly encouraging with the arrival of Jackie Stewart on the scene. Winning first time out at Crystal Palace, he was second to Jack Sears's Cobra in his second race, but beat the Cobra of Salvadori and the GTO of Mike Parkes.

Across the Atlantic, the XK-E's spiritual father, the E2A, had been raced in the US with some success, taking the flag at Bridgehampton with Walt Hansgen at the wheel in the factory-backed Briggs Cunningham outfit in 1960. But with the introduction of a new Jaguar sports car to America, it was inevitable that the XK-E would be tested in this arena before long. In the land of the big V8, motorsport was a well established and very popular pastime but without any official factory support, the XK-E was going to have to earn its stripes the hard way.

The first win by a production E-Type on the other side of the Atlantic was in the hands of Norman Namerow at St. Eugene, Montreal in a Canadian Racing Drivers Association (C.R.D.A.) event on 18 June, 1961. In another early motorsport outing at Santa Barbara, California, on 2 and 3 September, 1961, a lone E-type in the hands of Bill Krause was relegated to third spot in both of the two heats, behind a thundering Corvette and a Porsche. Upon reflection, this is perhaps not a bad result for the new Jaguar sports car in its debut season on the North American racing scene, as the E-type was scarcely six months old. ▨

↑ A Ferrari/Jaguar duel was what the crowds came to expect at race meetings in the early 1960s, and the 1963 Tourist Trophy at Goodwood on 24 August of that year was no exception. Here, the lightweight E-type (4 WPD) driven by Jack Sears is being harried by the rather sideways Ferrari 250GTO of Roger Penske.

The E-type – middle & old age

'We had an early GT40 when we were building XJ13, because we could see that that was where the competition was out on the race circuits.'

Brian Martin, Jaguar Cars (1949–67 and 1972–78)

  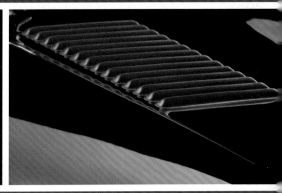

1966	1968	1970	1971	1973	1975
XJ13 ran for the first time	Series 2 launched in October	Series 2 production ceased in September	Series 3 launched in April	Series 3 FHC production ceased in September	Last E-type Series 3 produced in February

Jaguar XJ13 (1966)

It was realised, as far back as the mid-1950s, that the XK power plant had all but reached its development ceiling as a racing engine, and this awareness set in motion the design process for a far more powerful motor. In 1955 and with a possible return to Le Mans serving as additional inspiration for this development, Walter Hassan set about designing the ultimate Jaguar racing engine. This new engine would necessitate a whole new approach to racing, which by the late 1950s had become far more sophisticated and this required a new car into which to fit the engine. Code-named the XJ13, this car represented the most advanced racing project the company had ever been involved in.

The project, which was seen as vitally important for the company, proceeded in a rather stop–start manner for several years as during this time; Malcolm Sayer was still working on the production E-type, amongst other tasks. Tom Jones recalls: 'Well apart from this XJ13, he was doing all sorts of things, including investigating Grand Prix cars.'

Initially, the new power plant was conceived as a 5.0-litre V12 unit which was intended to be suitable for use in a road car once it had proved reliable at Le Mans. However, as priorities changed at Jaguar, development of the V12 engine project was dropped for a period only to re-emerge again in the early-1960s. As Jaguar was in the early stages of tooling up for their major new saloon car line, the XJ6, factory resources were stretched to the very limit and the XJ13 continued in development almost as a 'skunk project'.

With interest in sports-car racing once again high in Europe at this time, it was decided to revive the fabrication of this special, lightweight body to accompany the new V12 engine, a design task which naturally fell to Malcolm Sayer. In what must be regarded as Sayer's finest hour, the XJ13 emerged in June 1965 bearing a strong family resemblance to the D-type and of course E-type. Heavily reliant on aircraft assembly techniques just as in the D-type, the XJ13 first ran in March 1966, and with racing at Le Mans still a possibility, the future for the sleek racer looked bright.

The purpose of a race car is to win races, and so there is no place for niceties, and the ultimate performance package is all about compromise – efficiency versus weight. The screen of the XJ13 is ultra-low, just the correct height to deflect the wind over the head of the driver, while the sensuous bulges cover the wheels with the under body sloping upwards at the rear, as with the E-type. Most of the bodywork is only 20 inches (50cm) above the ground. With radiators mounted up front, the engine is installed behind the cockpit but ahead of the rear wheels in a typical mid-engined fashion as this layout had become the favoured set up for sports racing cars around this time. This mid-engined layout had the benefit of lowering the bonnet line to improve aerodynamic efficiency, while the optimal weight distribution vastly improved the car's handling.

↓ This early shot of the XJ13, taken in March 1966, shows how sleek and streamlined the racer was. The mid-engined layout allowed Malcolm Sayer to craft an ultra-low front end. The interior of this racer is surprisingly spacious as race cars go.

← Sayer again adopted his mathematical approach to the design of the XJ13, as this overhead shot illustrates. The bonnet slats allowed cooling for the radiators which were located up front.

Norman Dewis tested the XJ13 and he recalls, 'Of course the D-type was very low, 0.28 or something like that, but the lowest that Jaguar ever made here at the factory, the lowest coefficient was the XJ13.'

Under the skin of the XJ13, the major engineering challenge was to get the engine in its midship position with a suitable rear-suspension set-up. Mid-engined cars were foreign to Jaguar in the 1960s, and Tom Jones had Derrick White working on this set-up: 'Derrick White worked for me and he

completed the rear end; that was a big engineering job, then he left us and joined John Cooper.'

Following White's departure, Tom Jones drafted in Mike Kimberley who had been working for Jones on the limousines. Jones again: 'I transferred him to this racing job, and I said to him, just put the E-type front end on it to finish it off.' (Mike Kimberley, a very talented engineer, went on to become acting chief executive officer of Group Lotus plc). Kimberley then fitted the E-type front suspension

sub-frame onto the XJ13 which also carried the radiators in the sleek racer.

With the development of the XJ13 at an advanced stage and after some encouraging tests, a racing programme for the 1966 or at least the 1967 season seemed feasible. Although the car was complete, as a consequence of the uncertainties surrounding the outcome of the BMC amalgamation, the completed XJ13 lay sadly inactive in a corner of the factory for the next year and was taken out only in March 1967. Early one Sunday morning, and shrouded in secrecy, the new V12-engined racer ventured out for a run at MIRA, an operation that was considered very risky as it could have had a detrimental effect on the sales of the current six-cylinder XK-engined E-type should potential customers get wind of the powerful new engine waiting in the wings. At any rate, the XJ13 performed almost faultlessly requiring very little modification after race driver David Hobbs had achieved a speed of 175mph down the MIRA straight.

As mentioned earlier, it was not feasible to build a race car without an associated road-sports-car programme to share

the huge developmental costs, as the C- and D-type programmes had been able to do 10 to 15 years earlier. Sir William Lyons had always insisted that any racing programme should have benefits for their road-going range, and a stand-alone race car could not provide that, which meant that any XJ13 race programme would have been just that, a race car programme, and not something through which to promote the rest of the model range.

The XJ13 would have required further testing and development to have been competitive, and with no obvious benefit for the rest of the production models at that time, an expensive race programme could not be justified. Tom Jones remembers: 'We weren't quite good enough I don't think, because we were actually testing it against the Ford GT40.' With technology now too old to be considered competitive at Le Mans, the XJ13 was once again rolled away and covered up under a dust sheet in the corner of the factory. At best, it seemed that the XJ13 would serve as a test bed and experimental car at the factory, and the engineering staff

140

who had worked on the car could only imagine what might have become of the racer had it been given its chance at glory.

However, almost four years later on 20 January, 1971, the XJ13 was rolled out from under its dust cover at the factory and taken to MIRA. In 2006, 35 years later, Tom Jones still shakes his head at the memory: 'So it was brought out and they just pumped the tyres up.'

The aim of this exercise was to film the XJ13 speeding around the banked section at MIRA for a promotional film being produced to introduce the new V12 E-type due out later that year. The intention was to record a dramatic sequence of the car approaching at speed with the sound of the mighty V12 getting louder as the car approached, and then decreasing as it sped away into the distance – this would be the opening scene for the introduction of the new Series 3 E-type with the V12 engine which had started life in the XJ13, six years earlier.

With the film footage safely captured, test driver Norman Dewis rolled off a few additional laps on the MIRA banking at 160mph, when one of the racing alloy wheels suddenly gave way, propelling the car into the safety barriers, then down into the infield where it catapulted several times. The XJ13 was fitted with one of the first sets of magnesium alloy wheels available in the racing industry, as Norman recalls: 'The manufacturers didn't realise at the time, but the materials

they were using for the magnesium wheels, developed an inner corrosion problem.' The actual cause of the accident was the collapse of the magnesium alloy wheel. 'When we found the parts of the wheel, we sent them to the lab and what they found was that they had crystallised, and it looked like black coal dust.' he explained. Dewis feels today that had testing continued with the XJ13, the problem would have surfaced in a much less dramatic fashion, perhaps without the horrific results that occurred on the banking that day. In the MIRA accident, the XJ13 bodywork was all but destroyed, but fortunately the frame and most mechanical components were repairable. Happily, Norman Dewis emerged shaken but uninjured.

The wrecked car was returned to the factory and covered up under the same dust sheet for a further two years, after which time Lofty England decided that it was time that the car should be rebuilt. Fortunately for Jaguar, the original wooden body formers had been retained, and through the combined effort of both Jaguar and Abbey Panels staff, many of whom had worked on the prototype, the car was restored to its former glory. Tom Jones remembers with amusement: 'And it cost £20,000 for the new body.'

The wheels were a different story, however. The patterns used to form them had been scrapped and as two of the wheels had been almost completely destroyed in the accident, this left the engineers without a way of recreating them

← At 160mph, one of the magnesium-alloy wheels collapsed, somersaulting the XJ13 race car into the muddy infield. Jaguar's XJ6 track car can be seen in the background.

exactly as the originals had been. This dilemma was solved by the need for wider wheels and tyres, which in turn necessitated the widening of the wheel arches, or the 'eyebrows', as Norman Dewis refers to them, thereby completing the restoration of the car.

This monument to the excellence of Malcolm Sayer's design has fortunately been preserved for posterity and the magnificent XJ13 has thrilled thousands of enthusiasts around the world – it's a good thing that Mr. England decided to return the wreck to the factory.

Jaguar E-type Series 2 (1968–70)

Launched at Earls Court in October 1968, the Series 2 was offered in all three body styles simultaneously: open two-seater (OTS) or roadster, fixed-head coupé (FHC) and the two-plus-two coupé (2P2), all of which ran through to September 1970. The roadster and the fixed-head were still based on the old Series 1 eight-foot (96-inch) wheelbase,

while the 2P2 was built on the longer 8'9" wheelbase (105-inch) which offered limited rear accommodation.

On its announcement in the States, the Series 2 XK-E was seen by *Car and Driver* (May 1969) as one of the finest upgrades of the model yet. Although Jaguar had been trying to keep secret the fact that they were developing a V12 motor, it was obviously known by some in the motoring press. The opening lines of this road test read, 'All you Faithful Readers still holding your breath for the V12 Jaguar XK-F may exhale. It simply isn't time yet.' An XK-F? Well, there must have been really great expectations in America of some new model powered by a mighty big brute of an engine and draped in some radically new exotic bodywork, for it to have been branded an XK-F in the minds of those who thought they knew about such things.

There was some frustration in the media that Jaguar had perhaps over-used the XK power plant, and 20 years with one basic motor was perhaps a bit too long, and now would be the right time for something new. But despite some

→ As the cover of
Road & Track (June,
1969) suggests, the
new Series 2 had its
nose just in front of
the opposition in
the USA – not by
much, though.

obvious disappointment in this sector, the reaction to the revised XK-E in America was very positive. There was ample mention of the enlarged air intake (68% larger than the Series 1) citing the E's notorious overheating problems in heavy traffic as the reason for this, but in truth it was really for the twin cooling-fan set-up required for the improved air-conditioning system.

The trusty XK engine was de-tuned in compliance with US Federal emission requirements, and the effect of this was a substantial drop in top speed – it hardly seemed worthwhile building such an exotic sports car with all the performance potential it held, to achieve such lowly performance (maximum speed of 119mph in US spec). But then the XK-E was about much more than just top speed, it was presence and the knowledge that you had a 'Big Cat' under you with the handling to match anything else on the market.

Still possessing those drop-dead looks of the classic Malcolm Sayer design of a decade earlier, the XK-E was also all about enjoyment and that feeling of quality. The interior was still 'as well instrumented as a 707', according to the *Car and Driver* road tester, at a time when the Boeing 707 was king of the skies. But this was not an idle comparison as a full array of instrumentation had always been the desire of the enthusiast driver who liked to be kept informed and in control. The rake of the front windscreen had been softened resulting in a more streamlined slope to the windshield which

↓ For the E-type
Series 2 2+2 fixed
head, the base of
the windscreen
was moved
forward to give a
more streamlined
look to the car.

actually went some way towards improving the profile of the Series 2.

In much the same way that the original XK 120 progressed to the heavier and comparatively ponderous XK 140 and then the even more bulky XK 150, so the E-type too gradually

↑ The rear view of the Series 2 E-type shows the chromed full-width plate now housing larger tail-lamp clusters and a pair of reversing lights. This whole arrangement was now positioned beneath the bumper, the lower registration plate forcing the exhaust pipes to be re-routed either side.

SELECTED COMPARATIVE SPORTS CAR SPECIFICATIONS AND PRICES (1969/1970):

US Domestic models	Price*	Capacity	Engine type	Speed
Chev Corvette	5,073	5,737cc	V8	132mph
Chev Camaro Z28	2,743	5,736cc	V8	126mph
Shelby Mustang GT350	4,434	5,750cc	V8	119mph
Pontiac GTO	3,400	6,374cc	V8	110mph
US foreign imports	Price*	Capacity	Engine type	Speed
Jaguar XK-E Coupé	5,775	4,235cc	Straight six	119mph**
Ferrari 250 GT Lusso	13,375	2,953cc	V12	150mph
MG-C GT	3,350	2,912cc	Straight six	122mph
Lamborghini Miura P400S	19,750	3,929cc	V12	170mph
Maserati Indy 2+2	17,500	4,136cc	V8	155mph
Lotus Europa	4,695	1,470cc	DOHC 4-cyl	121mph
Aston Martin DBS	17,900	3,994cc	Straight six	143mph
Mercedes Benz 280SL	7,054	2,778cc	Straight six	114mph**
Porsche 911T Coupé	6,060	1,991cc	Flat six	122mph**

*Distributors Suggested Retail prices in US dollars including Federal Excise Tax **US spec

began to develop a middle-age spread as it grew older. Power-assisted steering was a new option on the Series 2, which was something Norman Dewis had been hoping to have ready for the late Series 1 car.

'You can only go so far with all these things, I mean, I'm a perfectionist and maybe it takes a lot to satisfy me. I just wanted to keep on improving things, but the time must come when you have to say we stop there otherwise you'll never get it into production. When you come to do the Series 2, you can say right, I wanted to put this on the Series 1 but I couldn't, so then I could introduce it on the next model.' recalled Dewis when questioned about the delay in introducing this typical American feature.

The changes to the exterior styling of the Series 2 E-type were perhaps the least pleasing of all, and the new lights,

front and back, did nothing for the looks of the car. If anything, the changes, which were the result of assorted engineering improvements, American legal requirements and a desire to meet new customer needs, were gaudy and reactive rather than proactive. The new light clusters that had been fitted at the back in order to comply with the American legislation left one with the feeling that they had been just stuck on without any real thought for the car's appearance and the same could be said of the front indicators, while the main headlamps, minus their Perspex covers, had been brought forward so far as to give the appearance that they almost sat on the wings rather than in them. Sadly, it looked as though the new light fittings had just been slapped onto the bodywork without any thought of retaining the earlier car's purity of line.

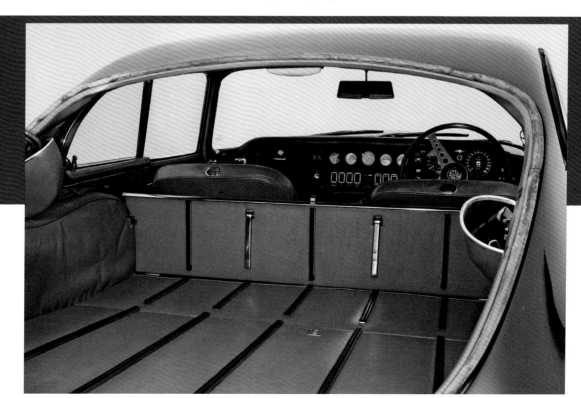

← **The Series 2 offered impressive storage space for a sports car, and could easily swallow two sets of golf clubs or allow sufficient luggage to be carried for that Continental vacation.**

Other improvements, although these styling changes could barely be called improvements, included wrap-around bumpers, which replaced the earlier, slim-line individual pieces and the removal of the 'ears' on the wire-wheel spinners. Deemed dangerous by the US authorities, these characteristic knock-ons had been part of the British sports-car scene for as long as most could remember.

An amusing incident recalled by Terry Cruse, parts manager at a Jaguar dealership in the London area, involved a Dutch customer who ordered a replacement E-type bonnet for his car in Holland. When the customer arrived to collect the bonnet, packed in an enormous wooden crate, he asked for some assistance in loading it onto his car. Terry picks up the story: 'When we went outside, he had a Volkswagen Beetle with no roof rack on it, and he was going to take this

E-type bonnet back to Holland in this huge crate on the roof. He had straps and string and was going to tie it on the roof and I said, "You won't get it out into the street, let alone down to Dove". But sure enough, he phoned us the next day, he had got all the way back to Holland with this E-type bonnet on the roof.'

Unfortunately, the Series 2 E-type had lost much of the original Series I's elegance, but the most alarming factor concerned the car's lack of performance. Perhaps it is fortunate then that Series 2 production lasted for only two years, because deep within the factory, a dedicated team of Jaguar engineers was busy developing a much more menacing beast. In March, 1971, Jaguar presented to the automotive world the final version of the E-type, the mighty 5.3-litre V12 Series 3.

↓ The Series 2 E-type even received favour from royalty. Here, Princess Grace of Monaco is being welcomed by an enthusiastic crowd in her Series 2 Roadster.

By 1970 the E-type seats and interior accommodation had been improved but the car still retained that distinctly British sports-car feel.

The Series 2 front end now included a bigger 'mouth' which fed an improved air-conditioning intake system, while the headlights were moved forward for improved illumination.

Jaguar E-type Series 3 (1971–75)

There were few significant changes during the life span of the Series 2 E-type, but towards the end of the 1960s, the Jaguar sports car was feeling progressively down on power due to additional exhaust emissions requirements and interior comfort features, and as a result it became heavier and slower.

However, with the introduction of the eagerly awaited and much overdue V12, the Coventry sports car had truly matured into a luxurious grand tourer. Almost ten years to the month since the launch of the sleek Series 1 in Geneva, the much loved E-type had lost that innocent image, with its pure and clean-cut styling of 1961; it had now taken on a more menacing presence and was fairly stating its intentions. The naïve schoolboy had become the mature graduate – yes sir, the E-type had grown up.

The Series 3 E-type was now available in only two body forms, the 105-inch-wheelbase roadster and the two-plus-two coupé, while the old 96-inch-wheelbase, two-seat body style was dropped. The longer wheelbase had nothing to do with the new 5.3-litre V12 engine; the chassis lengthening process had already been completed with the installation of the automatic transmission and the availability of the two-plus-two configuration in the late Series 1 cars, introduced in March 1966. The auto 'box frankly suited the V12 much better; as the old 4-speed manual 'box was at the edge of its torque limit coping with the 12-cylinder engine. When the wheelbase was lengthened by nine inches five years earlier, this had allowed not only the installation of two small seats in the rear, but it had also given front passengers more legroom.

↑ → The debut of the Series 3 was the first time a Jaguar E-type was launched in America before Britain or Europe. Once again, both *Road & Track* and *Car and Driver* seized on the opportunity, featuring the same car in different poses (May, 1971).

Although Jaguar had taken the decision to go with the large V12 unit, it did so with the knowledge that they would not be considering this engine for competition, but rather for the effortless consumption of miles and miles of motorway. The rationale behind this was to accommodate the plethora of emissions equipment required by the US authorities which was more comfortably achieved through a bigger-capacity motor, rather than a higher-revving and expensive DOHC unit of smaller capacity. This mighty engine was the work of the talented Jaguar engineering team of Bill Heynes and Claude Bailey and resulted in a slightly lower top speed than the early 3.8-litre Jaguar E-type, but still provided exhilarating performance. Considering that the Series 3 weighed around 20% more than the Series 1, most road test editors were unanimous in their admiration for this sports car, praising its quietness and smooth delivery of power to the road.

Such was Jaguar's desire to keep the V12 a secret that when the first press cars landed in the States, they were without any badging. Only an astute Jaguar enthusiast would have suspected that this car was any different from the old Series 2, as both the roadster and coupé now used the longer-wheelbase chassis, while the track had grown by over four inches at the front and three inches at the rear. The air intake, now fitted with a full-width grille, subtly hinted at some under-bonnet changes. However, when the engine was fired up there was no mistaking that this 'Cat' was no longer powered by the old XK motor, but that something else rather more powerful was purring under the long bonnet.

In fact the press cars used in America were so fresh off the assembly line at Browns Lane, that the factory referred to them not as production cars, but rather as 'final test cars', being released to the media a full two months ahead of the official Series 3 launch at the New York Auto Show.

At US$7,000, the new Series 3 E-type commanded an increase of almost 20% in price over its six-cylinder predecessor, but then as the Jaguar publicity department claimed at the time, 'a Jaguar is a Ferrari for half the price'. In reality, a Ferrari was more like three times the price, but Jaguar used this slogan

↑ **Diana Rigg tries out the Series 3 V12 E-type at the New York Auto Show. Rigg, from the TV show *The Avengers* (Diana Rigg starred as Emma Peel between 1965 and 1968), is being shown a few of the finer points of the new sports car by Graham Whitehead, the then president of Jaguar Cars Inc of America.**

→ An early Series 3 press photo showing the attractive detachable hardtop complete with neat side vents.

to good effect, as their research had also shown that just under half of E-type owners would have considered a Porsche before buying their Jaguar. Despite the popular Chev Corvette being substantially cheaper than the E-type, there were still sufficient customers who preferred the Coventry car as it offered the driver something out of the ordinary.

The Series 3 was now an altogether statelier car, and Jaguar no longer promoted the speedy image as they had done with the Series 1. When the XK-engined E-types were developed, it had been necessary to design a power bulge in the bonnet that would clear the front of the engine cam covers, but with the introduction of the V12 in the Series 3 E-type, the engine was much lower and didn't need the power bulge for the same

reason that its predecessor had. Geoff Turner explains: 'It wasn't necessary. We did cars with flat bonnets, prototypes, but they didn't look right. It just didn't look like an E-type.' Jaguar needed to continue the styling that it had created with the Series 1 and Series 2 cars, besides which, the power bulge gave much needed strength to the huge bonnet.

With the longer wheelbase and gentler windscreen angle, the lines of the Series 3 were undeniably more luxurious and reserved, giving the impression of a smooth, sophisticated ride in total comfort, rather than the out-and-out speed potential of the higher-revving Series 1 model. This was achieved through the increased body length and width as well as some subtle styling points such as the tinted windscreen and the

↓ Parked outside a typical English village shop, the Series 3 Coupé looked impressive.

wider wheel arches over new steel wheels (chrome wire wheels were optional). The full steel wheels moved the Series 3 slightly further away from the pure sports car image towards a more graceful, comfortable cruiser.

With the upsurge in vehicle safety requirements by the US authorities, it became apparent that the E-type would have to comply with increasingly stringent braking and safety regulations including certain crash criteria which involved

driving an E-type into a concrete block. Jaguar's rather tongue-in-cheek response was that the E-type was designed to avoid concrete blocks, not drive into them. They had to comply nonetheless.

But the introduction of the V12 was not all plain sailing. Geoff Turner remembers how it all started: 'In October 1968, my boss asked me to go down to Radford, the old Daimler plant, to put the V12 engine into production. So the old

↑ Longer doors meant easier access to the Series 3 interior which still looked familiar to owners of earlier E-type models. Wider seats, now fitted with adjustable headrests, provided a much more comfortable ride.

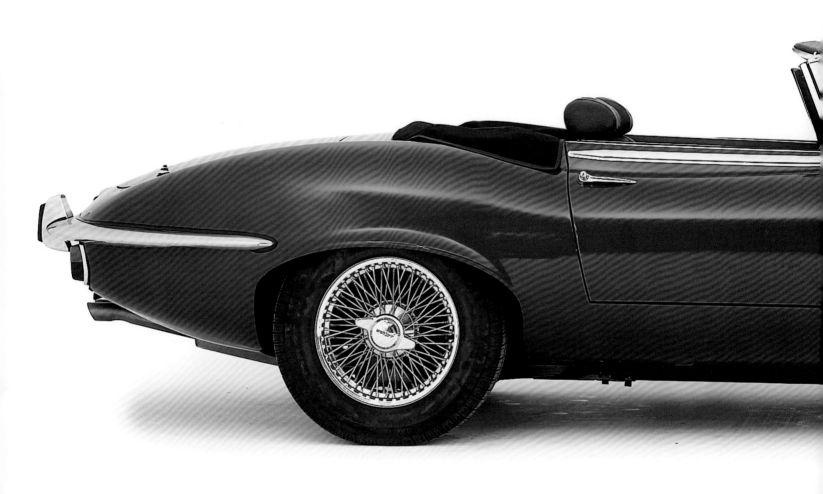

assembly hall at Radford was all stripped out and we put new transfer lines in for machining the blocks and heads and crankshafts and a new assembly track, a carrousel track, not just a straight track with a beginning and end.'

At the old Radford plant, the new carrousel track replaced the old straight track system because this allowed the engines to be assembled on individual fixtures which could be set at different angles, rotated and even turned upside down. The XK engine had always been built on trolleys which made it quite awkward to work on in places, forcing the workers to bend or kneel when assembling various components on the engine. But with the new engine 82lb heavier than the old XK engine, the rotating fixture on the carrousel line at Radford was a welcome change at Jaguar, allowing the workers to remain standing upright at all times. Geoff Turner again: 'It was all new for Jaguar, and a lot of investment. It was something like £7 million for all the new machinery and the new tracks which seems ludicrous today, but we thought it was a tremendous amount of money.'

While fitting out the Radford plant for V12 engine production, Turner got an urgent call from one of the fitters requesting that he get down there as quickly as possible. All of the new nut runners and stud runners and other machinery that had just been installed and connected up to the air supply now had brown, rusty water running out of the joints and air supply connections. The problem was that the area set aside for the V12 engine had previously been the assembly hall for bus and fighting vehicle assembly at Daimler, and although air tools had not been used on those larger vehicles, overhead air pipes had been installed throughout the factory. Through years of non-use, rusty water had built up in the whole system which now came out of every gap and joint possible, ruining the new overhead motors and machinery required for the assembly of the V12 engine. The problem had been caused by the air supply which actually ran across the main driveway at Radford from one building and into this assembly hall, resulting in the heavy accumulation of condensation in the overhead pipes. The old air pipes were subsequently dismantled and a

→ This shows the ingenious construction of the Series 3 fixed-head, which was the same as for the Series 1 and 2 cars that went before it.

new series of pipes was run under the roadway at the plant and a large air-conditioning dryer was installed to prevent a recurrence of the problem.

Turner again: 'Naturally the V12 engine was delayed into production. It wasn't ready for the saloon, which it was principally intended for, as there were various development changes going on with the V12 engine itself. Then we had a problem with the fuel system because it was going to be introduced with a fuel injection system and we had to go back to fitting a carburettor system. That threw the cat among the pigeons for a while, so it was quite late before we actually got the V12 engine into production and into a vehicle.'

By the early 1970s, computers were just beginning to make themselves felt in the motor industry. Jim Randle remembers his work on the V12 E-type: 'When I did the Series 3 E-type, I did computer modelling to work out the engine-mounting systems. The technology was fairly new, but the basic mathematics hadn't changed an awful lot.'

Once the engine assembly problems had been ironed out, testing could begin and the 'XJ6' saloon was fitted with the new V12 and sent out for assessment. On the car's return, the extreme heat generated by the large 12-cylinder engine had melted the battery casing in the engine and there was smoke pouring from under the back seat; the exhaust had also started a fire in the rear under-seat insulation and carpeting.

The solution for both the saloons and sports cars (Series

← In the foreground is the front end of a Series 3 E-type showing its larger grille, revised indicator-light clusters, bumper overriders and low-level air scoop. Just behind is the Series 2 with a slightly smaller front air intake.

3 E-type) was to fit heat shields in the engine and under the car between the exhaust system and the floor of the car. This only served to reflect all the heat downwards which caused another problem as Geoff Turner recalls: 'When we sent the cars to Japan, in their traffic jams and parking on their road sides and verges, they were setting fire to the grass and melting tarmac so that was when we had to fit under-shields to the Japanese cars, all underneath the exhaust system.'

Despite these development problems, the Series 3 E-type was the most sophisticated 'Cat' of all. Jaguar had learned that creating the right image for their grand tourer was paramount and in the early-1970s, it was all about horsepower, exhaust pipes and image. In fact the more exhausts a car had in the USA, the better, and the E-type had four of them. This image went some way towards beefing up the physical appearance and image of the E-type at a time when it had suffered at the

↑ → **Although the E-type had never been overly decorated, subtle chrome trim along the doors and front fender enhanced the visual impression of a long, sleek car.**

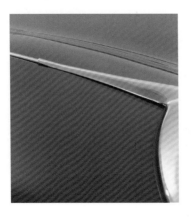

← The Series 3
E-type was fitted with
a quad exhaust-pipe
system – it made
beautiful music.

hands of American legislators. Most American cars in this market had big engines and featured large chrome exhaust tailpipes to affirm their presence, and Jaguar needed to do the same.

Tom Jones remembers with a smile: 'Well it was to give that appearance, yes. I remember designing that thing, I got two pressings and pressed them out and just shoved them onto the end of the tailpipes. It looked good, but actually the only criterion, really, was how it sounded.'

Besides giving the appearance of a big powerful engine, the quad tailpipes also produced a more muted sound, unlike the brash and loud exhaust note of the large V8-engined American performance cars. A Jaguar sports car should never sound that way, it was by nature a silent and stealthy beast, and it therefore needed to produce an aggressive purring sound rather than a loud bark – it was just a Jaguar thing.

Externally, the Series 3 E-type was immediately recognisable by the chrome air-intake grille and flared fenders. A larger grille opening was required for the bigger radiator which provided an increased cooling capacity for the huge V12 engine. It stood to reason that the E-type's larger mouth could not be left unadorned, as it was now simply too big for that, and this necessitated the fitting of a chrome grille to fill the gap. With the increased front screen height, the Series 3

→ A V12 boot
badge hints at
the powerful
5.3-litre engine
lurking beneath
the bonnet.

windshield could be swept by a conventional pair of wipers and so the triple-wiper set-up characteristic of the earlier E-types was dispensed with.

Designing and engineering a model to be slightly larger than, but essentially the same as, its predecessor is no easy task. It may sound a simple job to just add four inches to the front track and three inches to the rear track, but often in doing so one loses the styling purity of the model, and the car loses its sense of poise and proportion. Happily, this was not the case with the Series 3 E-type, and despite the still-awkward-looking rear tail lights, the car was even more stylish than the Series 2 which it replaced. The Series 3 car had gained a sense of maturity and presence, whereas the long-wheelbase version of the Series 2 model simply looked as though it had been stretched a bit too much.

From an engineering point of view this was no problem for Tom Jones: 'The engine was bigger so the track had to be widened of course and it was easy to do the frame; it was only the front cross member that had to lengthened, widened if you like.'

On the race track the performance potential of the powerful 5,343cc, which produced 272bhp in standard trim, was put to good use by several competitors on both sides of the Atlantic. Perhaps one of the most successful and best-known of the American racers was Group 44 racing boss, Bob Tullius. The Group 44 E-type V12 was a potent machine and in 1975, the factory-sponsored car won the Sports Car Club of America B-Class Production Car Championship.

By now the 'Big Cat' was approaching old age, but it had led a distinguished life and proved to be a remarkable export success for Jaguar. However, the Series 3 E-type was beginning to attract criticism for its outdated chassis, which had given good service for 14 years in all three models. There was no disguising the fact that the E-type was growing long in the tooth and in September 1973 production of the coupé ceased, while the roadster continued in production until February 1975.

Considering the style and popularity of the E-type, even in its final form in 1975, simply serves to highlight the huge impact that the Series 1 E-type had had when it was launched at Geneva 14 years earlier. It was in a league of its own and way ahead of its time.

→ The last of the line,
a black Series 3
roadster. 'HDU 555N'
was the very last
E-type made and was
retained by Jaguar
Cars, Coventry.
Today this car
performs at
numerous car shows
as an ambassador for
the company, and a
commemorative
plaque can be seen on
the lid of the glove
box, stating this
car's heritage.

A Series 3 E-type
roadster the way it
was meant to be
enjoyed – a picnic
with friends.

Jaguar E-type awards & achievements

There were some who considered the E-type to have had imperfections, but they were still complimentary in their criticism. Writing in *Car and Driver* in May 1961 at the car's launch, journalist Jesse Alexander had this to say: 'It's not beautiful from every angle, but wonderfully efficient nevertheless, and he [Sir William Lyons] and his staff have created a sports car that even Stuttgart will stop and look at.'

The measure of whether a sports car is successful or not is very often settled by taking a look at the results sheet of various motorsport events. Alternatively, if the car being assessed is a luxury model, then it would be deemed successful if it was bought by all the right celebrities and met expected sales targets. But if it wins its first race meeting straight out of the box, blows all sales targets out of the window, is snapped up by movie stars and is subsequently acknowledged by international design experts, then you can assume quite safely that it was an unmitigated success.

The E-type was selected for permanent display at the Museum of Modern Art (MOMA) in New York in 1996, and this just proves retrospectively what was already known back in the 1960s. The MOMA was in fact the first international museum to recognise the outstanding design quality of the E-type by placing it on permanent display, after its selection by the museum's assistant curator of architecture and design, Christopher Mount.

The model on display at the MOMA, a cobalt-blue 1963 roadster was placed prominently on the museum's top floor landing. Factors which led to the selection of the E-type for this display included the car's timeless styling and the fact that its designer, Malcolm Sayer, had achieved this style through a mathematical approach to design, rather than pure drawing and rendering. A journalist at the time of the exhibit's unveiling cited the E-type as, 'an enduring icon of the early 1960s and its eroticised popular culture'. Perhaps it achieved this notoriety in the minds of some admirers, but this was not what was in the mind of the car's creator at the time of its design.

Accolades abounded at the time of the car's launch in Geneva, even from as far afield as South Africa. A local publication there, *Motor Parade* (June 1961), elected the E-type as the 'Car of the Year' a mere two months after its launch. The publication went on to say that during the first few days of the New York Motor Show, Jaguar distributors around America had received over 1,500 orders for the new E-type.

The secret to the car's success lay not only in the superb design and outstanding performance, but also in the fact that, as an overall sports car, the Jaguar E-type was different from anything else on the market at that time. John Maries explains: 'We differentiated ourselves through styling, through performance and also through innovation.'

In August, 2004, the Design Museum of London, in conjunction with Jaguar Cars, held an exhibition at the museum celebrating 'The E-type – Story of a British Sports Car'. Charting the development of this great sports car, the museum exhibited the D-type, lightweight E-type and various other E-type models which had established this sports car as the 1960s cultural icon that it was. A press release put out by the Design Museum aptly described the moment when the E-type was launched – 'Speedy and stylish, with long, low lines and a voluptuous racing bonnet, it captured the glamour, dynamism and optimism of Britain in the early 1960s'.

Perhaps the greatest confirmation of an iconic design, however, is one which is voted for or chosen by the public itself; after all, motor cars are designed for use by a sector of the market and not just for museums or exhibitions. In a poll conducted in 2004 by the British newspaper, *Sunday Times*, the Jaguar E-type amassed 81% of the public's vote as the

← The E-type roadster on display at the Museum of Modern Art, New York. On the wall behind this permanent display can be seen the tabulation of the body co-ordinates as calculated by Malcolm Sayer.

Refining the Sports Car – Jaguar's E-type

The E-type has had a significant legacy as the first popular and large production car to evolve out of aerodynamic concepts previously used only on sophisticated racing machines. Recently the trend in automobile design has been toward a more aerodynamic shape. This type of styling – known as the 'jellybean shape', the 'lozenge shape', or even the 'worn-bar-of-soap look' – has dominated new designs in the United States, Europe and Japan. Prominent examples include the Ford Taurus, Buick Riviera, Chevrolet Caprice, Ford Contour and Oldsmobile Aurora as well as Mazda's recent redesign of its complete line. These curvilinear cars borrow heavily from the E-type, with their entirely rounded edges, bumpers intrinsic to the overall shape and head and tail lights cast into the body. Many, particularly the Mazda Miata, even feature the Jaguar's curved, mouth-like front air-intake vent. These cars replicate the E-type's overall sense of wholeness and unity of shape. The emergence of this kind of design clearly illustrates the demand for cars whose appearance in some manner acknowledges the laws of aerodynamics.

**Museum of Modern Art,
New York
April, 1996**

→ The regal and authoritative front end of a Series 3 E-type at the Jaguar Drivers Club 50th anniversary (April, 2006).

'UK's Best-Loved Car', with supercars like the McLaren F1 (66 %) and the Lamborghini Countach (62%) trailing behind. This poll just shows yet again how sensational the E-type was back in 1961, when 44 years later it was still regarded by the public as their favourite car.

As the creator of some of the world's most respected and sought-after fashion designs, Ralph Lauren is regarded as one of the foremost figures in the field of design. His keen sense of style and discerning eye have guided his passion in assembling one of the most important groups of vintage sports and touring cars in the world.

Speaking at the exhibition held at the Museum of Fine Arts, Boston (2005) – *Speed, Style and Beauty: Cars from the Ralph Lauren Collection* – Lauren said: 'These automobiles are moving works of art, embodying a functional beauty that can be inspirational, yet still purposeful.' In recent years, automobiles have been increasingly admired as art, as collectors and museums have come to recognise the remarkable craftsmanship of particular models, and the post-war years were an especially fertile period for design, producing cars that were both elegant and innovative.

Early in 2006, BBC 2 ran a television programme, The Great British Design Quest, as part of *The Culture Show* series which celebrated the design of British products. One of the products listed was of course the Jaguar E-type, and well-known British commentator, Jenny Éclair had this to say: 'There is something about this car that makes you want to lick it. This car conjures up what Britain used to be: it used to be sexy; we used to be optimistic; this is when we were just about to jet off here, jet off there. The Jaguar E-type, from the moment it was unveiled to this very second, has retained its gawp factor.'

You could hardly wish for greater affirmation of a design that has successfully held the motoring world in its grip ever since its launch in March, 1961. The Jaguar E-type has become what the author refers to as 'landmark car', which is basically a vehicle that, when it was produced, marked a change in automotive thinking. A landmark car represents an identifiable point in time that signals the beginning of a new era in design or production, or perhaps a dramatic step-change in market

August 2004, the Design Museum, London, hosted an exhibition celebrating the 'Story of the E-type'. Here, a Series 1½ FHC is displayed in the design tank outside the museum.

consciousness, which affects the buyer's use or appreciation of the motor vehicle.

A Bugatti Royale would not be such a vehicle, because as beautiful as it is, it was produced in such small numbers that very few people would ever see one in their lives, and the Royale did not have any significant influence over the design or manufacture of other automobiles which followed it. On the other hand, launched in 1948, the Porsche 356 represented a significant change in the packaging of sports cars, signalling that size was indeed not everything. Similarly, the Ford Mustang in 1964 heralded a new era in the market for sports and performance cars, in fact initiating the pony-car phenomenon, as did the Volkswagen Beetle, the BMC Mini and many other iconic vehicles that have gone on to become styling references in the market.

In the same way, the E-type ushered in a new standard of performance, affordability and styling, the likes of which had never been seen before in a volume-produced sports car. The landmark E-type became the sports car to which many potential customers around the world aspired, and that other manufacturers regarded with a combination of envy and respect. In short, a landmark car is a car of significance that is as important today as it was the day it was launched – the Jaguar E-type is such a car.

Demise of the E-type

It is really ironic that American legislators should be so obsessed with the exhaust emissions of specialised, low-volume sports cars, when it is their own domestically manufactured vehicles which have the largest engines, use the most fuel and which produce the highest vehicle emissions on the planet. With this backdrop, it is even harder to understand that it was America, Jaguar's largest and most lucrative market, which sealed the fate of the ever-popular E-type.

Overburdened with exhaust-emission equipment, the Series 3 V12 E-type had by 1975 become too heavy and slow to be a serious contender in the sports car market, and customers were now looking for something more modern.

↑ Inside the Design Museum, London, the E-type exhibition included several famous cars including (from left to right): HDU 555N (the last E-type ever produced, now owned by the JDHT), a lightweight E-type racer, a Series I roadster and a Series I FHC.

↑ In 2006, at the
Design Museum,
London, the E-type
was once again centre
stage at an exhibition
celebrating the best
of British design, as
part of the BBC 2
television series,
The Culture Show.

TOTAL JAGUAR E-TYPE PRODUCTION FROM 1961–1975:

Model	Quantity Produced	Roadster	FHC
E-type Series 1	38,389	17,369	21,020
E-type Series 2	18,848	8,641	10,207
E-type Series 3	15,292	7,982	7,310
Total	72,529	33,992	38,537

With performance of the Big Cat down and with a top speed of only 138mph, this was no longer considered very impressive for a mighty V12 and the additional bulk caused the car to appear spongy and its overall handling suffered notably.

72,529 E-types were manufactured between the years 1961 and 1974 of which 80% were left-hand drive. A total of 84% of the left-hand-drive E-types went to America, which represents a chunky 67% of the total production – that's two out of every three cars.

From the above table it can be seen that the FHC was a marginally better seller in the Series 1 and Series 2 E-types,

with the tables swinging slightly in favour of the roadster in the Series 3 model. The final Series 3 FHC was manufactured in September 1973 while the roadster ceased production in February 1975, accounting for the slightly better sales. With the anticipated arrival of roll-over safety legislation, Jaguar had begun work on the replacement XJ-S model, but this project was running well behind schedule and so the Series 3 roadster continued in service until 1975. In fact Sir William had considered a facelift for the Series 3, but was discouraged from implementing this as planning for the E-type's replacement model was well advanced. Tom Jones explains: 'Lyons wanted

→ Jaguar's magazine advertisements like 'Prowl Car' and 'Nobody's Pussycat' was an attempt by the company to prolong the public's perception of the ageing car's foreign mystique, power and grace.

↓ The end of an era – the final Series 3 V12 E-type takes its place in the JDHT Museum, Coventry. In the background are some of the prototype moulds of the later XK8 front nose section.

to do a face lift to the E-type, but we had gone too far along the line with the XJ-S and the tooling was all committed for it.' Tom Jones remembers making a model of the face-lifted E-type for Sir William. 'We only did a bit of titivating here and there, just something to regenerate the interest.' he laughed.

However, the E-type did not die a whimpering death, enjoying strong sales in its final year, thanks largely to a huge advertising campaign by the company which emphasised the car's animal instincts and stealth characteristics (with strap lines like 'Nobody's Pussycat' and 'Prowl Car'). The last of the E-Types brought to an end a run of sports cars that had started in 1935 with the SS90. The E-type had proved to be Jaguar's biggest-selling sports car even outselling the entire XK 120, 140 and 150 ranges combined. The final 50 Series 3 E-types produced were all painted black to mark the end of this remarkable era in the company's history, and each of these final batch of cars had a commemorative plaque affixed to the dashboard identifying it as one of the last produced. The very last E-type to come off the production line, 'HDU 555N', was retained by the company and appears regularly at events all around the world, in recognition of the part played by the E-type in the company's growth.

Despite its high performance and handsome appearance, the Jaguar E-type was not a specialised car produced in limited numbers, but one that attempted to appeal to as

large a segment of the population as possible. In an industry in which perceived image and performance are so often reflected in the price, the E-type provided a significant and affordable alternative. ▨

Life after the E-type

'There has got to be a spontaneity and creativeness about a Jaguar, it is a very, very emotional product. And that comes from a desire.'

Julian Thomson – Chief Designer, Advanced Studio, Jaguar Cars

  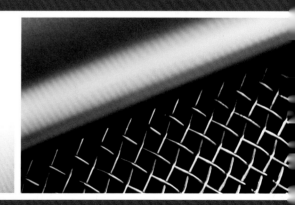

1970	1985	1988	1995	1996	1998	2000
Malcolm Sayer dies suddenly aged 54 years	Sir William Lyons dies 8 February	XJ220 prototype introduced at the Birmingham Motor Show	XK8 (X100) production commences	XJ-S production ceases	XK180 concept introduced at Paris Motor Show in September	F-type concept launched at NAIAS, 11 January
XJ-S launched September, 1975						

➜ The day the XJ-S was unveiled to the world – Frankfurt Motor Show, September, 1975.

JAGUAR XJ-S

When the new XJ-S was presented at the Frankfurt Auto Show in September 1975, the public and the media were expecting an E-type replacement. It was obvious from the start that the new car had an impossible task, as its predecessor had so totally captured the public's imagination since its launch in 1961. It is therefore hardly surprising that the XJ-S failed to stir the emotions in the same way as the E-type had done.

With the introduction of the new XJ-S, the old mystery of model naming once again reared its head. Post-war Jaguar sports cars had first followed the 'XK' family name, then came the 'E-type' borne out of a racing lineage, which was in turn followed by the 'XJ-S' – there simply appeared to be no logical sequence to the naming of the sports car line. Confusingly however, the 'XJ' refers to 'experimental Jaguar' which really applied to almost all of Jaguar's prototypes at one time or another, were they saloon or sports cars. What then did the 'S' stand for, 'sport'? 'Probably', laughed Jim Randle, 'That's what we thought, yes I think that is probably right.'

Certainly more of a grand tourer than a sports car, the XJ-S was a rather sudden departure from Jaguar's more traditional style of elegance and grace, especially in their sports-car range. Coming from the drawing board of Malcolm Sayer, the angular look of the XJ-S was quite unexpected, even to those working in the factory.

Geoff Turner recalls: 'Really, it was quite a shock after the E-type which was a sports car, although it had developed into a GT car in later years. The XJ-S was not what we were expecting. We were expecting something a bit different as a sports car so it was quite a shock when we looked at this body and said, "That's not a sports car, that's a GT-type car but its not a sports car".'

Just as the change in body construction from the XK 150 to the E-type had been quite revolutionary, so too was the changeover to the XJ-S quite marked, as the XJ-S was a very different beast to assemble from the Series 3 E-type. Based on a shortened XJ6 saloon floor pan, it had pretty much the same running gear as the saloon but with certain changes to suit the weight and road holding. Before the creation of the assembly development shop at Browns Lane, when preparing for the assembly of a new vehicle on the production line, Geoff Turner would talk to the fitters in the experimental shop in order to establish the best methods to be adopted on the assembly line. This would often give Turner a sneak preview of the new model long before many others, but as he remembers: 'We never really saw an XJ-S body until we got the first few delivered to assemble.'

However, the XJ-S began life on the drawing board as a mid-engined sports car, influenced in design by the XJ13. Turner again: 'There was a proposal following on from the XJ13 racing car to develop that theme into a road-going mid-engined car.'

These pre-XJ-S proposals would have resulted in a two-seater production vehicle rather than the two-plus-two configuration that the production XJ-S eventually became. Early drawings of this E-type replacement included an open roadster while the early full-sized body design drawings also showed the rear of the XJ-S with a hatchback just as in the E-type fixed-head coupé, with a similar opening rear door. This initial proposal was a development of the more familiar E-type theme but then later underwent a 'cut and shut' process to adapt it to the saloon floor pan for production.

In reality, Jaguar would not have considered building a mid-engined road car for several very good and practical reasons.

Firstly, a mid-engined layout did not offer the quiet and subdued ride Jaguar drivers were accustomed to, and a high-performance engine located immediately behind the driver's ear may have proved 'offensive' to many occupants. Secondly, a mid-engined car offered limited space for luggage and leaned more towards an out-and-out high-performance sports car rather than a grand tourer which Sir William preferred. Mid-engined sports cars offered quite distinct handling advantages for racing, but if intended as a comfortable motorway cruiser it offered limited advantages in ride and comfort, and even some disadvantages as mentioned earlier.

Geoff Turner again: 'The XJ-S was a quite a big change in market placing, and looking back, Sir William was right that the sports car market was dying off and the GT-type luxury car, the continental tourer type market, was a better market to go into at that time.'

The XJ-S was the last car that Malcolm Sayer designed, which surprises many people as it does not look like any of those that he had done before. 'Although,' as Keith Helfet explains, 'If you look at the original prototype you can see the connection, but he died before it was finished so that didn't help it.'

As explained elsewhere in this book, Malcolm Sayer had a unique manner in his approach to design, using mathematical formulae to calculate surface forms to position the body lines, as well as aerodynamic testing in wind tunnels and testing on

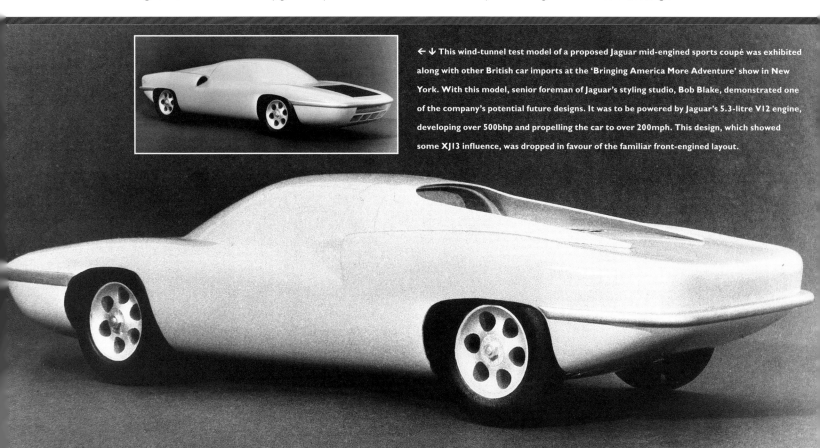

← ↓ This wind-tunnel test model of a proposed Jaguar mid-engined sports coupé was exhibited along with other British car imports at the 'Bringing America More Adventure' show in New York. With this model, senior foreman of Jaguar's styling studio, Bob Blake, demonstrated one of the company's potential future designs. It was to be powered by Jaguar's 5.3-litre V12 engine, developing over 500bhp and propelling the car to over 200mph. This design, which showed some XJ13 influence, was dropped in favour of the familiar front-engined layout.

the road with woollen tufts. Keith Helfet recalls: 'So in part, his designs were being developed from two perspectives, the one was in the aesthetic sense and the other was to meet his aerodynamic requirements. Arguably, he was one of the most talented car designers ever.'

In an attempt to understand how the very 'un-E-type' looking XJ-S came into existence, one must reconstruct the circumstances which surrounded the car's development at the time of its design. By examining other super sports cars

and grand tourers that were emerging onto the market at the time, it can be seen that the mid-engined format was becoming popular, certainly with certain Continental sports cars, and as the Americans showed huge respect for such thoroughbreds, Jaguar had to take this into account. Early designs for the XJ-S placed the engine behind the driver, hence the Ferrari-like buttresses behind the rear window, but this initial design was also much smaller than the eventual production model. Items to be carried over from the E-type model included the rear

ENGINE LAYOUT AND TECHNICAL SPECS FOR SELECTED SPORTS CARS FROM THE XJ-S ERA:

Car	Year	Capacity	Layout	Position	Output	Speed	Price*
Maserati Indy	1971	4,136cc	V8	Front	260bhp	155mph	$17,500
Lamborghini Espada	1972	3,929cc	V12	Front	350bhp	155mph	$24,500
Ferrari 365GTB/4	1973	4,392cc	V12	Front	320bhp	173mph	$25,350
Lamborghini Countach	1973	3,929cc	V12	Mid	375bhp	175mph	$52,000
Maserati Bora	1973	4,719cc	V8	Mid	310bhp	162mph	$26,900
Jaguar XJ-S	1975	5,343cc	V12	Front	285bhp	153mph	$20,000
Mercedes Benz 450SLC	1975	4,520cc	V8	Front	180bhp	136mph	$23,976
Aston Martin V8	1977	5,340cc	V8	Front	340bhp	140mph	$33,950
Chev Corvette	1977	5,765cc	V8	Front	210bhp	132mph	$8,648
Ferrari 512 BB	1979	4,942cc	Flat 12	Mid	339bhp	188mph	$85,000
Porsche 928	1980	4,474cc	V8	Front	240bhp	143mph	$37,930
BMW M1	1980	3,453cc	6 cyl	Mid	277bhp	162mph	$115,000

*All prices converted to US dollars for comparative purposes – these may vary slightly from actual showroom prices on the day

An early XJ-S prototype sketch, much closer to the final product at this stage.

suspension unit and the V12 engine which had started life in the XJ13.

To show how certain design cues are replicated by various manufacturers, the 1969 Chev Corvette Stingray (spelt as one word) Sports Coupé featured very distinctive buttresses, a trend which had started tentatively with the 1968 Corvette and which ran for about ten years. Around this time the Corvette, a model with which the E-type and XJ-S competed very strongly, had a very angular design with flat body panels, a feature which was again quite prevalent on the XJ-S, and one could argue that this was done to appeal to the American market.

However, the sports-car scene was showing ominous signs of change in America in the mid-1970s. Rollover legislation threatened the future of sports convertibles and this had an impact on early XJ-S plans so that it was offered only in coupé form at launch. This development constrained Sayer's plans which at that point included a soft top, but even the mighty General Motors ceased production of their convertible

Corvette in 1975, reintroducing it only ten years later when the threat of rollover legislation had evaporated.

Sadly, Malcolm Sayer died in 1970 just as the XJ-S prototype was beginning to take shape, and some of the momentum that had been established under his leadership, was understandably lost. As Keith Helfet explains: 'It just had an unfortunate background, but in fact if you look at an XJ-S it is very [sic] unique. It has a strong presence on the road; it has fabulous proportion and fabulous balance. It is a very impressive car, but it was not fair to judge it against an E-type.'

When the engine position was finalised in the XJ-S, it obviously influenced the front-end treatment of the car making it a relatively long feature, just as with the E-type. That is partly due to the fact that with a great big V12 up front, in order to ensure a 50/50 weight distribution, the engine had to be placed further back in the chassis, thereby creating a longer engine compartment. This overall increase in size of the XJ-S effectively limited any sporting pretensions owners may have had, thereby confirming its status as a grand tourer. Helfet

↑ This early publicity shot of an XJ-S was taken in June 1975 near Lac d' Orédon in the French Pyrenees, three months prior to the car's public launch at the Frankfurt Motor Show.

→ The XJ-S went on to become Jaguar's longest-running production sports car. The rear buttresses can be seen clearly on this 1979 model.

again: 'So, it lost all of the sculpture and the sexiness of the E-type, but some of that was in the original XJ-S prototype.'

The fact that Jaguar did not proceed with an XJ-S convertible at launch would seem to confirm that this car was once again aimed at the American market which is borne out by the company's observance of the pending rollover legislation there. The interior, which Sayer was not responsible for, was decidedly American and the XJ-S was available only with automatic transmission across the Atlantic, while in Europe, manual transmission was an option. The reason for this was not so much the American influence, but the fact that the tremendous power and torque generated by the V12

engine were best suited to the automatic 'box. Keith Helfet describes it this way: 'It was a difficult period and I think it had a mid-Atlantic look.'

Eventually the XJ-S was finished in the styling studio, but it is a car that means different things to different people, and is perhaps best likened to a good red wine, improving over time through constant refinement. 'It did get a bad press initially, but what a hard act the E-type was to follow.' Helfet pointed out.

The Coventry sales department was full of expectation for the new car, and when Geoff Turner was instructed to prepare the manufacturing engineering processes for the

Malcolm Sayer – a tribute
1916–1970

Malcolm Gilbert Sayer passed away very suddenly in 1970, aged just 54 years. Sayer, who was a student at Loughborough University's Department of Aeronautical and Automotive Engineering in 1938, was hailed by that institution as the designer of 'the most glamorous car in the world', the Jaguar E-type.

In a press release put out by the University in 2005, it said, 'He was one of the first designers to apply the principles of aerodynamics to cars with his scientific calculations, creating one of the most beautiful forms of the era.' This announcement was made at a special ceremony arranged by the University and the Jaguar Daimler Heritage Trust on 21 May, 2005, at which a bronze commemorative plaque was unveiled in recognition of his achievements.

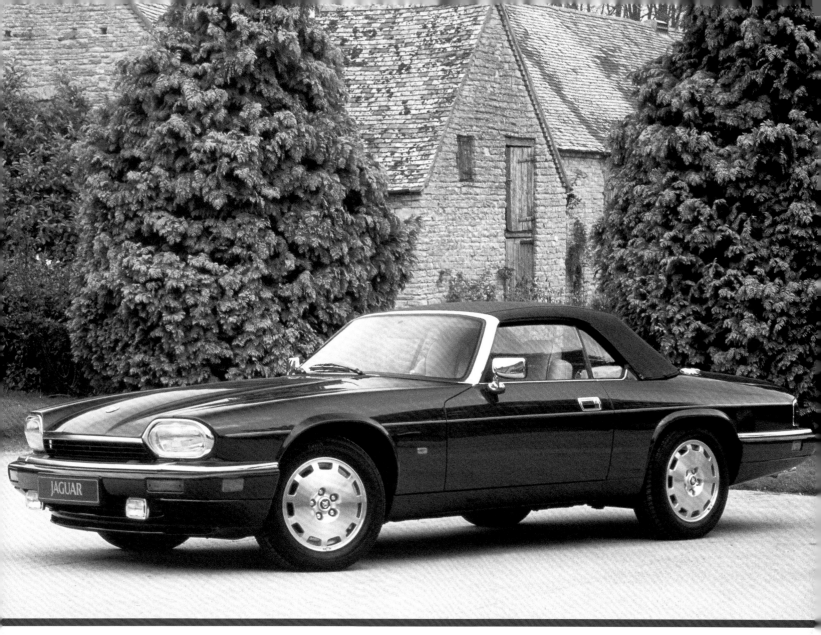

↑ This 4.0-litre convertible XJ-S is a 1995 model.

assembly line, his first question was how many cars the company planned to sell. A trip to the sales department served only to set the alarm bells ringing, as Turner was told, 'We'll want 500 per shift per week, and we'll need two shifts'. That amounted to a thousand cars a week for a single model, when the highest output the factory had previously produced was in the order of 800 cars a week across the whole range of Mark II, Mark X and E-type. 'Oh yes, we've got great expectations and plans for this car.' came the reply, 'It's going to sell like hot cakes and we're going to market it as a trans-Continental luxury express car.'

The production line was duly lengthened but according to Geoff, 'We never did get up to 1,000 a week and definitely not 500 a week, but we might have got up to about 280-ish for a few weeks.' By using the shortened floor pan and rear suspension of the saloon, the assembly method of the XJ-S was fortunately not very different from that of the saloon. However, although the car been developed and tested with carburettors, a last minute

decision was made to go with fuel injection, which further delayed the production of the XJ-S.

Once the XJ-S was in production and despite a rather slow start, Jaguar continued to develop the car, and a new fuel injection system in 1980 combined with the revolutionary May head with its 'fireball' combustion chambers, gave the model better fuel consumption. Introduced as the HE (High Efficiency), the XJ-S also came in for some interior and trim

JAGUAR XJ-S PRODUCTION:

Model	Years	Quantity
XJ-S V12 5.3-litre	1975–1993	82,384
XJ-S 3.6-litre	1982–1991	10,017
XJR-S V12 6.0-litre	1989–1993	837
XJ-S 4.0-litre	1990–1996	19,531
XJ-S 6.0-litre	1992–1996	2,561
Total		115,330

Figures supplied by Jaguar Cars, Coventry

upgrades. Tom Jones remembers with a smile: 'There was a new injection system which gave us about another mile and half, and the May head gave us another mile and quarter so they had to introduce them at the same time to show a big improvement, about two and a half miles to the gallon!'

It is interesting to note that although it is the E-type which is regarded as a design icon in the motor industry, the XJ-S was produced and sold in greater numbers, although admittedly it was Jaguar's longest-running production sports car. Looking at this comparison the other way around, it is equally interesting to see how favourably the E-type compares with the seemingly higher-selling XJ-S model which benefited from improved production methods and much more substantial marketing research. Although this is a very general comparison, as it groups together all the derivatives of each model, it just goes to show how successful the timeless styling of the E-type was at a time when marketing research was almost unheard of in Britain and Europe.

E-TYPE/XJ-S PRODUCTION COMPARISON

Model	Total production	Production period	Ave. annual production
E-type	72,539	14 years	5,180 cars p.a.
XJ-S	115,330	21 years	5,491 cars p.a.

XJ220 – An E-type 'supercar'

In 1988, after four years of development, Jaguar announced that they would be using the knowledge gained through racing the XJR-11 sports racer to launch their own supercar. The XJ220 made its debut as a concept car at the 1988 Birmingham Motor Show, and was undoubtedly the star of the show. However, when Jaguar was bought by Ford in 1989, they realised what a gem they had acquired in the deal and decided that the project should be produced through a joint venture between Jaguar and Tom Walkinshaw's TWR operation, thus creating the JaguarSport division.

Looking at the XJ220, one cannot help asking why Jaguar built this car in the first place, as it did not fit into an existing model line-up and nor was it a replacement for anything, and production volume was certainly not planned to be very high. The car's designer, Keith Helfet explains the justification: 'The rationale behind it was to take on the Porsche 959 and the 1984 Group B Ferrari GTO.' Helfet continues: 'Jim [Randle] said, "OK, Porsche and Ferrari have Group B cars, if we do one, I bet we will be able to start a racing series because others will follow". So, it was designed as a Group B car originally, virtually right until a couple of weeks before we launched the thing, it was known as the "Group B".'

The XJ220 must rank as one of Jaguar's finest automobile designs, arguably occupying a place alongside the XK 120 and

➔ Geoff Lawson and Mark Lloyd with the XJ220 prototype in the studio at Park Sheet Metal in Coventry where the body was made. The vehicle pictured here was the actual prototype show car, and at that stage, the only full-size XJ220. The final production bodies, however, were made by Abbey Panels.

Sir William Lyons – a tribute
4 September, 1901 – 8 February, 1985

Sir William Lyons was an extraordinary man. He ran his company with a no-nonsense attitude and demanded the very best from all of the workers, from the most menial right to the very top. Some have said he was even tight fisted with his money, but it was that autocratic approach that got the company to where it was.

Born on 4 September, 1901, in Blackpool, William Lyons began his business life there too in 1922 as a partner together with William Walmsley manufacturing Swallow sidecars. It was, however, only ten years later that William Lyons would realise his dream, to manufacture his very own brand of motor car, the S.S.I and S.S.II. In the mid-1930s, Walmsley left the partnership, a move which set young Lyons on a path to the top.

From those very early days, William Lyons was able to surround himself with talented and hard-working personnel, a quality which stayed with him throughout his working life. Jim Randle explains: 'Sir William didn't do it all on his own, he got some super people around him, that was his brilliance, he would get some really tremendous people, Bill Heynes, Bob Knight, Wally Hassan and all of those guys were really brilliant. It was an era when people cared more about cars than they cared about making money, but yes, you have to have them both balanced.'

Sir William remained a driven individual who settled for nothing but the best in everything he did, as Jim Randle

→ Sir William and Lady Lyons photographed at their home, Wappenbury Hall in the early 1980s.

remembers: 'The Old Chap, he was always in the shop, and even back in the 80s, I used to see him almost everyday. He would come along and look at what we were doing, point out with his stick and say, "Do you think that is right there Randle?", and you'd say, "Yes, I think so Sir William", and he would go away and you would think about it overnight and you would think, "Oh the old sod is right you know", so you'd change it and he would come back and say, "Yes that looks better", ... Oh yes, he was a great man, I loved him dearly.'

Right to the end, Sir William showed commitment and was involved even from his home. Randle again: 'I had instructions from him the day before he died. We were doing XJ41 at the time, the day before he died, from his death bed he rang me up and wanted to know how things were going. But, he was always dead bloody straight. Whatever was going on, you knew exactly where you stood. He was just so committed to the company and he had such talent. Right to the end he was committed to the company. It's a pity a few more others weren't. Yes, I gave the eulogy at his funeral, his memorial.'

the E-type. But this car almost never made it to production, as Jim Randle was emphatic that the 220 should not interfere with any other work being done, as he could not be seen to be diverting resources away from the company's core business. In short, it was a 'Saturday Club' car, being designed and developed after hours when time permitted and on weekends.

'When I was doing the 220 that was done after hours. I had a full-time job and this was done after hours in the Saturday Club. That could not be done in normal hours, which is why again I had a free hand; I was doing it off my own bat.' Helfet explained.

Just as the XK 120 was very different from the SS100 which came before it, in the same way, the E-type was a huge step forward from the XK 150, which followed the XK 120. The XJ-S was also another big leap in design, being totally different from the design and styling of the E-type. In each of these successive sports car generations, the design language progressed significantly, creating a new standard in the

industry and a new set of expectations and desires for the customer with each new model. The challenge with the XJ220 concept for any Jaguar designer, would be to take the elements from these past designs and incorporate them in a new model without appearing to be backward-looking. None of the creators of the cars mentioned above sought to take too many elements from its predecessor forward into the new model, as this would have defeated the object of a having a new model. That way, it would just have ended up being a revised version of the earlier model.

The most difficult thing for Helfet was that the XJ220 was to be the spiritual successor to the XJ13, and this served as both a challenge and as a help for him. The challenge was that the XJ13 was such a hard act to follow, yet it also provided such a wealth of design inspiration which provided significant motivation for the designer.

Keith Helfet gives an insight: 'It caused me both agony and ecstasy, because conceptually the 220 was going to be the successor to the 13, a modern successor to it. And there was

'Creating an object of desire; I think there can be no greater prize for any designer. Certainly that is what I was trying to achieve. Malcolm Sayer was my mentor, I never met him; he died before, but he was my inspiration. He was one of my design idols for want of a clichéd phrase.'

Keith Helfet on the XJ220

← Jaguar designer Keith Helfet stands proudly amongst the sports cars he designed. In the foreground (from left) are the XK180 prototype, XJ220 and XK8. Behind is the actual design-studio scale model of the XJ220, used to approve the full-scale mock-up.

part of me thinking that this is an impossible act to follow because the 13 is just a work of art. It is absolutely magnificent. Therefore, following that is unbelievably daunting; on the other hand it is a piece of inspiration.'

When the XJ220 was designed, there was nothing else like it on the market, but as we have seen above, that was the Jaguar tradition in pushing the design envelope with each successive new sports model. Helfet again: 'To me the 13 was not about taking a few clichés or styling features from it and simply drafting it onto something else. To me that is not what Jaguar is all about. Malcolm Sayer did not try to do that.

'There was an essence to that which I thought was still relevant. One of the things was the use of sculpture and form to make the design statement. There were some design features like the exposed engine at the back which I thought was great and there was no reason why not to do that again. And of course the oval mouth which was styling cliché, but it made sense.' Helfet added.

183

↑ One of Helfet's design objectives was to recreate the exposed-engine feature as seen in the XJ13, a sports racer which he used as inspiration in the design of the XJ220.

XJ220 PROTOTYPE AND PRODUCTION MODEL SPECIFICATIONS:

Vehicle details	XJ220 Prototype (B'ham Motor Show 1988)	XJ220 Production model (introduced 1991)
Engine configuration	V12 mid-engine	V-6 twin turbo mid-engine
Engine capacity	6.2-litre	3.6-litre
Gearbox	Hewland 5-speed	Manual 5-speed all-synchro
Maximum output	530–550bhp (est.)	542bhp
Maximum speed	200mph plus (est.)	220mph claimed (213mph measured)
0–60mph	3.5 secs (est.)	3.6 seconds
0–100mph	8 seconds (est.)	7.9 seconds
Length	5,141mm	4,930mm
Width	2,203mm	2,220mm (includes mirrors)
Height (roof)	1,237mm	1,150mm
Weight	1,590kg	1,470kg
Quantity produced	1	350*
Price	£ n/a	£413,000 (including VAT, June 1992)

*Maximum 350 planned – approximately 300 built including prototypes and race cars
Details and specs supplied by Jaguar Cars, Coventry

In developing his appreciation of automotive design and styling, Keith Helfet had the benefit of Sir William Lyons's experience for almost five years. Although Sir William died before the 220 was even proposed, Keith Helfet is convinced that he would have approved of it. 'I was influenced by him because he was there and I was influenced by him even when he was not there. I remember doing the 220, and he never saw the 220, that happened after he died, and thinking I had the ghost of Sir William on my shoulders, thinking "would he approve of this or not?" – that was important to me: how he would have done things. I believe he would have approved of the 220', commented Keith Helfet.

The XJ220 was constructed around a bonded and riveted monocoque chassis formed from lightweight, corrosion-resistant aluminium-alloy sheet, and reinforced by aluminium honeycomb sections in highly stressed areas. When the first 220s rolled out of the factory in 1991, they quickly earned the soubriquet of 'The World's Fastest Car'. Initially, the prototype XJ220 was fitted with a massive 6.2-litre V12, 48-valve, fuel-injected engine developing 530bhp mounted on a four-wheel-drive, active-suspension set-up with a top speed in excess of 200mph. The production car however did away with much of this hardware, and was instead fitted with a twin-turbo V6 motor of 3.5-litre capacity producing no less than 542bhp. This awesome combination propelled the supercar to that magical figure of 220mph, making it the fastest production car in the world, and thereby meeting one of its important design targets.

But herein lay another important departure by the Coventry manufacturer, as they once again reverted to naming their latest sports car in accordance with its potential top speed, namely 220mph, just as they had done 40 years earlier with the Jaguar XK 120. Where previously the engineers had opted for a traditional front-engine layout for the production XJ-S, rejecting the mid-engine configuration, the XJ220 now boasted a mid-engine layout. However, this was at the cost of luggage space, but that did not matter when the car could claim the performance statistics of the XJ220.

Available in five metallic colours, silver, grey, green, maroon or blue, the XJ220 was equally impressive inside the cabin. Creature comforts extended to air conditioning, full leather interior and a stereo, but the proof of the pudding was in the eating, as the cabin was luxuriously fitted, comfortable and yet not lacking in that supercar feel. In June 1993, the two well-known British motoring journals, *Autocar* and *Motor*, road tested the XJ220 for the first time and they reported the car's performance as 'astonishing'.

The final test for the XJ220, however, lay not only in the car's performance, the write-ups in various world-renowned motoring journals or even the positive acclaim of the wider media world. The ultimate test was to be found at a regular Jaguar car club meeting back in little old England, where the

↓ **The profile of the production XJ220 offers one of the most pleasing, streamlined shapes of the entire Jaguar sports car range. The success of this design encompasses elements of the D-type and other traditional Jaguar styling cues and will stand as a testament to Jaguar's sports-car heritage for many years to come.**

XJ220 was to be displayed to ordinary, mature members of the Jaguar enthusiasts' fraternity.

Keith Helfet was to be in attendance and he was more than a little nervous. 'The original concept car was on display at the Coventry Motor Museum a few months after the official launch of the 220 in front of all of these Jaguar aficionados, the real devotees and I would fear them judging the 220. The prospect of that was frightening. I could just imagine these guys saying, "Well of course Jaguar stopped when Sir William left the company" or whatever, and I was not expecting them to embrace and approve the 220. To my complete amazement, they did and they just saw it as a real Jaguar. But in a way these were the ultimate compliments, because to get the approval of that crowd who really know their stuff and really know what Jaguar is all about, that was the ultimate endorsement.'

Such was the public's approval of the new supercar from Jaguar that the company received 1,450 confirmed orders for the XJ220, each accompanied by the required deposit of £50,000. That amounted to an attractive tally of £72,500,000 just for the deposits, a massive over-subscription of 1,100 cars.

'It was a phenomenal success. The competitor by comparison, the McLaren F1, I think the original orders were a few dozen; there was just no comparison. You know, that is the bit that got lost in the headlines. We could not believe it, and nobody had even driven the car. People started to say,

"Right, I desire that, I want one, I don't care about anything else", and handing over blank cheques. Talk about the ultimate emotional purchase.' commented Keith.

The development of the XJ220 took almost six years from concept to production model, as Keith Helfet explains: 'The design scale model took a year and it took three years from there to the '88 car [Birmingham Motor Show prototype] and then it took a further two years to production.'

In the same way that the E-type inherited its fundamental design and layout from the racing D-type, so too did the XJ13 strongly influence the design of the XJ220, and one can trace the unmistakable lineage of this supercar back to the E-type itself. However, as the 220 was initially intended as a Group B race car, the super-sleek, aerodynamic shape was perfectly suited to the race track, but as a road car it can arguably be regarded as a limited edition, E-type supercar.

XK8 – A reworked XJ-S?

Following the unexpected success of the XJ-S grand tourer after a 21-year life cycle, the company needed to inject a bit more 'Jaguar' into their sports-car line-up. That is perhaps a slightly unfair statement to make, because despite a rather wobbly start, the XJ-S sold in greater numbers (115,330 cars over 21 years) than any other sports-car model in the company's history. But one could argue that the XJ-S had lost some of the curvaceous lines that Jaguar sports cars

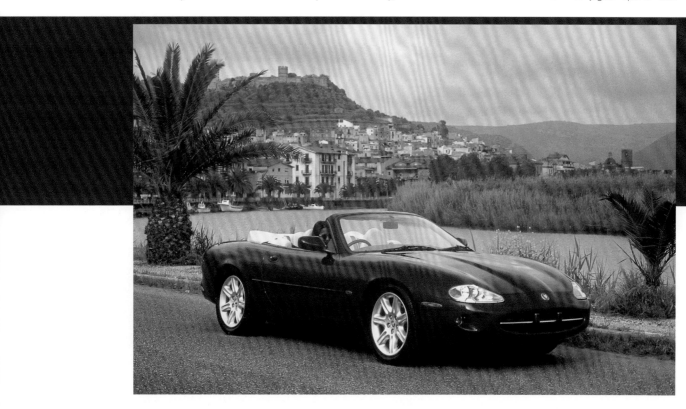

← ↑ A pair of handsome XK8 models at launch (1996), in both Convertible and Coupé form.

← ↑ A pair of handsome XK8 models at launch (1996), in both Convertible and Coupé form.

→ 'New Jag E-type' – Autocar's take on the new XK8 (6 March, 1996).

had become famous for and the time was right for a return to that styling.

Code-named the X100, the XK8 used the basic underpinnings of the XJ-S, but unfortunately this model was the subject of some rather unpleasant corporate politics. Now under the control of Ford, the XK8 design was initially influenced by Manfred Lampe from the company's headquarters in Dearborn, Michigan. As so often happens in large corporate design institutions, a new design initiative is sometimes accompanied by an unwelcome political agenda within the company, and the XK8 was not exempt from this unpleasantness. Ford's design interpretation was bombed out after a series of disastrous clinic trials in the USA, leaving the design proposal by Geoff Lawson and Fergus Pollock (Jaguar UK) as the only one on the table.

In order to try and smooth over all of the unpleasant in-house politics and in an effort to keep the concept alive, Keith Helfet was asked by Lawson to come up with an alternative design so that the Ford design bosses had more than one

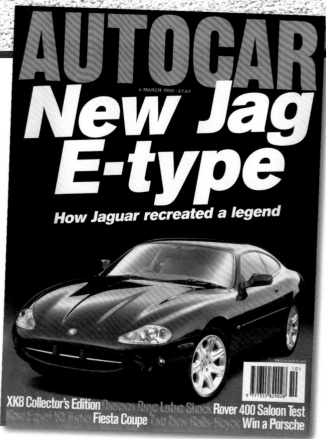

AUTOCAR

6 MARCH 1996 · £1.65

New Jag E-type

How Jaguar recreated a legend

XK8 Collector's Edition Daewoo Buys Lotus Shock Rover 400 Saloon Test
New Ford V2 turbo Fiesta Coupe Two New Rolls-Royce Win a Porsche

design to consider. This development was not one that Keith Helfet went into blindly, as he saw the possibility of a potentially very damaging career situation arising should his design win over that of Geoff Lawson, his boss. As it happened, Helfet's design was the preferred model and he was given the go-ahead to complete the job.

Although it was principally his design that was eventually approved for production, Keith gracefully withdrew from the project towards the end of the design phase when he felt it was becoming politically too messy. The XK8 was finished off by the newly created styling department, and Helfet is not too complimentary about the 'big mouth' that was stuck on the car.

The XK8 made its debut at the Geneva and New York shows in 1996, and was highly acclaimed by both the press and public alike. 60% of the production was allocated to the American market while 70% of total sales were expected to be convertibles. The XK8 has gone on to become one of Jaguar's best sellers, but ironically it shares more design and

styling heritage with the E-type than it does with its predecessor, the XJ-S.

A press release (2 October, 1996) issued at the time of the car's launch states, 'A new car in just 30 months'. The release goes on to say that this was achieved due to the benefits of simultaneous engineering teams and advanced quality planning techniques, which is really only half the story. One of the main reasons for the short '30 months from approval' timeline, is because the XK8 was really only a re-skinned XJ-S. Like most other new cars of the time, the wheelbase was the starting point: 'All of that existed; it was an XJ-S basically. All of the engineering package was there, fixed, so we were just draping this thing [new body] around it – it was a re-engineered XJ-S. That was just a draping exercise, but it turned out very successful.' Helfet commented.

The body-panel count on the XK8 was reduced by 30% over the XJ-S with a torsional rigidity increase of 25%, a far cry from the days of countless panels being welded up on jigs as with the early assembly of the E-type. Apart from the

↑ The XK8's interior stylishly finished in 'Sports' trim (2003).

structural and engineering improvements, Jaguar made a massive effort to re-invent themselves through this new model, trying to drop their ownership age by ten years, from the traditional 55-year-old male to 45-year-olds, but now also aiming at the female market. Retaining the classic cockpit theme, interior trim options included the standard 'Sport' finish and the extra cost option of the 'Classic' Jaguar interior. It is interesting to note that the 'Sport' interior was the standard no-cost option which was intended to appeal to the younger set, while the extra cost 'Classic' option would appeal to the older and slightly more traditional customer. It was the classic look that would have been standard in the old days, which demonstrates Jaguar's attempts to attract the younger market segment.

In Jaguar's press pack, the 'Sport' option, which was intended to widen the appeal of the XK8, was described as follows, 'The darker tones of the standard Sport interior reflect contemporary tastes in fashion, art and furnishing and provide a more functional, state-of-the-art appearance. The optional Classic trim epitomises the traditional Jaguar walnut-and-leather environment with elegant colour coordination'.

The boot could now accommodate two sets of golf clubs which placed the new XK8 more firmly in the 'our car' category, as opposed to the 'his car' category which was traditionally aimed at the sporting male Jaguar driver who tended to do things on his own, such as playing sport, or going for a fast drive in the country. The XK8 was a fast, executive, sporting two-door with very civilised manners and all the

↑ The 2003 XK8 convertible strikes a handsome pose even with the hood raised.

↓ This front three-quarter view of the XK8 clearly shows its E-type lineage, having abandoned the boxier styling of the XJ-S, its immediate predecessor (2003).

comforts of a saloon, including power-operated front seats, power windows, air conditioning, electronic driver aids and a portable telephone facility.

Extensive market research had revealed that the world-wide luxury sports-car sector in which the XK8 would compete accounted for around 55,000 sales in 1995, of which American customers made up almost half this figure. Germany accounted for another 25% while the UK made up 8% and Japan 6%.

The XK8 was powered by only the third generation of Jaguar engine ever, the first being the old pushrod engine in the pre-war cars, followed by the Claude Bailey XK unit which powered Jaguars to victory at Le Mans and the new AJ-V8 which was now fitted to the XK8. However, as much of this heritage was lost on modern Jaguar customers, the company identified two types of reluctant buyers to whom they needed to appeal in order to successfully broaden their market. The first group was called the 'rational rejecters', made up of those who had rationally considered the new XK8 but had rejected it in favour of another manufacturer's product. The second

group, 'image rejecters', consisted of those potential buyers who felt that the XJ-S portrayed a somewhat old-fashioned image. Although the XJ-S had been significantly modernised and upgraded during its lifetime, these image-conscious buyers felt that the longevity of the model meant that it no longer met their selection criteria.

The technical advances made by the new XK8 went some way to addressing the rather stuffy image which Jaguar had acquired in recent years, but the return to a more pleasing, curvy, sexy E-type body style certainly did the rest.

XK180 – A Jaguar with cleavage!

'The 180 was a car that we did very quickly, which is just a modified XK8, a shortened XK8.' recalls Keith Helfet.

The creation of the XK180 concept roadster, hand-built in the company's special vehicle operations workshops at Browns Lane, Coventry, was to celebrate the 50th anniversary of the introduction of the Jaguar XK sports car. Created for the 1948

Earls Court Show in London, the XK 120 was initially fabricated in aluminium as it was intended to be a limited-production sports car. In the same way, the XK180 body was crafted from aluminium by Abbey Panels, the same company responsible for building the body panels for the C-type, D-type, XJ13 as well as the awesome XJ220 and so it seemed appropriate that they should also do the XK180.

The engineering team was given just ten months to come up with a jaw-dropping show car, in time for the Paris Motor Show in September 1998, 50 years after the introduction of the XK 120. In the light of the significance of the anniversary that it was to mark, the XK180 was made into a bit of a special car. At thirteen and a half inches (345mm) shorter overall than the XKR, the XK180 was not simply a modification of a stock car. Five inches (125mm) was taken out of the wheelbase, making the XK180 strictly a two-seater which necessitated a substantial reworking of the suspension, especially as the shorter car would now have to handle even more power. The engineers took the mighty 370bhp supercharged version of the AJ-V8, and boosted output to a whopping 450bhp.

In order to create a distinctive yet easily recognisable shape, the XK8/XKR body styling was modified by Helfet to incorporate design cues from the company's earlier racing cars. Notably, the shorter, more-rounded nose and the headrests behind the seats were reminiscent of the D-type, while the interior, which took four weeks to design, was also styled in

such a way as to reflect the racing cockpits of old, and followed Helfet's specific theme of 'metal or leather' in the cabin.

Designers must draw their inspiration from somewhere, and factors which can typically influence design direction include fashion, nature and other engineering structures such as buildings, aviation, furniture or even other automotive designs. These influences are more subconscious than conscious factors as Helfet explains: 'I try not to be [influenced]. I try to just do it from first principles and do it my way, because I try and keep my stuff different from other people's. Because I like to do my own; I like to break the mould.'

Fashion is a styling element which changes constantly, and following contemporary styling and influences can draw comments like, 'Oh he is just copying so and so.' Helfet again: 'I have done some slightly bizarre things like the cleavage in the screen on the XK180, which as far as I know has never been done before or since.'

When Helfet proposed the idea at Jaguar, his boss Geoff Lawson wasn't so convinced. 'Geoff nearly freaked out. He said, "You can't be serious!" I said, "Why not?" He said, "How are you going to wipe it?" I said, "Well, if you have got a single wiper, it won't have a problem." He was very nervous. I said, "Be brave, Geoff, it is only a show car." Helfet recalled the incident with amusement.

Although it was diplomatically dubbed the 'double bubble' by the company, the cleavage form on the XK180 windshield

← In the foreground is the XK180 concept car with Jaguar's D-type race car in the background. The fin behind the driver of the D-type served as an inspiration for the rear humps behind the occupants of the XK180 which Helfet blended into the overall styling of the concept car.

→ The XK8 heritage can be clearly seen in the XK180 body, but the 'double bubble' windscreen cleavage was a distinct departure for Jaguar. This photo was taken at Silverstone during a test session at the track.

did more than just raise a few eyebrows. In Keith's words, it is 'form following function', which in this case has a certain logic because each occupant has his or her own windscreen bulge through which to see ahead. Technically speaking, the centre point is lower than the two high points and it might arguably result in slightly less wind resistance and therefore better aerodynamics, but the XK180's windscreen cleavage was Helfet's interpretation of a beautiful and natural form, the female body. This form is carried through to the two humps behind the heads of the occupants, so, 'There is logic to it, which is why it does not just look bizarre.' added Keith.

Designed in seven weeks, the 180 was certainly an example

of what can be achieved when a lateral-thinking designer is given a free rein. 'Geoff, I think, saw it twice.' smiled Helfet, adding 'I try not to follow the fashion and copy other people, and that is because it is fun for me; it is fun to do it that way.'

Although the XK180 was only a show car, a one-off styling exercise, it had a spin-off model which nearly resulted in one of the most stunning sports cars of all time. Wolfgang Reitzle, head of the Premier Automotive Group in Ford at the time got the opportunity to show off the 180 to some of his BMW friends at Goodwood: 'And I think that made him decide to say: "Let's do another one and let's do it for production".' commented Keith Helfet.

↘ The double-breasted windscreen theme of the XK180 was carried through into the twin humps behind the occupants, just as the D-type had done to streamline the airflow behind the driver's head in 1954. A neat rear wing finished off the back end in a stylish manner.

F-type (2000)

Geoff Lawson approached Keith Helfet once again and put the Reitzle proposition to him. With a completely blank canvas, Helfet had absolute freedom with all aspects of the new concept. 'It was up to me, and that was the brief. I could have put the engine wherever I liked, I had no restrictions. In fact I had absolutely no-one telling me what to do. I just did my own thing.' explained Helfet.

Helfet was given eight months in which to do the car but in just eight weeks the design was complete. Unfortunately, two weeks into the project, Geoff Lawson died very unexpectedly, leaving Keith without a boss for the remainder of the project which meant that he was almost without supervision, which is extraordinary in the design industry, especially in a large multi-national corporation. During that time, the then Jaguar design boss, Ian Callum, succeeded Geoff but it was J. Mays, Ford's Director of Design who approved of Helfet's progress on the F-type. 'J. Mays from Ford used to pop in occasionally, but he did not tell me what to do.' recalls Keith.

Conceptually, the F-type was intended as a smaller production version of the XK180 study, which had in turn been created as a lean version of the XK8/XKR. The F-type would act as the perfect little brother to the XK8 in the same way that the Porsche Boxster was the entry-level model to the more expensive 911 range. The cheaper Boxster carried the same important core brand values, but was within reach of those for whom the 911 was too expensive. As Helfet spelled out, the F-type was meant to be a stripped-out, back-to-basics sports car in the true sense of the word, and a car that could have put Jaguar back on the global sports-car map in the same way that the E-type had done 40 years earlier. This was not to be a tourer, a sort of all things to all men, as Keith explains: 'This was the car I wanted, an enthusiast's car that puts a smile on your face when you drive it. Not for posing.' Not that the F-type would have done your image any harm should you have wished to pose in it, but that was not the object of the exercise.

The conceptual starting point for the F-type, or X600 to

↑ Keith Helfet discusses some detailing aspects of the F-type's front end with a modeller in Jaguar's design studios.

← The F-type concept inherited some design and styling features from the E-type roadster, like the muscular wheel-arch lines and the stylish, seductive rear end. The dashboard style is modelled on the Spitfire wing shape and reflects Helfet's instruction to be simple, functional and modern.

give it its correct internal project designation, was in fact both the XK180 and XK8 models but only in so far as transferring the 'signature' of these two cars to the new project was concerned. In the same way that the Boxster fitted into the Porsche model family beneath the 911 range, so too would the F-type slot in neatly below the XK8 without poaching any sales from its bigger brother. For this reason, Helfet based the F-type on the Boxster's wheelbase which made it much smaller than the XK8 and therefore strictly a two-seater. This move would give Jaguar a product that could compete head-to-head with the Boxster in the lucrative small, affordable sports-car market.

'Originally I called this project the Roadster, no nonsense, stripped out, this was going to be all new, and I thought that this was something that could compete with the Boxster.' Helfet pointed out. The heritage of the E-type and its successors can be clearly seen in the nose and air intake styling, while the front oval lights were reminiscent of those on the E-type. The front driving lights also matched the rear round light clusters which helped to keep the styling simple, as per the design brief. The dashboard, taken from the XK8, was in the classic 'Spitfire' wing shape although in a much faster design in the new F-type.

The new sports car had lost the rear wing configuration of the XK180, but had grown small, stylish buttresses which served to continue the window line rearwards, while the rear

end of the car was small and neat, yet powerful in style, which all helped to give the car a dramatic, agile stance so familiar in Jaguar's earlier sports cars. The occupants were seated just in front of the rear axle which allowed the engine to be positioned further back in the chassis giving the car that critical 50/50 weight distribution, and with a relatively long bonnet, the F-type had those all-important, traditional sports-car proportions.

'I'm very proud of the back end; it captures quite a lot of E-type, it's maybe a bit more muscular than an E-type, because it's quite a powerful thing, but it's got a lot of sculpture.' Helfet explained.

Just as the sports-car market changed at the end of the E-type Series 3's life when Sir William Lyons introduced the XJ-S in a more 'grand tourer' style, so now the market profile was changing once again at the start of the new millennium. With safety features much improved in recent years, convertible and open-top sports cars were once again flourishing in a rejuvenated global market and an F-type Jaguar would have been just the right car to exploit such an opportunity. At the time, the Boxster was selling for around £34,000 which is where Helfet envisaged the F-type to be positioned in the market.

The car had been packaged around existing Jaguar components and was designed to accept the 240bhp AJ-V6 S-type engine, while a 300bhp supercharged version was

↓ The Keith Helfet F-type concept car (2000) was one of the most evocative styles to come from Jaguar's design studios in many years (below and below left).

also a later possibility. This made the project all the more convincing as it always looked like a credible car, except for the screen and the greenhouse, which, in Keith's own words, 'was bit exaggerated'. With all of the design bosses happy with the progress, the future looked rosy and so the F-type was shown at the North American International Auto Show in Detroit, 2000. In fact, plans for the car were that advanced that Jaguar included it in their publicity for the show, mentioning that it would be competitively priced with the Boxster and even giving the car's performance figures.

'The F-type Concept is a clear signal of Jaguar's intent to return to the true sports car market in which we were so successful in the 1950s and 1960s.' commented Jaguar's managing director, Jonathan Browning at the car's launch on 11 January, 2000.

The press release went on to say that Helfet wanted the new design to have its own personality. 'Designing-in the Jaguar style is an instinctive process.' he said, adding, 'Heritage is an inspiration, but not more than that.'

A second official F-type press pack was published on 4 January, 2001, carrying the strap line – The Art of Performance – communicating the very clear message yet again that this little beauty was going to transport Jaguar back into the realms of sports-car performance once more. The press release was headlined, 'Jaguar F-type Roadster Is Go!', and the announcement was made by Jaguar's Chairman, Dr.

↓ **Ian Callum's attempts to redraw the F-type (2001), after it had already received widespread acclaim from both inside and outside the company, resulted in a much squarer model.**

Wolfgang Reitzle, at the 2001 Los Angeles International Auto Show that the F-type would be delivered to market within three years.

Accompanying this press release was an alternative set of sketches introduced by Jaguar's new design supremo, Ian Callum, offering a more bulky and heavier look to the F-type than the Helfet model which already had broad management approval. This proposal progressed to full a scale model stage, but the press pack prepared for the media which publicly introduced this alternative design served only to confuse the market and the whole project began to unravel, with many of the advance orders drying up. Within a week of Nick Scheele seeing the alternative proposal, the F-type project was cancelled.

If ever there was a car that could have pulled Jaguar ahead of its competitors in the market, the original Helfet F-type was that car. It is the opinion of the author, and a great many Jaguar enthusiasts around the world for that matter, that the cancellation of the F-type project represented one of the most costly about-turns in Jaguar's history and will probably go down as one of the biggest lost opportunities the company will endure for many years to come.

As Keith Helfet explained in an interview, one of the most important contributing factors in the wide acclaim of this project was the fact that he had had free rein to design what he thought would be wanted by the sports car market, a car that he would himself like to buy. It is through this approach, rather than design by a committee, that a car like the F-type had such a strong identity and character, because it was the interpretation of one inspired designer.

When questioned about how he felt after the F-type was cancelled, he replied: 'Obviously I was really upset and disappointed, because you put your heart and soul into these things for one, and the other thing is particularly with the F-type, I wanted one. I was fed up that I could not get one. After all these years, this was the car that I wanted. This was the car for me and, unfortunately, lots of other people too.' ■

↑ The compact, no-nonsense F-type concept (2000) would certainly have drawn a significant number of sales from competing models such as the Boxster, BMW's Z3 and others, while also giving potential buyers an opportunity to get their foot on the first rung of the Jaguar product ladder.

The E-type legacy

'If the proportion of the car is right and the wheels are in the right place then that makes a great sports car – the performance is almost secondary.'

Ian Callum – Director of Design, Jaguar Cars

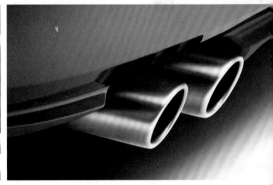

1996	1998	2000	2005	2005	2006
XK8 introduced in October	XK180 shown in Paris in September	F-type shown at Detroit Motor Show in January	Advanced Lightweight Concept introduced at Geneva Show	First XK produced 20 December at Castle Bromwich plant	XK introduced to the media in Cape Town in January XKR launched London ExCel in July

→ The Advanced Lightweight Concept, or ALC, was introduced to the media in Detroit in 2005.

Advanced Lightweight Concept (ALC)

With the announcement of the Advanced Lightweight Coupé (ALC), Jaguar were talking about a new 'design direction', which promised to show the company's future thinking. One could be forgiven for having expected something that was radically new, a totally new Jaguar sports car shape, so when the ALC show car appeared, there were lots of polite comments. Striking and purposeful it certainly was, but a new 'design direction' was maybe pushing it a bit.

The Advanced Lightweight Coupé made its design debut at the 2005 Geneva Show and the company's press release touted it as the 'star of the show'. No doubt the car did attract a lot of attention because of the high expectations created by the marketing hype that had been put out through the media prior to the show, but what the press release didn't spell out was the crowd size around the 1961 E-type show car which shared the same stand with the ALC. Sources close to Jaguar suggested that just as many people were drooling over the 44-year-old E-type as came to see the new Advanced Lightweight Coupé.

Heralding a new generation of Jaguar sports cars and

↓ From the front, the ALC is distinguishable by its large lower air intakes, which on the production car are replaced by driving lights.

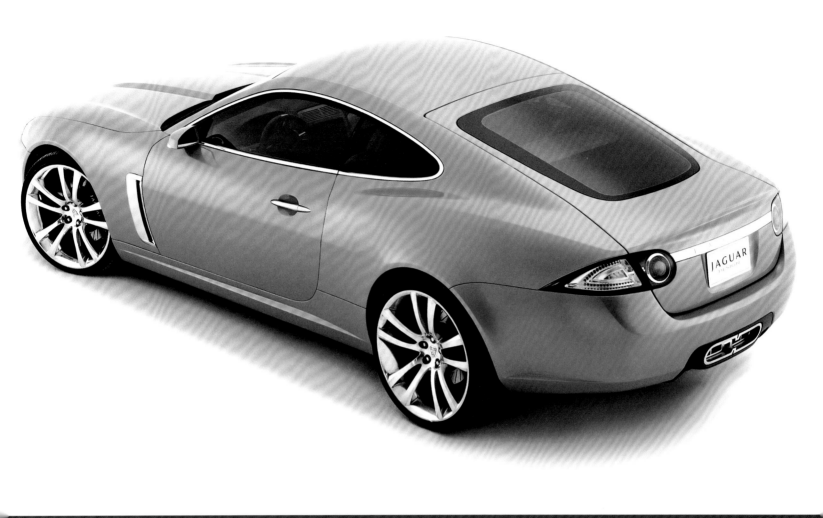

sports saloons at the Geneva Show, Jaguar Chairman and CEO, Joe Greenwell commented: 'The Advanced Lightweight Coupé represents the very essence of Jaguar, its heart and soul. If you want to know what lies ahead for us, what direction we will take – this is Jaguar's answer.'

The 2005 event signalled the 75th show and 100th year anniversary of the Geneva Salon, and Jaguar chose their 1961 show car to remind showgoers just how significant an impact the E-type had made, in the hope that the new ALC would repeat the performance. 'The E-type is a very special car.' explained design director Ian Callum. 'Its lines are unashamedly geometrical and still remarkably contemporary, yet it possesses a sensuality and litheness that is unmistakably Jaguar. It was a source of great inspiration when we began work on our next generation of sports cars.'

That was a different era, though, and the E-type then was revolutionary and sensational. Its simple, flowing lines and long, purposeful bonnet captured the glamour, dynamism and optimism of Britain in the early 1960s, and the E-type

symbolised Jaguar's interpretation of beautiful, fast cars. The Advanced Lightweight Coupé, however, is a physical expression of Ian Callum's new direction for the next generation of Jaguar sports cars, which, like the 2+2 ALC show car, would have purposeful and seductive exteriors to bring Jaguar design firmly into the 21st century.

'I firmly believe that Jaguars should appear powerful as well as elegant.' Callum said. 'Look back at the great cars from our past and you will see that they were as muscular and taut as they were subtle and curvaceous. That's what confident Jaguar design is all about.'

The Advanced Lightweight Coupé was certainly an attractive, aggressive and sophisticated-looking sports car, but too much talk and hype can just as quickly bring a model down as poor quality or any other disappointments. Scheduled for production later that same year, the new XK sports car was going to have to deliver the goods once the media and first customer drives began to take place, if the model was to live up to expectations.

↑ The rear view of the ALC is also different from the production version with the dominant central exhaust outlet cluster being replaced by a more modest twin-exhaust system.

Jaguar XK (2006)

→ The XK convertible was launched in Detroit in January 2006.

At approximately 11:30am on Tuesday 20 December, 2005, the first of the new XKs rolled off the production line at Jaguar's Castle Bromwich manufacturing centre, Birmingham. A liquid-silver 4.2 XK coupé with charcoal interior and burr-walnut fascia, was duly handed straight to the Jaguar Daimler Heritage Trust to take its place alongside the 1961 E-type Geneva show car as well as the last Series 3 V12 E-type, HDU 555N, in the Trust's collection.

Based on the Advanced Lightweight Coupé exhibited at the Geneva Show, the new Jaguar X150, or XK to give it its marketing name, made its global public debut just six months later at the Frankfurt Motor Show in September 2005, with the XK convertible making its public debut at the NAIAS Detroit Motor Show in January 2006. The media were let loose in the new cars at the XK's international press launch in Cape Town in the February of the same year, just two months ahead of the first customer deliveries.

The new XK convertible was designed first, before the coupé, as this was to ensure that the convertible body structure was sufficiently strong and rigid (1,595kg), and not just a converted coupé which might lack the strength needed to live up to its tin-top sibling. This was a welcome change in design process, which meant that the convertible already had an exceptionally strong body before the coupé was even considered. The beautiful lines and clean surfaces were crucial

in defining the all-new XK's more sporting character and the powerful looks are clearly a continuation of the style of the Advanced Lightweight Coupé.

Arguably, in one respect the all-new XK has more in common with earlier cars like the original XKs and the C-, D- and E-types than it does with the most recent XK8, notably in the way in which the shape wraps more tightly around the mechanical underpinnings. The front-wing power vents are a new Jaguar styling signature, while the distinctive oval grille opening, prominent bonnet power-bulge and practical rear lift-back door all echo the E-type of old. But it is interesting to note how much more centrally the cabin is located on the new XK model than on the old E-type which used a long

↓ The first XK rolled off the production line at the Castle Bromwich plant in December 2005, and was handed to the JDHT for posterity.

muscular-looking bonnet to convey a message of power, thereby forcing the cabin position much further back in the vehicle layout. The XK is also a much wider vehicle which makes it appear shorter, but at the same time it communicates a very strong presence on the road.

While the new sharper-looking design and styling hit one first, it is undoubtedly under the skin where much of the new technology is found. The most far-reaching engineering feature in the all-new XK is its use of Jaguar's 'Lightweight Vehicle Technology', the all-aluminium architecture that was introduced recently with the latest-generation XJ saloon. Fifty years ago, it was inconceivable that an all-aluminium structure could ever be stronger than an all-steel structure, but with technical developments in the field of welding and engineering, this is now a reality. Developed from aircraft-industry construction methods just as with the earlier C-, D- and E-types, the new XK manufacturing process produces a massively strong but light structure that is both riveted and epoxy-bonded. Even before going on sale, the new XK had

already been awarded the Engineering and Technology Award at the prestigious Prince Michael International Road Safety Awards, in recognition of its all-new industry-leading feature, the pedestrian deployable bonnet. The XK's 'Pyrotechnic Deployable' bonnet system is an industry-leading safety feature and was created to comply with phase one of the new European safety legislation.

In the cabin, the layout is driver-focused and sportingly modern in nature; the seats are set low against the high waistline to give a strong 'cockpit' feel reminiscent of the E-type. With a longer wheelbase, wider track and taller roofline, the 2+2 layout has more interior space than the XK8 that it replaces.

As already mentioned, early consideration was given to developing a single 'Coupé Convertible' (CC) model with a folding steel roof; however when stowed this structure all but eliminated what little boot space there was and so a two-model programme was subsequently followed, namely a coupé and a convertible.

↑ An opportune moment for the new XK Convertible while on the car's UK press launch in the Cotswolds, as an older XK8 Convertible passes by in the background.

↑ Despite the company's attempts not to make too many references to the past, this rear view of the XK Coupé shows a distinct likeness with its predecessor, the E-type.

Initial driving impressions in the press were positive although some journalists were somewhat cautious about the car's new styling, and questioned whether it was as radically different as the model had been hyped up to be. On first impressions, it is undoubtedly a world apart from any preceding Jaguar sports car but this is a car that the company had needed five years earlier. Power, ride comfort, safety and looks all get a big affirmative, but boot space in the convertible is very limited. With the hood retracted, one would get little more than an overnight bag or a briefcase in the boot, but then the enjoyment is all in the ride.

If one asks the question – is this the new E-type? – one would have to mentally draw a line under the XK's predecessor and tell yourself that this is the first new sports car to come from Jaguar since the disappearance of the E-type in 1975. In looks, it is not too far removed from the XK8 series, but to

JAGUAR'S SPORTS CAR RIVALS (PRICES 2006):

Model	Price Coupé	Price Convertible	Engine Config.	Engine Capacity	Max. Output	Top Speed
Chev Corvette C6	£46,595	£52,595	V8	5,967cc	404bhp	186mph
Jaguar XK (X150)	£58,995	£64,955	V8	4,196cc	300bhp	155mph
Porsche 911 Carrera 4	£62,930	£69,900	Flat 6	3,596cc	325bhp	174mph
Aston Martin DB9	£109,750	£118,750	V12	5,935cc	450bhp	186mph
Ferrari 612 Scaglietti	£170,500	-	V12	5,748cc	540bhp	199mph+

Figures supplied by each manufacturer

leave it there is also to do the newcomer a disservice. The new XK is a stunning and very advanced vehicle, but the final decision will have to be left in the hands of the public as its success will ultimately be determined by the car's sales.

Will the XK do for Jaguar what the E-type did for the company back in 1961? That is almost an unfair comparison to make because the two cars were produced in two totally different eras. The new XK shows off new, more modern technology in a world where safety regulations play a huge part in new-car design, whereas the E-type impressed the market with a combination of performance and affordability. The XK needs to impress a very different buyer today, a far more sophisticated and better informed buyer. The new XK is certainly the most driver-focused grand tourer to have come from Jaguar since those early E-type days, but the question remains, does it deliver that unique, magical Jaguar feeling?

↑ The new XK Coupé certainly makes a handsome picture, with its tensed haunches. In the language of its designer, Ian Callum, it has 'attitude'.

What makes a great sports car?

Some performance-car manufacturers have been so successful over the years in creating and maintaining an element of anticipation and excitement in their sports cars, that it is almost expected by the market before a new model is even produced. In the 1960s, this was certainly true of cars like Jaguar, Ferrari, Porsche, Lamborghini, Maserati and others. But the secret behind this magical element is to know what those special qualities are that contribute to this perception in the first place. This unique and distinctive character is rather like that illusive term, 'goodwill' in accounting, but in a sports car it is usually the combination of several important attributes such as reputation, performance, a certain amount of mystique and, of course, quality, all of which should be consistently present in order to attract buyers over a long period of time. Some of these qualities can be built into the vehicle, such as quality and performance, but there are many sports cars which claim these characteristics to varying degrees, but

which do not have that certain magic. It is these intangible qualities which are the hardest to identify, because they are created in the minds of the buyer, and cannot be built or bought, but are earned over time through consistent delivery of the right product.

Today, most major manufacturers' marketing departments possess huge influence in the decision-making process, which determines what is 'in', and what is 'out' of fashion in respect of their car, and consequently what is on and what is off the drawing board. In the past, it was the engineering prowess and technical innovation present in a sports car that more often than not swayed one's purchasing decision, but public tastes have changed because so many cars today are technically capable of high performance. Fifty years ago, you could list the high-performance-car manufacturers in a single breath, but today most motor manufacturers have a high-performance model in their range that is relatively affordable to a large section of the market. No longer is the motorsport adage 'win on Sunday sell on Monday' valid alone; it's all about communicating the right image to your social group or peers, and so vast amounts of market research money are spent in trying to pin down what it is that appeals in a certain market.

Strange though it may seem, the automaker's marketing researchers need to take into account the lifestyle habits of an increasingly broad range of personal preferences, such as a decrease in the demand for leather upholstery and trim. It is the motivation for such a change in taste that is so interesting: a movement which has developed from the growing trend in the eating preferences of some of the younger population. Through an increasing interest in wildlife conservation and vegetarianism, some people do not want leather or wood interior finishings in their car, and this preference may well be the result of the customer's lifestyle choices, such as an objection to killing animals or felling trees. All this can affect the trim options in a product range, but it is not a trend that would have overly concerned motor manufacturers 50 years ago. Today you ignore these market signals at your peril, because if you don't notice the changes in the market, the competition will, and your company may have lost a potential sale.

Essentially, a sports car must have strong performance characteristics and handle well because a sports car is all about fun; it must give the owner freedom and in today's terms that also means convenience. Defining these convenience factors is none too easy, because some drivers want their sports car to be a head-turner and a show piece, others want it for investment purposes or as a tax write-off while some are out-and-out enthusiasts who just like to drive it with the top down in the middle of winter with the heater on full blast.

One can draw a parallel with those adventure seekers who go skiing or sailing and when you ask why they do it, the answer is usually because they like the thrill of it all. For them, it is just the exhilaration of doing something different, and that alone is a reason for buying such a car and those who can afford that kind of leisure-filled lifestyle will no doubt want a car to give them the same thrills. It's a far cry from the oil-smelling, fume-filled cockpits so familiar in the sports cars of old that required warming up and tinkering before you were able to set off down to the shops to buy the Sunday papers. Its all about convenience, you push the starter button, a warning light tells you to buckle up, the roof folds back at the push of a button and the multiple-speaker surround-sound system pushes out as many decibels as your ears can handle. Today this owner is more likely to be quite young, perhaps a thirty-something who has a fast pace of life and enjoys the social status that his or her sports car radiates.

The other group of drivers is today's 55-year-olds who can afford to treat themselves to a bit of enjoyment in their second youth. For this reason, some manufacturers have

↓ **What makes a great sports car? Certainly charisma, style, quality, performance – and emotional desire. It's hard not to be impressed by these characteristics, as this Series I roadster shows.**

→ One could argue that the interior trim of the new **XK** is somewhat sterile, but then Spitfires no longer rule the sky either. The **XK** has moved on and its controls are more akin to a stealth fighter, with high-tech finishes and electronic controls.

introduced a lot of retro features and styling into their cars as this appeals to this older group in the market for whom these features would be familiar, while the styling still remains 'cool' with some of the younger set. Today there is wider acceptance for the justification of personal 'indulgence and reward' in the mind of the buyer and the need for originality and authenticity enters more strongly into their sports-car buying decision.

Understanding the Jaguar customer – 1990/2000s

The profile of the traditional sports-car buyer in the 1930/40s was a fairly clear-cut one, comprising mostly males of above-average means with a sporting or social inclination, and a good deal of recreational time on their hands. However, the most

→ The XKR version of the X100/XK8, introduced in 1998, packed a mighty 370bhp punch with its supercharged 4.0-litre V8 engine. This early convertible is in pristine condition.

influential elements that contribute to the successful design of a sports car today are quite different, this being an area of development that has changed perhaps more than any other in the motor industry in the past 50 years.

No longer does a buyer seek out a sports car solely for the purpose of racing, and nor is it a status symbol in the same way that it was in the early post-war years. Today's sports car buyer may be either male or female and range in age from 20 years to 60 or 70 years, be a high-earning professional or even a young person just starting out in their career. With the boundaries between the traditional car-buying segments having fallen away, this makes life more difficult for the manufacturer and especially more difficult for the car designer.

As a starting point, design has become an increasingly important factor in the buyers' perception of what that product is worth to them, to the extent that it may be decisive in whether they might buy that product or not. This appeal pulls all the right strings in the buyer and is termed 'emotional desire', but building this into a car like a Jaguar is not as simple as it might be for some other manufacturers, because of the perceived traditional values that Jaguar sports cars must maintain. Jaguar sports cars must still be elegant, although this is regarded as an old-fashioned word in the modern world of paddle shifts and electronic aids.

It is a fact that people are getting bigger, and this places constraints on the designer when increased interior space must be considered, as does the raft of safety regulations which must be taken account of. It is not an exaggeration to say that sports-car design today is as much influenced by these regulations as it is by any other issues, what with increasing passive, active, passenger and pedestrian safety requirements.

However, there are still several fundamentals that a car designer must include when developing a sports car for today's market. Ian Callum, Jaguar's Director of Design, gives his view: 'Emotional desire is number one, but the constraints within which you have to work are very, very tough – and

↑ The rear view of this XK8 coupé and the Series 1½ E-type roadster provides an interesting comparison, on the occasion of the XK8's launch in South Africa in 1996.

→ XK coupé as featured in the Jaguar 2006 'GORGEOUS' calendar, showing the familiar 'Spitfire wing' window line.

↓ XK roadster in Jaguar's 2006 'GORGEOUS' calendar, in a stunning setting.

they get tougher by the day. And to get that emotional desire, the proportions of the car are the most important thing; how the car sits architecturally and how it sits relative to its wheels.'

If the composition of these design elements is present in the right proportion in a sports car, then regardless of how the car is finished, its quality will always shine through. However, if the proportions are not there in the first place, it doesn't matter how well it is adorned, it will never work. Callum continues: 'Get the proportions right, get the stance right and especially the way it sits on the road, then everything else falls into place and everything else happens a lot easier. So that is number one in emotional desire; its proportion.' Get these things right and the emotional desire kicks in, pushing the performance aspect down into second place, as the car has managed to create the image that owner seeks. For the development engineer, performance is a lot easier to build into a car today through electronics and tuning. It is a factor that is still important but is becoming less significant in the final buying decision.

Understanding the customer's reactions and responses has today become a science in itself, helping the designers and engineers to interpret these factors in order to successfully build the required elements into their sports car. But many customers are not able to articulate these subconscious ideas, thus placing the responsibility for creating the necessary emotional elements in the product fairly and squarely on the shoulders of the manufacturer. Because of the bewildering range of choices and flexibility of vehicles today, the customer needs to be 'told' what he likes as this is no longer an easy task for him to do personally, and the successful conveyance of this message is largely down to targeted advertising and clever marketing and events promotion.

Ian Callum explains: 'It is about drama, it's about excitement and it is aspiration and that gets into branding more than anything else. And it is about being exotic.'

Exotic – strikingly different or unusual and often exciting, suggesting unfamiliar or rare origins.

Author

In the modern world of marketing and advertising, the word 'exotic' is bandied about frequently in the promotion of many different types of products, from refreshments to motor cars to holidays, and pretty much everything in between. The basic term is intended to describe a product or a place that is different, special and exciting, but to create an exotic feel in a sports car is a difficult science. A big engine in a bland body style is not exciting, and equally, the most fantastic shape with a puny engine will also disappoint; it is

the marriage of all of the above elements that creates the sense of something extraordinary. Jaguar's customers have come to expect this in the sports cars from Coventry, but it cannot be assumed by the car's designers that their customers will automatically sense this quality in their sports car range, based on the badge alone.

'Exoticism' is the strangest of qualities to look for in a sports car, because when you are paying top dollar for your pride and joy, you are aware that the purchase will involve

↑ There is a definite family resemblance to its predecessor as well as to its Aston Martin cousin, but make no mistake, this pussycat has its own character.

213

compromise. Why pay so much for something that is a compromise? On a scale of one to ten, the mid-point of five would represent comfort, space and a reasonable amount of power. Moving towards the lower end of the scale, say three and below, one could expect less power and style but perhaps better fuel consumption due to a smaller engine and a low purchase price. However, moving towards the top end, one would expect, with a higher price, an increase in engine size and power together with greater performance. It is the combination of a more potent engine with greater performance that brings about the compromise, because at the extreme end of this top group is the truly exotic, sleek, bullet-shaped, high-performance sports car. A striking and aerodynamic shape in this league means a low roofline which compromises cabin space and usually means two seats, but then these cars attract attention because they are dynamic

to look at – which is what the driver wants at this level of car ownership. So for the car to be exotic, one can expect a certain element of compromise in the car's composition, but where it may be short on space and ease of entry and exit, it will be big on style, big on looks and big on performance – and also big on price.

Ian Callum explains: 'Subconsciously I think what it is, is this car is compromising my basic needs and therefore there is something exotic about it – it says my emotional needs are more important. I think that is what it is about and therefore my emotional needs become more important than my basic functional needs. That's exotic, and that's what sports cars are all about.'

Sitting in the car must create the same feeling of power, command and authority. The driver is expecting to be fed information on the performance of his car, and therefore the styling and functionality of the interior are just as important as the exterior. Callum again: 'If you get the proportions of the car right and the feeling when you sit in it is exciting and inviting, that to me is what makes a good sports car.' None of the elements described above can be sufficient in isolation, but the successful marriage of them all will ensure the right composition.

Did the engineers and designers think about these factors during those pre- and post-war years? Probably not to the same extent, because that era was all about technical development, but today's sports-car buyer is far more demanding and sophisticated, and therefore the designer has to interpret what it was in the heritage of the brand that attracted customers in the first place, and then interpret those values in order to recreate them in the current model.

There is of course the danger today of always trying to modernise an old style or vehicle design, because it once was successful. It is especially difficult when the heritage of the brand is as strong as Jaguar's, as there is so much success to draw on, but when one examines the creations of Sir William Lyons and Malcolm Sayer, they were always moving forward, both technologically as well as in terms of design. In those early years, they may have developed a particular design or styling cue in order to retain brand identity, but they would not for one moment have considered reinventing past designs. Many automotive designers today, across the industry, attempt to create new models based on reviving styling cues from the 1940s/50s/60s, forgetting that those styles appealed back then for a specific reason – you can recreate the style but you cannot recreate the circumstances in which those styles were once popular, and they are therefore likely to be short-lived.

Importantly, Jaguar has today sought to recreate the values that existed in their early sports cars, rather than trying to build a modern E-type. If the company did build a

↓ Jaguar engineers spent a lot of time getting the interior sound effects just right, to the extent that the exhaust note is fed back to the cabin through a special valve in order to deliver the right level of engine feedback under acceleration. For a performance car, adequate engine 'growl' when accelerating is necessary to provide the driver with the sensation of power and speed in an otherwise well-insulated cabin.

new E-type fashioned around the 1961 car, it might be a success story fuelled by nostalgia but for a limited time only, because the circumstances around which the original car was created have long since gone. The social setting into which a sports car is born plays an enormous role in the success of a vehicle that eventually attains iconic status, proving that this quality cannot be built into any car at any time – this recognition and acknowledgement by the car-buying public is acquired only over time.

There are some who feel that too many cars today all look the same because they are based around similar design parameters, and this is to a large extent quite true as manufacturers all seek to satisfy the customer's needs in the same way. However, in 2001, Jaguar displayed their 1961 E-type show car once again at the Geneva Motor Show, and the crowds were ten deep just as they had been forty years earlier, which just goes to show that a good design never dies.

The values which Jaguar speaks of today include proportion, stance, purity of lines, simplicity, integrity, honesty, fun and all things that are intrinsically British. Ian Callum again: 'We have consciously made these into our new products, because we are trying to move on now at a much greater pace than we have in the past. We will be moving away from clear individual cues and we will be using "values".'

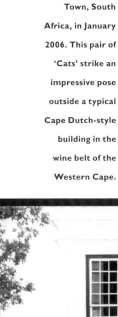

↓ Jaguar launched the new XK coupé and convertible to the media in Cape Town, South Africa, in January 2006. This pair of 'Cats' strike an impressive pose outside a typical Cape Dutch-style building in the wine belt of the Western Cape.

The difference between Styling and Design

Owning and driving a sports car is all about conveying a message. What the car is saying about its owner is that they want to be a little different and they choose to show it through what they drive, but this is only possible if the sports car in question successfully captures the owner's own interpretation of those qualities.

What is it that draws some sports-car lovers to one style of car, while others are drawn to another very different type of style? The design language of the 1961 E-type Jaguar attracted the eye of most sports-car enthusiasts in its day, but the sleek and smooth lines of the sultry cat was not everybody's cup of tea in America, where a more chunky and angular design was popular. It's all about design and styling language; and language speaks, so design language conveys a message about the car's owner and what he or she is saying about themselves.

A sports car cannot convey a message of moderation or conservatism, it must be about power, speed and performance, all wrapped up in an attractive, sporty-looking body. It's all about 'proportions and the evocation of power' – in the words of Jaguar's director of design, Ian Callum.

Creating this evocative or expressive element in a car draws on the very nature of what appeals to humans in the opposite sex: a healthy, attractive and well-proportioned body. As humans beings, we admire the collective elements of strength,

power and the authority that this form or shape brings, suggesting an overwhelming ability to perform at a higher-than-average level. When evaluating this analogy between a fit, strong human being and a sports car, one would expect the car's body to be similarly formed into a muscular physique representing speed, strength and power. The distinctive automotive design and styling treatment of 'muscles and shoulders' is an important tool for the designer to exploit in achieving such a look in a sports car.

Ian Callum expands on this concept: 'There is a lot of human analogy here. If you build cars that way, with the proportions of the big wheels sitting on the ground and on top you have the cabin moving inboard of that, it gives this impression of muscular power – which is about shoulders, and that is the killing factor. It's got this essence of confidence and power to aspire to, they want to feel this way, so they compensate by buying one.'

But what is the difference between styling and design? Design is about understanding the architecture of the vehicle visually and creating the initial structure which can then be engineered to become what the designer intended. Ian Callum says, 'We create the architecture, we create the stance of the car and it is that balance of components in making it all work, to create something that is aesthetically exciting, that is what design is about.'

In an automotive sense, styling is more about 'joining the dots', as Callum puts it. By taking fixed parameters such as the roof line, wheels, bonnet line and vehicle dimensions, one can then create a style within those boundaries. Callum again: '[As a stylist] you would have no influence over the fundamental structure or architecture of the car and how it sits and relates to the rest of the world. You have just adorned it, and therefore to me that is styling.' ■

←There can be no doubt about the powerful message being conveyed by the new **XKR**, as it shows its muscular lines at the London ExCel launch (June, 2006).

'Designers are just more conscious about creating an entity which is a sum of the parts, rather than just joining the dots.'

Ian Callum – Director of Design, Jaguar Cars

Into the future

'You bought a sports car in the old days because it got you to your destination faster and quicker, and that is the long and the short of it.'

Julian Thomson – Chief Designer, Advanced Studio, Jaguar Cars

↑ Table Mountain
presents an
impressive backdrop
to an equally
impressive XK
convertible at the
car's media launch
in Cape Town
(January, 2006).

Jaguar sports cars – the future

'When Jaguar's revered aerodynamicist Malcolm Sayer created the E-type he didn't sculpt the car, but devised its remarkable shape from pure geometry – it is a series of ellipses.' commented Giles Taylor, Jaguar's senior design manager. 'By designing the E-type that way he gave it a mechanical purity that we wanted to reflect in this car's face [XK – 2006]. That meant the grille had to be perfectly symmetrical in both a horizontal and vertical plane, and by doing that we have made a focal point from which every line can stream backwards.'

So many customers, admirers, enthusiasts and general commentators over the years, have marvelled at the pure lines of the E-type, but it must be remembered that it was designed and produced in a time frame that can never be repeated. Certain market conditions were present then that will never be experienced again – post-war technological developments enabled people to really dream big, but today we expect things to happen instantly. Today's customer has

become a lot more critical if something is not absolutely perfect, whereas back in the 1960s, it was good enough if it was just British.

In Jaguar's language, it has done 'retro for too long', and according to Ian Callum, Jaguar's design boss, the new XK represents the future for the company. 'Attitude' is a word that Callum uses a lot, and he is striving to build this into his current and future cars at Jaguar. Certainly, for too long Jaguar has rested on its heritage and a fresh direction and styling signature must be injected into the sports-car range just as they were with the introduction of the XK 120 and the E-type. At no stage did any of those revolutionary models borrow from earlier designs, as Sir William Lyons sought constantly to renew a current model's image. Looking backwards and borrowing from a predecessor's design was taboo as early designers were forward-thinking and not interested in retro-styling – it would even have been looked down upon in the industry. There is today a tendency to get new models into the limelight by submitting them for an increasing number of design awards around the globe, in the hope that winning such awards will help promote sales. Unfortunately, many of these awards are lost on the public because they are not familiar with their significance or relevance, which would suggest that they are for the benefit of the designers and manufacturers alone. Such self gratification rather misses the point, as the ultimate judge of a good design will be the buying public; it is they who will part with their money to buy the vehicle if it appeals to them.

Studying the market today, there is a plethora of similar-looking cars in almost all sectors of the industry, and one might reasonably assume that this is driven largely by regulations. But Jim Randle explains: 'Not entirely; it is driven by fear. People don't want to move too much from where they are, because of the fear of getting it wrong.'

He continues: 'It is lack of self confidence. The "Old Chap" [Sir William Lyons] never ever did that; every car was different. He kept looking at "how do we move it forward?" If you look at the latest XK, it is hardly any different because they are too fearful to move on.'

In fairness, much of what is available on the road today is driven by packaging. 'The thing about those cars was that they were styled and then packaged because the "Old Chap" drove everything. I mean that is what made a Jaguar what it was. It just had such a sleek style because we accepted compromise, because that was part of the character of a Jaguar. But under

Ford they have what was called an "18-panel chart" where you have to be at least equal if not better than "best in class" in all areas. What you do then, is design a perfectly competent car that has no character. When their own career prospects [the designer's] are supreme relative to the product; I mean that's what happens.' explains Randle.

Keith Helfet adds his concern: 'I would love Jaguar to be successful, but they have lost that competitive advantage of style.' The difference between the XK 150 and the E-type was so marked in 1961 that the two cars might just as well have come from two totally different manufacturers. The challenge facing the Jaguar designers today in moving forward with innovative quality is how to inject that E-type sparkle into their modern creations.

↑ The E-type was never happier than when being driven – this is a Series 1½ roadster in the leafy suburbs of northern Johannesburg, South Africa.

A gorgeous E-type Series I roadster basking in the sun at the JDC's Prescott Hillclimb.

Julian Thomson gives his thoughts: 'You look at the historical values and you have to write down things like – these cars were very glamorous, they had very pure forms, they had excellent proportions, they had excellent stance and they looked very [sic] unique – and that is almost the brief that you give to your designers. You don't tell them, "Go and create a new E-type".'

Today's designers at Jaguar must look at what the E-type did for the customer in 1961, and interpret what was important about those emotions. 'That is the sort of brief you give. The thing which is difficult to really put your finger on is this "shock" value that the car had. And again when I talk about having so many more cars in the market and so much diversity, to create that sort of stir which is also very aesthetically pleasing and non-challenging like the E-type did, is quite difficult.' adds Thomson. 'I want a car that when we pull the covers off at the Geneva Motor Show, it is as good as when we did that with the E-type. That is the ultimate briefing that you give, and to make sure that you do that is another matter, but that is where you would like to be.'

Equally, in a global market, a premium motor vehicle must be distinct from the other models in the market, and for Jaguar that is its Britishness, or more specifically its Jaguar-ness. In the XK and E-type days this was not as much of a problem as Sir William Lyons did what he thought was best and that was largely different from anything else on the market

anyway. In the 1950s and 1960s, Britain was regarded as the sports-car capital of the world, but even within the British market, all sports cars could be easily identified as design similarities were positively avoided. Control of design today is not in the hands of the individual designer and cars therefore have a more corporate feel and some new models are even predictable ahead of their launch.

However, in order for Jaguar to maintain its innovative distinctiveness, they have attempted to analyse the sports-car buyer's emotions evident in the 1960s, and to build these factors into the modern-day sports-car requirements. For Jaguar, part of that distinctiveness is being British but those traditional British qualities that were relevant in the 1960s have changed over time and Jaguar has to keep pace with what its target market perceives to be 'British' today. During the age of elegance, Jaguar was all about wood and leather; today's customer is more interested in the technical look of carbon fibre, and titanium appeals more than traditional or natural materials. To paint all of its cars in traditional British racing green and to create the interiors with the old-fashioned 'club-room feel' would be the wrong way to go, but to modernise the values around which Jaguar has developed is essential. The exterior of a British car should be emotional, and it has got to have a bit of charm about it too, but, according to Thomson, Jaguar must work to 'bring the values forward, not the design'.

Three generations of Jaguar sports cars – at the rear is an XK 140, with a Series I E-type ahead and a C-type up front.

Recent Jaguar marketing research has shown that some customers, for example conservationists and vegetarians, prefer not to buy a car with leather upholstery because the hides come from animals that have been slaughtered for general food consumption. Where previously leather upholstery was regarded as a top-spec interior finish, now some manufacturers are having to think twice about this, as traditional quality finishes are under scrutiny in the market. This development is not because of price, but rather from the market pressure of a certain group whose principles are playing a deciding role in their purchasing decisions. This was certainly not a factor back in the 1950s and 1960s when leather was the upholstery finish of choice, irrespective of one's social conscience.

Creating this mix in a new sports car while maintaining the history that Jaguar has created is without doubt a fine balancing act. Unless they do so, they run the risk of reducing their unique marketing advantage and competing on level terms with their competition, such as Mercedes or BMW.

Maintaining this emotional appeal is what sets Jaguar sports cars apart from the rest of the market and as Julian Thomson says, 'It is a case of how much you turn up the volume on the heritage aspect of the car. How much do you do a modern car and how much do you do a heritage car, and how much you play with those factors? And then, how do you actually communicate that to the person buying the car?'

In the 1960s, manufacturers went out of their way to differentiate their product from those of others. Besides competing on the track and in the showrooms, arch rivals Aston Martin and Jaguar were poles apart in terms of price and the thought of sharing components or design knowledge was unthinkable. More recently, until early 2007, Aston Martin and Jaguar were owned by the same company and while the price gap was still quite wide, it narrowed noticeably during the years under Ford's control. This development has been made possible through the sharing of components, materials, processes and even market knowledge.

↑ The timeless lines of a Series I E-type. This shot of a relaxed group of motoring enthusiasts could have been taken back in the 1960s; in fact it was taken at the JDC's recent Prescott Hillclimb (2006).

JAGUAR

Reflections on Jaguar

↑ They say a picture
paints a thousand
words, and rightly so
because the
differences between
the XJ220 (1990) and
the XK 120 (1948)
couldn't be more
marked. The
horizontal grille and
mid-engine layout of
the XJ220 results in a
roof height just above
the XK 120's bonnet.
Equally noteworthy is
that the top edge of
the 220's grille is
below the bumper
line of the 120.

One of the challenges facing Jaguar, a company very conscious of its past and heritage, is to recreate themselves as a modern, relevant and appealing brand. For a manufacturer founded on high-profile, high-quality engineering and the wood-and-leather club room feel, it is not easy to reposition themselves in the high-tech world of titanium, carbon fibre and electronic driving aids. Shaking off a long-term image is not an easy thing, but then do they really want to? After all, such a reputation has been hard-earned and it is the bedrock of their customer perception.

However, while the XK 120 or the E-type is today one of the most desirable sports cars and a favourite of collectors the world over, they were also once at the cutting edge of technology. The XK 120 was modern, high tech and one of the few cars that could actually do 120mph in its day. Similarly, the E-type represented a giant leap forward in the market and the industry was collectively quite envious of this model when it was launched.

For the last 45 years, Jaguar sports cars, apart from the XJ-S in 1975, have faithfully followed the styling laid down by Malcolm Sayer; the XK8 in 1996 and the recent XK (2006) have both continued with this styling in an easily identifiable theme. Is this style still relevant today? Would Sir William Lyons and Malcolm Sayer have continued with this style in the same manner? This is a question that will often be asked but for which we will never have an answer. Perhaps an indication of where they might have taken the sports-car line could be gleaned by looking at the history of the sports-car line up.

The late-1930s saw a bold move forward by Lyons with the launch of the SS100, but the introduction of the XK 120 in 1948 took the company in a completely different direction, again with cutting-edge technology and performance and drop-dead looks. Following the XK 140 and 150 upgrades the E-type was once again an incredibly brave, adventurous and creative move by the company which did not borrow on any previous production-model styling, apart from the handful of D-types which were produced for racing. It showed a completely new direction in the design thinking of the company.

In the 1950s and 1960s, the company built and marketed their products under the slogan, 'Grace, Pace and Space', terms that were modern and relevant for the time. Today, one does not talk of 'Grace' as it is a quality associated with a bygone era, especially in the context of the ride and comfort of a sports car. A modern rendition of this slogan would more likely be 'Roadability, Ergonomics and Comfort', and so Jaguar has had to face the challenge of modernising its reputation of quality and the club-room feel. Their latest marketing slogan of 'Fast Beautiful Cars' is certainly more appropriate in the modern world of increased customer demand for motoring relevance and personal image.

While the table below is a rather general assemblage of models over the whole production life of each model, and while it groups left- and right-hand-drive with fixed-head and open-top cars, it is nevertheless an interesting account of how Jaguar sports car production has developed over the years. The X100/XK8 model produced between 1996 and 2005 showed a remarkable jump over its predecessors, even the XJ-S, but if the new XK model is to revive Jaguar's fortunes, it will have to sell in even greater numbers than the XK8 series. If it is volume that Jaguar is looking for in their sports car line-up, a resuscitated F-type model would undoubtedly draw in a whole new market sector, while still maintaining Jaguar's brand image. Unfortunately the opportunity created by the F-type concept of 2000 has now gone, as Jaguar's decision to pull the plug on that model after preparing the market for its arrival may have done some damage by creating uncertainty amongst potential buyers – it's the old adage: 'once bitten, twice shy'. Perhaps the possibility does still exist for this model type to be revived by Jaguar, but it will involve some fancy footwork on the part of the product planning and development engineers. The XK is not the fun, affordable sports

JAGUAR SPORTS CARS PRODUCTION FIGURES:					
Model	No. of Years	1948–1961	1961–1974	1975–1996	1996–2005
XK 120/140/150	12	30,504			
E-type	14		72,529		
XJ-S	21			115,330	
XK8	9				90,616
Ave. Annual Prodn.		2,542	5,180	5,491	10,068

Automotive Hall of Fame

Sir William Lyons was inducted into the Automotive Hall of Fame in Detroit, Michigan, in 2005, the highest honour that can be bestowed on automotive industry leaders in the United States. Such recognition is given only to those people, typically between four and eight per year, who have helped to shape the direction of the industry in a very significant way. Sir William's grandson, Michael Quinn, today a patron of the Jaguar Daimler Heritage Trust, was thrilled to receive the honour on behalf of his grandfather.

Although the name of Jaguar has remained, the company is now owned by automotive giant, Ford. Despite the ups and the downs over the years, the name of Jaguar still commands respect wherever it is mentioned, but no matter which way you want to look at it, there will always be a little bit of Lyons in every Jaguar. One couldn't wish for a greater legacy.

← This statue of Sir William Lyons stands in the grounds of the Jaguar plant at Browns Lane, Coventry, a fitting tribute to a great man. He was inducted into the Automotive Hall of Fame in Detroit, Michigan, USA, in 2005.

↓ **Included in the press launch material was this image of the F-type concept in 2000, with the ghost image of a Series 1 E-type roadster in the background. It just shows what an influence the E-type has had on the design of those Jaguar sports cars that followed it decades later.**

car that Jaguar created with the E-type in 1961; it is too sophisticated a car for that and some have even said that it is too big. But there is a market waiting for Jaguar to sit up and take notice of this opportunity, and to produce an exciting sports car for the motoring enthusiast, once again.

What is the measure of a successful sports car? Certainly one can expect an impressive sales record where it has achieved its production targets and gone on to enjoy a long model life in markets around the world. Even a limited-run, highly specialised car can achieve global sales and admiration. But in order to be classed as a truly outstanding sports car it should be a landmark car on which others are modelled, and whose design perceptibly changes the direction of sports-car styling, setting new standards in the automotive industry in the process.

The E-type Jaguar has done this and then some. The accolade is evident even in the voices of the current Jaguar designers, as despite their deafening efforts to convince the media and the public that they have not set out to create a new E-type, they constantly refer to Sayer's creation as though it were the benchmark against which they measure their current offering. There are design cues evident in the XK8 and the current XK that are so clearly inspired by the 1961 E-type. By their actions the designers are paying the E-type the highest compliment possible. Words cannot add to the brilliance of the E-type created by Malcolm Sayer some 45 years ago; it is a design so significant and yet so simple, that it is destined to be an automotive landmark for many more years to come. ▪

↑ **In side profile, the sleek window line of the new XK really sets the style for the whole car.**

→ **Created by Malcolm Sayer in 1954, the horizontal 'mouth' of the D-type is still evident in the styling of the XK, half a century later.**

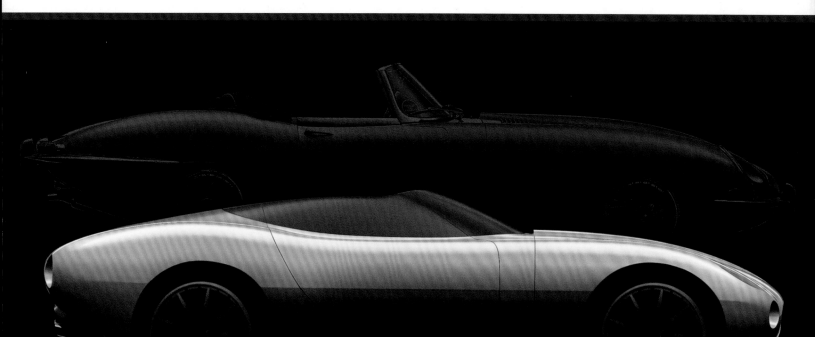

'Jaguar should have a line that comes from the front, whooshes back to the rear, that's very important. It might go into a Coke bottle, it might be straight, it doesn't matter as long as it has got a dynamic to it – it is these values that we need to understand. But these [new] cars are quite different and therefore getting back to the values, we need to fit these into the modern cars. The next generation will be a move on from what you might recognise today.'

Ian Callum – Director of Design, Jaguar Cars

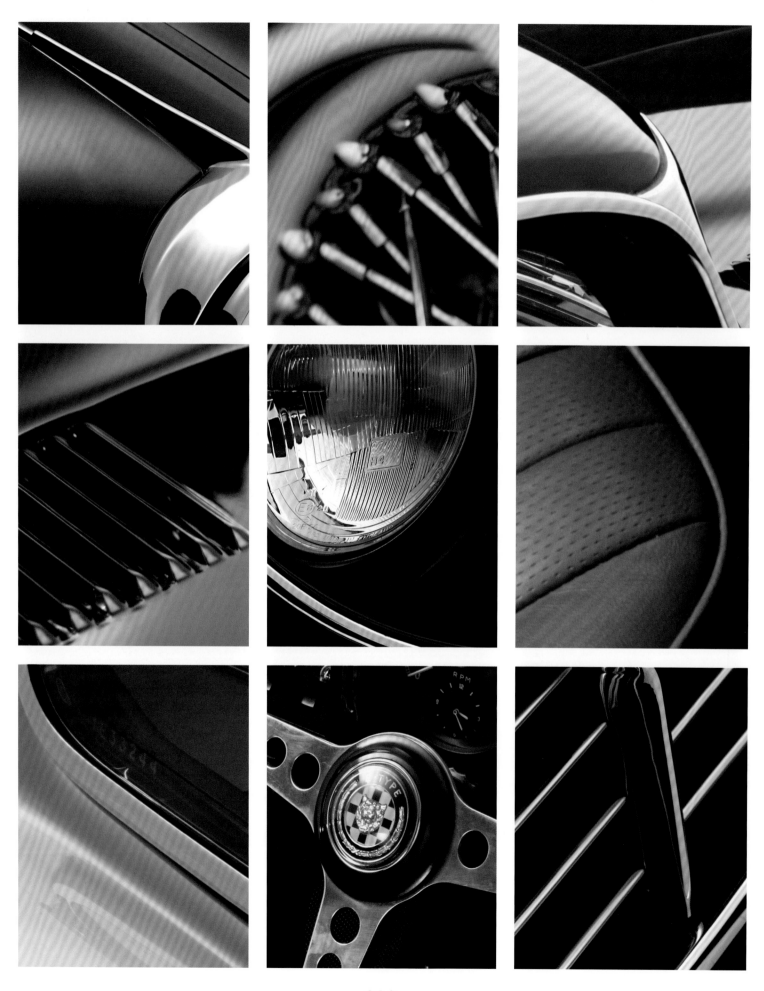

Bibliography

Porter, Philip, *Jaguar E-type, The Definitive History*
(G. T. Foulis & Co., 1989)

Skilleter, Paul, *Jaguar Sports Cars*
(Haynes Publishing, 1988)

Wood, Jonathan, *The Ultimate History Of Fast Cars*
(Paragon Books, 2002)

Thorley, Nigel, *Jaguar E-type, A Celebration of the World's
Favourite '60s Icon* (Haynes Publishing, 2006)

Other Publications & Organisations

Jaguar Cars (UK), Press and PR dept.,
Coventry

Jaguar Daimler Heritage Trust,
Coventry

Heritage, a JDHT magazine – various

Jaguar Journal – a Jaguar Cars Ltd
publication

Autocar – various

Road & Track magazine – various

Car and Driver magazine – various

Jaguar Quarterly magazine – various

Motor Parade magazine – June 1961

Sunday Times newspaper

Design Museum, London
– Press and PR dept

Ralph Lauren, New York
– Press and PR dept

Refining the Sports Car
– Jaguar's E-type: The Museum
of Modern Art, New York

Museum of Fine Arts, Boston
– Press and PR dept

Public Relations Office,
Loughborough University

BBC 2 Publicity – *The Culture Show*

Index